YALE STUDIES IN RELIGIOUS EDUCATION

XIX

THE MOTHER'S ROLE IN CHILDHOOD EDUCATION:

NEW ENGLAND CONCEPTS

1830–1860

THE SAMUEL B. SNEATH
MEMORIAL PUBLICATION FUND

The publication of this volume has been aided by The Samuel B. Sneath Memorial Publication Fund. This Foundation was established on October 19, 1922, by a gift to the Divinity School of Yale University from Mrs. Laura S. Sneath of Tiffin, Ohio, in memory of her husband, Samuel B. Sneath. He was born on December 19, 1828, in Tiffin, where he resided until his death on January 7, 1915. As merchant, manufacturer, banker, and organizer of public utilities he made, throughout a long and public-spirited life, a substantial contribution to the development of his native state.

"THE NEST AT HOME."

"Compared with maternal influence, the combined authority of laws
and armies, and public sentiment, are little things."

THE MOTHER'S ROLE IN CHILDHOOD EDUCATION: NEW ENGLAND CONCEPTS

1830-1860

BY

ANNE L. KUHN

NEW HAVEN

YALE UNIVERSITY PRESS

LONDON · GEOFFREY CUMBERLEGE · OXFORD UNIVERSITY PRESS

1947

PREFACE

ON the shelves of small town libraries and secondhand bookstores throughout New England are to be found scores of dusty, insignificant looking little volumes which tell the story of the beginnings of parent education in this country. These books and periodicals, published in greatest number during the period 1830 to 1860, are addressed to young women as prospective homemakers, and to mothers and fathers concerned with the physical, mental, and spiritual welfare of the rising generation. They were written by clergymen and doctors, social reformers and educators, some of whom are remembered today in other connections: Heman Humphrey, president of Amherst College; William Alcott, cousin of Bronson; Lydia Sigourney, literary lady and "sweet singer of Hartford"; Lydia Maria Child, active in antislavery circles; and Samuel Goodrich, publisher of children's literature. These authors and others of their time were zealous for fireside reform. The focus of their interest was the American mother and her responsibilities with respect to the nurture of the young.

It was on discovery of this vein of literature and its availability in the Sterling Library at Yale University that the present study was undertaken. Its purpose is to portray the mother's educational role, not as it actually was, but as it was seen through the eyes of a group of socially minded New England writers. The childhood education in which they were interested had reference to the young child from infancy to approximately six years of age, or the period during which character was molded, in the mid-nineteenth century, largely by fireside influences. "Domestic" or "fireside" education as they defined it was said to include "all the rights and duties of parents, in the government and instruction of their families." [1]

The ideal maternal role they sought to portray was apparently considered applicable to all American mothers regardless of social or economic status, all mothers, that is, whose association with their children was not totally disrupted by industrial labor. Dr.

1. Heman Humphrey, *Domestic Education* (Amherst, J. S. and C. Adams, 1840), p. 15.

43172

William Alcott maintained, for example, "that the MOTHER, whether wise or ignorant, learned or unlearned, healthy or sick, pious or impious, is the most efficient educator." [2] The province of reform appears, for him, to have extended downward as well as upward on the social scale. Stress was placed for the most part, however, on the middle- and upper-class mother, presupposing for her the capacity for self-improvement and the opportunity to put into practice the principles extolled by fireside moralists. Furthermore, the predominant emphasis of the didactic writers was upon urban rather than rural conditions, since many of the social problems of the period were urban in origin.

The concepts of New England writers have been singled out for study principally because it was in this section of the country that social reform took its strongest impetus during the mid-century years. Yet it is evident that the American ideals and patterns which emerge from the literature studied were current in a wider area, geographically, than New England. A sampling of contemporary literature [3] for parents issued from other centers of the Eastern United States reveals material of so similar a nature that sources might be used interchangeably.

The peculiar interest of a study of this sort for today lies in the fact that "mothering," after being held in some disrepute for several decades, is coming once more into vogue. Ironically enough, scientific sanction for some of the earlier modes of approach to home nurture of the young comes at a time when the American mother has almost forgotten how to function with respect to these modes. Throughout nearly a century of community expansion and scientific developments contributing to family dispersal she has seen her duties taken over one by one, by the school, the church, the clinic, the nursery, and social agencies of the neighborhood. While parent-teacher associations have welcomed her to the school, and nursery staffs have instructed her in their methods of child management, they have reduced the educational function of the home to a minimum, even taking over, in some cases, such primary duties of nurture as the provision of

2. William A. Alcott, *The Young Housekeeper* (4th ed. Boston, George W. Light, 1839), p. 26.

3. See especially *The Mother's Journal and Family Visitant* (Utica, New York and Philadelphia), Vols. VIII–XXV, 1843–60; and *The Mother's Magazine and Family Circle* (Utica and New York, S. Whittelsey), Vols. I–XIV, 1833–46.

food and of rest. While the church and the Sunday school have stressed the importance of daily growth of children in spiritual concerns, they have tended to place the guidance of this growth largely in the hands of the Sabbath school teacher or young people's leader, appealing to mothers for aid in other channels of adult enterprise. While the clinics and health centers have done much to educate mothers with respect to the physical needs of children, they have tended to foster maternal dependence upon agencies outside the home for skilful ministration to these needs. Meanwhile, the great machinery of the press and radio has conditioned the mother to think of herself, principally, not as the guardian and guide of the rising generation, but as a good consumer.

There is evidence, however, that this state of affairs is changing. Public interest in parental roles and responsibilities is increasing. Bolstering this interest is a growing awareness on the part of teachers, sociologists, psychologists, and pediatricians of the unique part which the home and early relationships in the home play in the adjustment of the growing individual. Some students of personality [4] even go so far as to say that the stabilizing process, which can be effected only by love and intelligent guidance provided in early childhood within the family circle, may be the only cure for hostile, aggressive, destructive conduct which imperils the future of society and of the civilized world.

It is helpful, therefore, to look back to the time in our history when the family was considered a bulwark of democracy and when mothers were regarded as custodians of morals, capable of pulling society up by its "bootie" straps. An excursion of this sort into the past does not purport to yield specific answers to today's complex problems, but it does provide a useful historical perspective on the task which confronts parents in each new generation.

A. L. K.

Matinicus, Maine, 1946

4. See especially Lawrence K. Frank, "The Fundamental Needs of the Child," *Mental Hygiene*, 22:372, July, 1938.

ACKNOWLEDGMENTS

The study on which this book is based was a dissertation presented to the faculty of the Graduate School of Yale University in candidacy for the degree of Doctor of Philosophy. For sustained interest and guidance in every stage of this work I am warmly grateful to Professors Bessie Lee Gambrill and John S. Brubacher of the Department of Education at Yale. As teachers and friends over a period of years they have contributed immeasurably to my thinking and have passed along to me their own zest for educational exploration. To Professor Ralph H. Gabriel of the Department of History, I wish to express appreciation for counsel and suggestions generously accorded, and for the inspiration of his lectures on "American Thought and Civilization." My sincere thanks go also to the reference librarians and others on the staff of the Sterling Library at Yale for their many courtesies, and for the privileges granted to me in the use of library facilities.

I am particularly indebted to Dean Luther A. Weigle of the Yale University Divinity School for his encouragement and support in the publication of this volume. His sponsorship, and the assistance rendered by the Samuel B. Sneath Memorial Publication Fund, made the publication possible.

For permission to quote from the sources indicated I wish to thank the following:

George Allen & Unwin Ltd. (London) : Max Weber, *The Protestant Ethic.*

Citadel Press: V. F. Calverton and S. D. Schmalhausen, editors, *The New Generation.*

Arthur H. Clark Company: Arthur W. Calhoun, *A Social History of the American Family,* Vol. II.

D. Appleton–Century Company, Inc.: E. Douglas Branch, *The Sentimental Years;* Gilbert H. Barnes, *The Antislavery Impulse;* Edwin G. Boring, *A History of Experimental Psychology.*

E. P. Dutton & Co., Inc.: Van Wyck Brooks, *The Flowering of New England.*

Emerson Books, Inc.: Ernest R. Groves, *The American Woman.*

Charles Fred Heartman: George Livermore, *The Origin, History and Character of the New England Primer.*

Harcourt, Brace & Co.: Vernon L. Parrington, *Main Currents in American Thought,* Vol. II.

Little, Brown & Co.: Odell Shepard, *The Journals of Bronson Alcott.*

Liveright Publishing Corporation: Lorine Pruette, "Why Women Fail," in *Woman's Coming of Age,* edited by S. D. Schmalhausen and V. F. Calverton.

The Macmillan Company: Carl R. Fish, *The Rise of the Common Man;* Willystine Goodsell, *A History of Marriage and the Family;* Una B. Sait, *New Horizons for the Family.*

New England Quarterly: Bertha Stearns, "New England Magazines for Ladies," in *New England Quarterly,* III, October, 1930.

Science Press Printing Company: Emma L. Bolzau, *Almira Hart Lincoln Phelps.*

Yale University Press: Sandford Fleming, *Children and Puritanism.*

CONTENTS

ILLUSTRATIONS

PART ONE

BACKGROUNDS: MOTHERS AND YOUNG CHILDREN
IN MIDNINETEENTH CENTURY NEW ENGLAND

THE MOTHER'S ROLE IN
CHILDHOOD EDUCATION

CHAPTER I

CULTURAL SETTING

LITHOGRAPHS and engravings of the ideal family of the midnineteenth century reflect none of the bustling activity and mental turmoil of the period. The mother is usually depicted sitting peacefully in one corner of an unpretentious living room, sewing or attending to several young children who cluster around her. The father, seated in the other corner, reads aloud to the family group or is engaged in instruction of an older child. S. G. Goodrich, in setting the keynote for his text, *Fireside Education,* makes use of a picture which has significant symbolism. The mother is shown placing the arms of her small son around the neck of his little sister, while the father, standing by a window, textbook in hand, points out the heavenly bodies to an older child. The caption beneath reads: "The mother sways the dominion of the heart, the father that of the intellect." [1]

More significant still is the symbolism of a picture in which an entire family, dressed in outdoor garb, stands on the veranda of their home, gazing upon a rainbow which extends from one corner of the horizon to the other.[2] There is no glint in the father's eye for the pot of gold, nothing but hope in the eyes of all, hope for the glorious future which they, an ideal family, may help to achieve for their country.

Certain trends of the period are discernible through the rosy haze of these wishful pictures—the drive toward a "united family" ideal; toward self-culture in the form of family reading; toward fresh emphasis on home education of children, and the respective functions of parents; toward regard for the needs of individual family members; and, finally, toward "millennialism," that useful concept which served as a magnifying glass for nineteenth century ideals.

The actual conditions which gave rise to these stresses in New England society were far from ideal, however. To begin with,

1. See illustration p. 150.
2. *Mother's and Young Lady's Annual* (Boston, Cyrus Stone, 1853), p. 18.

family unity had, since the beginning of the century, been exposed to the disruptive influences of increased urbanization and industrialization. Small towns became cities overnight and bustling business enterprise claimed the full attention of fathers who, under the old rural economy, would have spent much time with their families. The Reverend John S. C. Abbott wrote in 1842, "Paternal neglect is at the present time one of the most abundant sources of domestic sorrow. The father . . . eager in the pursuit of business, toils early and late, and finds no time to fulfill . . . duties to his children. . . ."[3] These conditions placed new responsibilities on mothers and also brought the hurry and tension of the outside world into the family circle. Thus we read:

How often has the faithful wife to conceal her disappointment . . . while, after toiling to render *the only hours of the day* that bring her husband and the little ones . . . together—the occasion of happy domestic enjoyment, of mutual improvement, and of a father's instructions and discipline—she finds him full of a restless impatience to have the meal ready even before the appointed time; hurrying through it himself in silence, or if speaking, using only the necessary household words. . . .[4]

This state of affairs is noted by Calhoun[5] as a typical evil of the day. Together with the growing emphasis on formality and "gentility" in family life, it tended to erect barriers between wives and husbands, between fathers and children. Fathers were said to interfere in family affairs with only "a brief and occasional word of authority, or a surly lamentation over . . . intolerable expensiveness,"[6] and mothers to teach their children "to be quiet and still"[7] in their father's presence. Calhoun quotes a European commentator as saying that mothers, while they were passionately devoted to their offspring, maintained for their husbands " 'a sort of half distant respect.' "[8]

3. John S. C. Abbott, "Paternal Neglect," *Parent's Magazine*, 2:148, March, 1842.
4. "The Father," *Parent's Magazine*, 2:174, April, 1842.
5. Arthur W. Calhoun, *A Social History of the American Family* (Cleveland, Arthur H. Clark Company, 1918), II, 131.
6. President Wayland, "Paternal Duty," *Mother's Assistant*, 12:110, May, 1848.
7. John S. C. Abbott, *The Mother at Home* (2d ed. Boston, Crocker & Brewster, 1833), p. 76.
8. Calhoun, *op. cit.*, p. 133.

Attendant on this evil were those of the effects of material wealth on the unity of the family. Except for a brief period of depression in the 'thirties, national prosperity increased by leaps and bounds, and with it came a host of "fashionable follies." Many families strove to acquire "gentility" and a place in society. Children were sent to school at a tender age to be out of the way,[9] or were turned over to hirelings while mothers devoted their time to a round of daily calls and evening parties. Mrs. Graves, writing in 1843, claimed that this fashionable class had an extensive influence "in our cities, towns, and villages, and even in the green retreats of our rural abodes,"[10] and that the evil was of especially startling magnitude in its effect upon *"wives and mothers*—beings possessing fearful responsibilities."[11] As the concept of feminine delicacy took hold, many considered it unseemly for young women to spend their time in the nursery, this work being suitable only "for the poor and the plebeian."[12]

It should be noted at this point, however, that mothers of the lower middle classes, in their attempts to ape the fashionable rich, were thrown into closer contact with their children as a result of their need to economize. Dispensing with servants, they observed "the strictest economy in their internal regulations" to keep up "an outward show before the world."[13] This of course took its toll upon family nerves and health and raised new problems of family management for the overworked mothers. Theodore Sedgwick, New England commentator, whose views were reprinted in *The Family Magazine* of 1837, stated that this class, which he described as the *"fashionable, expensive poor"* embraced in the United States "a larger proportion of the people than in any other country whatever."[14]

Catherine Beecher referred to the "mingling of all grades of wealth, intellect and education" even in the "stationary portions of the community." Movement and change and the flow of wealth

9. Lydia H. Sigourney, *Letters to Mothers* (Hartford, Hudson & Skinner, 1838), p. 112.

10. Mrs. A. J. Graves, *Woman in America* (New York, Harper & Bros., 1843), p. 94.

11. *Ibid.*, p. 95.

12. "The Good Dinner," *Ladies' Magazine*, 6:38, January, 1833.

13. Graves, *op. cit.*, p. 37.

14. Theodore Sedgwick, "Poverty of the Manufacturing Class," *The Family Magazine*, 5:255, December, 1837, quoted from Theodore Sedgwick, *Public and Private Economy* (New York, Harper & Bros., 1836), Part I, p. 114.

were affecting New England as well as the frontier, with the result that there was, among people of humble means, "a constant temptation presented to imitate the customs and to strive for the enjoyments" [15] of those who possessed larger wealth.

Intemperance began to be recognized as a disruptive influence in the family, operating at all social levels. It was during this period that T. S. Arthur wrote his *Ten Nights in a Bar Room*, and much of the contemporary fiction was weighted with sad tales of the broken family brought to disgrace by a drunken father or son. Poor widows of inebriates were driven with their children to factory labor in order to subsist.[16] At the other end of the social scale, the indulged and intemperate newly rich evaded home responsibilities by living in hotels [17] and attending a round of social events.

Poor health and a high mortality rate struck heavily at the roots of the family. Although these will be dealt with in a later chapter, it is well to note here a New England woman's comment on the health question:

. . . why are we, as a general rule, thinner, smaller, paler, more nervous, head-achy and dyspeptic, than the women of the olden time . . . ?

The increase of luxury, which tempts to indulgence, while it devolves all active labor upon the servants—the high and enervating temperature at which we keep our houses during the cold months . . . the weakness with which we yield to the prejudice against active out-of-door sports and exercises for girls,—these may be some of the causes. . . .[18]

One might suppose that this applied only to the indolent upper-class woman, but Bunn claimed that dyspepsia was "the besetting malady of the entire country, in both sexes," stating that a woman was set down as "old at twenty-seven" and a man as old at forty.[19] A contributor to the 1842 *Parent's Magazine* estimated the number of female deaths as about one in thirty-six annually in cities,

15. Catherine E. Beecher, *A Treatise on Domestic Economy* (Revised ed. Boston, Thomas H. Webb & Co., 1842) p. 40.

16. Theodore Sedgwick, *op. cit.*, pp. 254–55.

17. Sigourney, *op. cit.*, p. 175.

18. "Health," editorial, *Mother's Assistant*, 1853, p. 174.

19. Alfred Bunn, *Old England and New England* (London, R. Bentley; Philadelphia, reprinted by A. Hart, 1853), p. 266.

and one in seventy-five in the country.[20] An astonishingly high mortality rate of infants and young children may be assumed from the frequent reference to death in religious and poetic writings [21] on mothers and children, and confirmed by an examination of contemporary medical treatises and the mortality statistics for the midcentury period in the New England States.[22]

While family unity was being disrupted by these manifold evils, family government was weakened by the shortcomings of young wives who, having rushed prematurely into marriage, found themselves ill prepared for household responsibilities and regarded their children either as burdens to be turned over, if possible, to domestics, or as "pretty playthings" to be shown off to the "best advantage." [23]

It is necessary, before going further, to differentiate between the faded mother of forty with a large family, and the young married woman of sixteen or seventeen, since their conditions were vastly different during this period. With the rapid increase of wealth, it was natural that mothers of growing daughters should wish to spare them the hard life of household toil and of self-abnegation which had been their own lot. An essay written in Bangor, Maine, deplores as a serious fault of the times that "the daughters of our land resemble too closely their sister 'lilies of the field,' " [24] while their mothers are literally servants to them. Mackay claimed that society was under the absolute sway of young ladies in their teens, and that family efforts were bent toward providing a fashionable milieu from which they might be married in style.[25]

20. Willis G. Clark, "Education of Young Ladies," *Parent's Magazine*, 2:149, March, 1842.

21. See especially, *Mother's Assistant*, 1846–53, *passim*. The 1851 volume, for example, contains such titles as "To My Mother in Heaven," "The Infant in Heaven," and "The Angel and the Child."

22. See especially, William A. Alcott, *The Home Book of Life and Health* (Boston, Phillips Sampson & Co., 1856), p. 17; Catherine E. Beecher, *Letters to the People on Health and Happiness* (New York, Harper & Bros., 1855), pp. 121–33; and J. D. B. DeBow, *Mortality Statistics of the Seventh Census of the U. S., 1850*.

23. "Responsibility of the Mother," *Parent's Magazine*, 1:155, March, 1841.

24. Mary A. Bright, "How Children May Make Their Parents Happy," *Mother's Assistant*, 9:126, December, 1846.

25. Alexander Mackay, *The Western World, or Travels in the U. S. in 1846–47*. (Philadelphia, Lea & Blanchard, 1849), I, 134–35.

In 1830 the *Ladies' Magazine* reprinted an article describing the superficial education of young women which enabled them to " 'play, sing, dress, glide down the dance, and get a husband, but not to be qualified to render his home quiet, well ordered and happy.' " [26] The household chores which had formerly been their portion were turned over to servants, or, in less affluent homes, to the overburdened mother. One might assume that this ambition existed only in cities, but mention is made of the fond father who, coming in from the plow, found that his " 'ruined favorites' " refused to serve him.[27]

Much of the material with which this study is concerned was addressed to young women who, trained to be delicate ladies, found themselves after a year or so of marriage overwhelmed by the change in their condition and the family problems which they were badly equipped to solve. According to Mackay, many of these younger matrons who had once been the center of attraction disappeared altogether from the social scene, to reappear years later with faded cheeks to introduce their own daughters.[28] Early marriage and large families were the rule, and it is small wonder that mothers wished their daughters " 'to enjoy life while young,' " for " 'they would have to work hard enough when they should come to have families of their own.' " [29]

The servant problem cannot be overestimated as an aggravating factor during this period. Many of the better class of American "helps" who had assisted in the skilful management of New England households before the increase of industrialization, were drawn into factory work, being supplanted by a lower type of domestic recruited frequently from the new, unskilled immigrant population. This had serious results for family felicity. Irresponsible young mothers were confronted with new problems of discipline, not only with children, as a result of their mismanagement at the hands of hirelings, but with the hirelings themselves, who were impudent and highhanded. "Hence," wrote Mrs. Graves,

26. "Fashionable Follies" (reprint from *Western Monthly Review*, 1830), *Ladies' Magazine*, 3:182, April, 1830.

27. *Ibid.*, p. 184. This comment, coming as it does from a Cincinnati periodical, cannot be taken as being necessarily applicable to New England, but the editorial preface accompanying its appearance in the *Ladies' Magazine* hints at similar follies to be checked in New England. See *ibid.*, p. 181.

28. Mackay, *op. cit.*, I, 137.

29. Bright, "How Children May Make Their Parents Happy," *Mother's Assistant*, 9:127, December, 1846. See also Graves, *op. cit.*, p. 40.

"we find many a mistress of a family who is almost afraid to reprove even where reproof is necessary . . . lest she should lose a servant whose aid is valuable to her. . . ." [30] This state of affairs is likewise noted by Catherine Beecher, who devoted one chapter in her treatise on *Domestic Economy* to the "care of domestics." [31]

Another factor in the weakening of family government was the growing indifference with which worldly parents regarded their religious duties. Old family observances began to drop out —grace at meals, daily Bible reading, and morning and evening prayers, formerly conducted by the father of the family. Miss Goodsell attributes this break from the old Calvinistic practices to the "spread of tolerance and knowledge through public education," to the progress of science, and to the growth of machine industry, with its emphasis on worldly interests and the amassing of wealth. [32] These factors, however, are only partially responsible for changes in religious attitudes during the nineteenth century. The many aspects of these changes will come out in the chapters to follow. Meanwhile it is sufficient to note that family life was invaded by a new laxity of government which had been impossible in the older church-centered society. Religious education of the young, once supervised by the father of the family, became the function of the Sabbath school or of the mother, who, if engrossed in the pursuit of "fashionable folly," was apt to neglect her duties.

This will perhaps suffice to give a background for the problems of family life. It is difficult to determine how many of these social evils penetrated to the small towns and villages of New England. Judging from the idyllic accounts of such writers as Lucy Larcom, [33] Harriet Beecher Stowe, [34] and Mrs. Susan Lesley, [35] home life in the solid, substantial families of the rural section went on,

30. Graves, *op. cit.*, p. 73.

31. Beecher, *A Treatise on Domestic Economy*, chap. xviii. See also Humphrey, *Domestic Education*, p. 63.

32. From Willystine Goodsell, *A History of Marriage and the Family* (New York, Macmillan Company, 1934), p. 464. By permission of the Macmillan Company, publishers.

33. Lucy Larcom, *A New England Girlhood* (Boston, Houghton Mifflin & Co., 1889), *passim*.

34. Harriet B. Stowe, *Oldtown Folks* (Boston, Fields, Osgood & Co., 1869), *passim*. While this is fiction, it is also judged to be semi-autobiographical and authentic in background detail.

35. Susan I. Lesley, *Recollections of My Mother* (Boston, Houghton Mifflin & Co., 1899), pp. 416–20.

externally at least, in its usual peaceful fashion during this hectic period of social change. Mothers, while released from the drudgery of spinning and weaving, were taken up with large families and with the many homely chores of country life. One has only to examine Mrs. Child's *Frugal Housewife*,[36] widely sold cookbook of the 1830's, to discover what were the multifarious duties of the good housekeeper of the period. Children were frequently cared for by older brothers and sisters, or by relatives and domestics, but received a generous share of firm parental guidance. The father was recognized as head of the family and usually took charge of family prayers and religious instruction. Young girls, not yet lured by the fashionable follies of city cousins, learned to cook and sew and care for children. In conservative homes, the pale and delicate heroine of current novels had not yet supplanted those wholesome English models of feminine deportment set forth by Hannah More and Mrs. Chapone. Harriet Martineau, critical commentator on American life, wrote, after visiting a small town in Massachusetts, "Never may its peace and security be invaded by those social abuses which are more hateful than foreign spies. . . ."[37]

Still, it is not possible to draw a sharp line between the old and new orders in New England society. Looking beneath the surface, one sees at least three great forces operating on the mental temper of rural New England. These were: (1) the activities of the clergy; (2) the spread of ideas via the press and travel; and (3) the new zeal for learning.

New England ministers had, since the early part of the century, been caught up in that revolution of thought which marked the transition from eighteenth century rationalism, which conceived of human nature as evil, to the nineteenth century flood of romanticism, which grew stronger as the democratic movement strengthened "with its humanitarian emphasis on the potential excellence of man and the equality of human rights."[38] The orthodox clergy had at first resisted every aspect of the new liberalism, which they identified with the Unitarian movement. Vehemently reaffirming their Calvinistic faith, they denounced

36. Lydia M. Child, *The American Frugal Housewife* (Boston, American Stationers' Company, 1836).

37. Harriet Martineau, *Society in America* (London, Saunders & Otley, 1837), I, 270.

38. Vernon L. Parrington, *Main Currents in American Thought* (New York, Harcourt Brace & Co., 1927), II, 271.

the "Boston religion" and injected new life into their own dusty creeds. But the new ideas had too much popular appeal for the rising generation of the young republic to withstand. The eloquent sermons of Dr. Channing were spread far and wide, carrying their protest against "a pietistic rigor in private life, against interminable prayers and ministerial cant," and their religious justification "for the social conscience—'good works,' humanitarianism, benevolence; . . ." [39] By 1836, most of the Congregational churches in the cities of New England had, according to Branch, "voted Calvinism out and Unitarianism in." [40]

It is important for this study to understand the effects of this revolution upon the small town clergymen of New England. Although many of them retained their orthodoxy so far as outward observances went, their doctrine and beliefs had undergone significant changes. The leaven of liberalism and tolerance had worked in them to produce a new zeal for social welfare and improvement. Doctrinal differences were not forgotten, but they were supplanted by the goals which all clergymen had in common, those of communicating their visions of "a new heaven and a new earth," and of indicting the social evils of a "Yankee world given over to materialism." [41] This was the ethical spirit of the Puritan faith, reawakened after two hundred years, and its most fertile seedbed was the New England village. Mrs. Stowe spoke of the small town clergyman as the intellectual center of his own district, attributing to him the stimulus which was later to come through a thousand other channels to people remote from the currents of social change.[42] If we are to accept her *Oldtown Folks* as semi-autobiographical, we may conclude that her own inspiration as a social reformer grew through contact with such personalities as that of Mr. Avery, minister of Cloudland.

Many activities of the clergy involved active participation by families. Religious revivals,[43] occurring periodically, featured the conversions by thousands of women and children. The Sabbath school was spreading rapidly, and this served the double purpose of redefining the goals of religious education and of focusing at-

39. E. Douglas Branch, *The Sentimental Years, 1836–60* (New York, D. Appleton–Century Company, Inc., 1934), p. 326.

40. *Loc. cit.*

41. Parrington, *op. cit.*, p. 385.

42. Stowe, *op. cit.*, p. 453.

43. Sandford Fleming, *Children and Puritanism* (New Haven, Yale University Press, 1933), p. 16, and *passim.*

tention on children. Missionary work and benevolent enterprises were undertaken which put many demands upon the women of the community. Harriet Martineau commented upon the way in which religion was made an occupation of the women, saying, "I was perpetually struck with this when I saw women braving hurricane, frost, and snow, to flit from preaching to preaching; and laying out the whole day among visits for prayer and religious excitement, among the poor and the sick." [44]

The spread of ideas through the press and travel cannot be underestimated as an influence in the broadening of the rural mind during the midcentury period. It is true that the press made slow progress in many of the conservative homes of the inland regions. Van Wyck Brooks states that the books read in such homes were of a somber, religious nature, except for those of Sir Walter Scott and Maria Edgeworth, which were respected for their moral tone.[45] There is evidence, however, that the reading of periodicals of both a religious and secular nature increased widely even in these regions during the 1830–60 period. Said Jacob Abbott, writing in 1835, "You can hardly find a dwelling in New England, be it a framed house or a log cabin, in which some periodical print is not taken." [46] Mrs. Lesley, in describing the daily schedule in the Lyman household, stated that both her parents settled down regularly after breakfast to the reading and discussion of current printed matter.[47] Mackay was struck, on his American travels, by the "extraordinary number" of newspapers. Towns numbering two thousand inhabitants had several daily papers, and many families in rural sections were not contented with one "but must have two or more, adding some metropolitan paper to the one or two local papers to which they subscribe." [48] There can be no doubt that this wide sale of periodical literature affected general book sales and the spread of literary culture in all sections of New England. Farmers and business men, who bought their almanacs and daily sheets for the advertisements and current news, were exposed also to more solid matter of social or religious import, as anyone may discover who

44. Harriet Martineau, *op. cit.*, III, 268.

45. Van Wyck Brooks, *The Flowering of New England* (New York, E. P. Dutton & Co., 1940), p. 56.

46. Jacob Abbott, *New England and Her Institutions* (Boston, John Allen & Co., 1835), p. 25.

47. Lesley, *op. cit.*, p. 417.

48. Mackay, *op. cit.*, II, 239.

dips into almanacs and daily papers of the midnineteenth century. The book trade increased and libraries increased in all New England towns. Bunn observed that there was scarcely a village where there was not either a library or some institute for the formation of a library.[49]

The spread of ideas by travel affected New England villages in two ways. The seaboard towns were influenced by tidings brought to them from the great outside world. Maritime commerce had widened their horizons and broadened their mental outlook. Brooks speaks of the "buffer generation" who grew up during the mid-century period, lawyers, ministers, scholars and seamen who, while preserving the "faith in discipline and standards that had marked the older culture . . . yet . . . encouraged in their sons and daughters a free mind, a knowledge of mundane things, the study of languages, music, drawing, dancing, an education of the eye and ear which, from the point of view of the inland regions, savoured of the frankest paganism." [50]

Inland towns, while sheltered from these influences, were, nevertheless, with the improvement of the railway and perfecting of other means of transportation, laid open to invasion by the travel of merchants and their families who, it is said, often "made tours across New England, to Stafford Springs, through the Berkshire hills, . . . perhaps on their way to Niagara or Trenton Falls," visiting country relatives en route and bringing with them new ideas and new standards of living.[51]

To suggest that the zeal for learning and for self-improvement came to rural regions by these same channels of communication would be to postulate the carrying of coals to Newcastle. The love of learning which made Boston the intellectual hub of the universe during the midcentury had its roots deep in the soil of the New England villages, where, from Colonial days onward, the schoolhouse had been second in importance only to the church. But the new channels of communication helped to give a social direction to the thinking of the rural people during this period of intellectual awakening. Thought once turned inward on the problems of individual salvation now turned outward to the pressing social problems of a growing democracy.

49. Bunn, *op. cit.*, p. 29.
50. Brooks, *op. cit.*, p. 52.
51. *Ibid.*, p. 56. By permission of E. P. Dutton & Co., Inc., publishers; copyright, 1936.

Lectures and lyceums exerted a powerful educational influence, even in small villages, where, lacking funds to erect a hall, the inhabitants made use of the churches and schools for this purpose. Bunn was impressed by the activity "in remote and comparatively insignificant places." Thus, he wrote, " 'Going to lecture,' is the next important duty to 'going to church'; and he who seeks to impart information must be well read (or, as they more mercantilely express it, well 'posted up') in what he talks about, or he will find many amongst his hearers who can correct him, and put him to rights." [52] He further commented on the solid content of the lyceums, which were called into existence during the midcentury "by the doctrines which religion and learning respectively inculcate." [53]

The rise of the common school throughout New England is a story in itself. It is important to note here the way in which this movement contributed to the spread of learning in rural families. The famous McGuffey readers, which have reached the hundred million mark [54] in publication, were written during this period and circulated by the hundreds of thousands. Noah Webster's *American Spelling Book,* and the numerous texts of "Peter Parley" [S. G. Goodrich] also found their way into remote homes to take their place on the family reading shelf, next to the Bible and heavy religious texts. This new secular influence served to whet public interest in American publications and in the cause of common education. When Horace Mann and Henry Barnard began their campaigns for free schools, they found staunch supporters in the rural areas. From small towns in New England came, during the midcentury years, the famous pioneers of higher education for women, Mary Lyon, Catherine Beecher, Emma Willard, and Almira Phelps.

There is evidence that school attendance was almost universal. Harriet Martineau, writing in 1837, remarked that "The provision of schools is so adequate, that any citizen who sees a child at play during school-hours may ask 'Why are you not at school?' and, unless a good reason be given, may take him to the schoolhouse of the district." [55] Jacob Abbott, in describing a typical farm

52. Bunn, *Old England and New England,* p. 30.

53. *Ibid.,* p. 34.

54. "William H. McGuffey," *American Authors, 1600–1900* (New York, The H. W. Wilson Company, 1938), pp. 495–96.

55. Martineau, *op. cit.,* III, 163.

family of the period, stated that an evening visitor would find
the children, one and all, seated at their lessons, and the father
likewise engaged in reading.[56]

So much, then, for the avenues of innovation in rural New England. It was through these agencies, the church, the press, and
popular education, that the more or less "stable" element of society was drawn into the intellectual and social ferment of the
period. Thus, the social problems of family life in urban and
semi-urban society became part of the social consciousness of the
public at large. A recognition of this diffusion of awareness is
essential to an understanding of the body of literature with which
this study is concerned. Answers to domestic problems came not
only from city lectures, lyceums, books, and periodicals, but from
thinkers and writers in country byways where there was leisure
and detachment from which to view social problems. Every social
development of this renaissance period had its leaders who came
from quiet towns and villages, bringing with them a body of wise
tradition with which to temper the materialism or the arch
romanticism of the new urban generation.

To give a fair impression of New England's mental climate during this period of fervent awakening, it is necessary to glance
for a moment beyond the social scene and its problems to that
movement which has come to be looked upon as New England's
peculiar contribution to midnineteenth century American thought.

It was transcendentalism, in its Americanized version, which
gave newness and creativeness to reforms of the period. Transcendentalism was, as Mason Wade points out, "the spirit of a
new age in a new country," [57] though it had its origins in German
idealism, and stemmed from many ancient traditions.

The essence of the new spirit was its faith and confidence in
man as the child of God, in man possessing the power of daily rebirth, and in man called to a life of high purpose by the voice of
God within him.[58] In emphasizing the godlike in man, this doctrine went beyond the faith of the Enlightenment and beyond
the practical zeal of liberal Unitarianism. It clothed in romanticism three tenets of the democratic faith, concepts already dom-
inant in the more restrained thought of New England as a whole,

56. Abbott, *op. cit.*, p. 201.

57. Mason Wade, *Margaret Fuller, Whetstone of Genius* (New York,
Viking Press, 1940), p. 63.

58. Parrington, *op. cit.*, II, 382.

namely, the concept of the free individual,[59] of the perfectible individual, and of the responsible individual. Consequently, despite the fact that transcendentalism won only a relatively small body of converts in its own time, it had tremendous influence upon the formulation of the democratic credo which emerged during this period, giving it a romantic and idealistic superstructure which it has never since entirely lost.

The connection between transcendentalism and the domestic concerns of mothers and young children in midcentury New England is, while indirect, of considerable significance. The new faith embraced a doctrine of "plain living and high thinking" which highlighted many of the intimate details of domestic life. Dress and food reforms, as we shall see in a later chapter of this study, were at least partially inspired by this doctrine. Daily occupations were influenced by idealistic emphasis upon the world of nature and communion with God in nature. And finally, those "apostles of the newness" who sought to influence their generation were, many of them, active in educational improvements of the period, contributing directly or indirectly to a philosophy of domestic education.

59. Ralph H. Gabriel, *The Course of American Democratic Thought* (New York, Ronald Press Company, 1940), p. 19. Professor Gabriel mentions three doctrines of the democratic faith, the concept of the fundamental law, of the free individual, and of the "mission of America."

CHAPTER II

GROWING RECOGNITION OF THE SOCIAL IMPORTANCE OF MOTHERS AND YOUNG CHILDREN

TO understand how recognition of the social importance of mothers and young children grew during this period, it is necessary, first of all, to consider some of the philosophical, scientific, and social concepts which influenced their status from the early part of the century.

In his *Social History of the American Family*, Calhoun treats of the "emancipation" of childhood, while he uses the milder term "emergence" with respect to women of the midcentury period. To determine which came first would be difficult, but the qualifying descriptive terms and the order of Calhoun's chapters would seem to suggest that a public recognition of the child as a socially significant being somewhat antedated that of the woman or mother.[1]

In the realm of philosophical thought, at least, speculation on child nature and destiny was exerting a leavening influence upon popular concepts of childhood several decades before the midcentury period.

The *Christian Disciple*, accepted religious publication in New England, had found occasion in its second volume, 1814, to set forth a "Dissertation on the Sinfulness of Infants," affixing to the article this apology from the editor:

The preceding dissertation has been admitted, from a conviction that the subject is interesting to all; and that it is one which has occasioned much anxiety to many pious christians, and one on which good people are divided in opinion; and from a hope that a candid discussion may be a means of affording light and promoting kind affections.[2]

1. Calhoun, *Social History of the American Family*, Vol. II, chaps. iii and v.

2. "Dissertation on the Sinfulness of Infants," *Christian Disciple*, 2:249, August, 1814.

Its plea was for a new and clement attitude toward child nature. "I ask . . . if children were demons, fit for hell, would God have given them that attractive sweetness, that mild beauty which renders them the most interesting objects on earth, and which compels us to shrink with horror from the thought of their everlasting ruin?" [3] This was one of the points on which the clergy had taken issue since the beginning of the century. Lyman Beecher, despite his opposition to the new liberalism, had felt it necessary to deny that Calvinists teach infant damnation.[4] Theodore Parker, preaching against this as well as the doctrines of infinite wrath and total depravity, held these views as particularly repugnant to women, stating that "celibate priests, who never knew marriage, or what paternity was, who thought woman was a 'pollution' . . . invented these ghastly doctrines." [5]

Those who reacted most violently to the austerity of the older views adopted an extravagant romanticism in their definition of child nature. They embraced the concept of childhood as a state of purity and innocence "which speaks to us of heaven; which tells us of those pure angelic beings which surround the throne of God, untouched by sin, untainted by the breath of corruption." [6] Mothers mourning infant death were assured of everlasting joy and bliss for their little immortal beings. Poems and lithographs dealt with sentimental themes such as "The Little Hand," [7] "The Little Foot," [8] and "The First Prayer," "The First Ride," "Peek-a-boo," and "Little Emmie." [9] In its worst extreme this view of childhood was to produce the spoiled and pampered pets of the age, the little overdressed and overindulged dolls of urban society, fed on sweetmeats and smothered with the fond caresses of doting parents.

At its best, however, the romantic approach, despite its haziness and vapidity, made one important advance for the cause of

3. *Ibid.*, p. 248.

4. Calhoun, *op. cit.*, II, 57.

5. Branch, *The Sentimental Years*, p. 317.

6. "A Sketch from Life," *Ladies' Magazine*, 6:258, June, 1833.

7. Lydia Sigourney, "The Little Hand," *Parent's Magazine*, 1:95, December, 1840.

8. Miss H. F. Gould, "The Little Foot," *Parent's Magazine*, 1:71, December, 1840.

9. Arnold Gesell, *The Guidance of Mental Growth in Infant and Child* (New York, Macmillan Company, 1930), p. 48. Gesell lists here other generic portraits and prints of children of the period.

the child; it focused attention on childhood as such, and helped to remove the "miniature adult" from the scene. By 1841 children were being recognized as unique individuals. Quoting a contributor to the *Parent's Magazine:* "Young children remember things but a moment. . . . Their impressions are like the little white clouds that flit over the summer landscape. . . . They like to be free as the fawns that play upon the mountains . . ." but "to be all day under marching orders . . . outrages every feeling of childhood." [10] This was the sort of sentiment which was to make easy the transition to more scientific attitudes regarding child nature.

Perhaps the most typical New England approach to concepts of child nature during the midcentury years was that which grew out of a compromise between the orthodox view of the church and that of the romantic liberals. This compromise stemmed, strangely enough, from the empiricism of Locke in combination with its direct antithesis, nineteenth century "millennialism." Going back again to the *Christian Disciple* of 1814, we read, "Human beings come into the world in a state of total ignorance. They have not one idea of God or duty, of virtue or vice, of truth or error. . . . In a state of childhood they are necessarily dependent on their parents and others around them for the instructions they receive." [11] These implications of the Lockian philosophy penetrating slowly into the popular consciousness were forceful arguments against infant sinfulness, even for the orthodox diehards. If Locke's *tabula rasa* was to be accepted, then children could not be held responsible as moral agents until impressions either for good or for evil were imprinted on their minds.

For a time theologians had been content to keep the soul and the senses safely apart, so that it was entirely possible for them to accept the *tabula rasa* theory of the mind while thinking of the soul and its salvation, or unregeneracy, as a separate process. The nineteenth century challenged this separation by exalting man to a new position in relation to the Godhead.[12] The Unitarian teaching had made Christ the link between the human and the divine, thereby vesting man with a new dignity.[13] Man's body with its

10. H. Rood, "The Government of Children," *Parent's Magazine*, 1:106, January, 1841.

11. "On the Influence of Education as a Source of Error," *Christian Disciple*, 2:264, September, 1814.

12. Branch, *op. cit.*, p. 331.

13. *Loc. cit.*

432172

mind, its senses, its faculties became, instead of a base hindrance to him, an instrument capable of moral use, fit indeed to work to the glory of God. Carried to one extreme, this exaltation of man led, in the midcentury, to perfectionist manifestations such as "Millennarianism" [14] and other movements featuring the establishment of heaven on earth. Many conservatives, on the other hand, went on declaring, far into the century, the total depravity of man and his native bent toward evil.

The middle ground, or compromise, is seen in the literature of the semi-orthodox, and shows how singularly able was the shrewd New Englander to keep one foot in hell and the other in heaven. Briefly, his solution was this: the child is born with a blank mind and is a potential inheritor of heaven or of hell. He is not a moral agent, but he fast becomes one, and the parent is supremely responsible for imprinting pure images on the waxen tablet of his mind. The line between mind and soul is thinly drawn. Mrs. Sigourney, writing in 1838, exclaimed, "The soul, the soul of the babe, whose life is nourished by our own! Every trace we grave upon it, will stand forth at the judgment. . . ." [15] In the same volume she speaks of the waxen state of children's minds.[16]

Perfectionist hope of heaven is strangely linked with the Calvinistic fear of unregeneracy. Thus, in writing to mothers, the same author exclaimed, ". . . to be the guide of a spirit which can never die, to make the first indelible impressions on what may be a companion of seraphs, and live with an unbounded capacity for bliss or woe, when these poor skies under which it was born, shall have vanished like a vision" [17] is an honor for which every mother may hope, but she also warns ". . . if there is, in your church-yard, one grave shorter than your child, hasten to instruct him in religion." [18]

Reverend Heman Humphrey, sober educator and Congregational divine of the period, showed the same tendency to add a dash of bitters to celestial hopes. He warned, ". . . however it might have been with our children . . . had sin never entered the world, we know how it is now. 'They are prone to evil, as the sparks fly upward,' " [19] and further, addressing the liberals, "We

14. Branch, *op. cit.*, p. 337.
15. Sigourney, *Letters to Mothers*, p. viii.
16. *Ibid.*, p. 21.
17. *Ibid.*, pp. 24–25.
18. *Ibid.*, p. 34.
19. Humphrey, *Domestic Education*, pp. 118–19.

can leave the twig without a touch in the *right* direction, but, if we do, we cannot hinder its being bent the *wrong* way." [20] He urged that children be converted to God in childhood and early youth, and yet he rejected the forcing process of older practices and insisted on the gradual expansion of the moral faculties. His position is best expressed by this passage on the infant; "It is just waking into an endless life. Its destiny is onward. It will rise and shine and sing with cherubim and seraphim, or sink and wail with the outcast and the lost, forever and ever." [21]

The doctrine of "Christian nurture," as set forth by Horace Bushnell in 1847,[22] was the most clearly worked out and forceful statement of the middle position with regard to child nature which was devised during the midnineteenth century. Fleming, in his work on *Children and Puritanism*, gave Bushnell credit for marking "a turning point . . . in the place of the child in the life and thought of the New England churches." [23] To what extent Bushnell's ideas were influencing other domestic reformers of the period is hard to determine,[24] but his views on nurture were profoundly important in the progress of religious education. Briefly, his position was this: Parental guidance is of paramount importance, not just to fill the empty cup of the child's mind, but to impart to it the Christian spirit. This nurture is not negative, not a mere warding off of evil, but an out-pouring of good from parent to child. Thus, "every hour is to be an hour of duty, every look and smile, every reproof and care, an effusion of Christian love." [25]

In the Bushnell philosophy, infant baptism is important to the organic unity of the family, for by this sign is the child made acceptable as a member, or potential member, of the church fold. This point of view had a significant effect in removing the con-

20. *Ibid.*, p. 139.

21. *Ibid.*, p. 71.

22. The date of the original treatise, "Discourses on Christian Nurture" was 1847. These discourses enlarged and rewritten were published in 1861 under the title *Christian Nurture*.

23. Fleming, *Children and Puritanism*, p. 207.

24. Mrs. Horace Mann recommended the reading of Bushnell's *Christian Nurture* in her *Moral Culture of Infancy*, a series of letters written in 1843, but not published until 1863. While her note was probably added to the letters in the interim, it is possible that she was familiar with the "Discourses" in the early period.

25. Horace Bushnell, *Christian Nurture* (New York, Charles Scribner & Co., 1867), p. 59.

cept of the child as a "miniature adult," for it accepted infancy as such. Bushnell objected to the religious conversion which is deferred to adolescence, since it placed the child outside the fold prior to conversion, and thus ignored the laws of nurture which operate on soul and body from infancy upward. In place of the unnatural "spirit of conquest" common to religious revivalism of the period, Bushnell stressed the acquisition of grace by nurture, by "internal growth." [26] He condemned alike the "no government" or "ostrich government" [27] of children advocated by the liberals, and the harsh concepts of the orthodox, whose methods promoted "hopeless despair" in the tender souls of young sinners. Yet Bushnell was not able to relinquish the doctrine of depravity. He made the point, definitely, as Fleming remarks, "that the doctrine of growth is not an infringement upon the doctrine of depravity." [28] It insists, rather, that depravity is "best rectified when it is weakest." [29]

This was Bushnell's middle position. It was obviously more than a cautious compromise. It heralded a new day for the child, and set him in a new light, as a being linked inseparably with the family and with the church from infancy upward. And yet it was a position acceptable to many of the orthodox, because Bushnell claimed that he was returning to the older orthodoxy and making it practical and consistent.

Many other examples of the middle position will come out in later chapters. Its significance here is that it accounts for the agreement which prevailed among parent educators of the mid-century period with regard to the importance of childhood. Whether they looked backward to sin or forward to the millennium, whether the infant was innocent or corrupt, its early years were most important. Purity, if there at birth, had to be preserved, and sin, if originally present, had to be weeded out. The common meeting ground, the educability of the child, made possible the mingling of strangely different approaches to child nature.

No definite line can be drawn between philosophic and scientific concepts of child nature. The ideas of the gradual expansion of the child's faculties, of his onward progress toward a higher

26. *Ibid.*, p. 61.
27. *Ibid.*, p. 67.
28. Fleming, *op. cit.*, p. 198.
29. *Loc. cit.*

"There are many birds which in twelve hours after they are hatched, run about and pick up seeds, selecting them from amidst the earth and gravel among which they are scattered. How different is it with the infant! How many efforts must it make before it can even pick up a pin."

destiny voiced in Humphrey's work, were, apparently, partially scientific in origin, since, in speaking of them, he called attention to the "footsteps of progression" [30] in the animal kingdom and urged comparison of infant and animal development. Samuel Goodrich, stressing the potentialities of man's prolonged infancy, embraced the concept of progress and of man's onward march toward immortality.[31] Childhood was to him an object of scientific study. Thus, he wrote: "The chemist delves deep in search of hidden acids and alkalies; the botanist climbs to the top of the Alps . . . the mineralogist plunges into the cavern. . . . I refer the reader to a more fruitful source of the wonderful and the beautiful. Study childhood." [32] Calhoun, in describing qualities of childhood during the midcentury years, remarked that "the new country was not ready for the 'prolonged infancy' that marks advanced civilization." [33] Children were prematurely old and thrust into commerce and society in their early teens. These new theories of child nature and growth were, consequently, to be of social significance.

Progress made in the sciences of physiology and medicine contributed vastly to changed concepts of child nature. Works [34] by European physicians such as Andrew Combe of Edinburgh were quoted in New England.[35] American treatises on the management and feeding of infants and children appeared in Philadelphia in the first quarter of the century. As the teachings which these embodied were popularized by lecturers, journalists, and health reformers, they were seized upon by champions of the child and applied to domestic goals. Mrs. Sigourney wrote in 1838, "Let us educate a race who shall have room to breathe. Let us promise, even in their cradle, that their hearts shall not be pinioned as in a vice, nor their spines bent like a bow, nor their ribs forced into the liver." [36] The old acceptance of disease and death as visitations of Providence was beginning to be questioned. Miss Sedgwick

30. Humphrey, *op. cit.*, p. 72.

31. Goodrich, *Fireside Education*, p. 47.

32. *Ibid.*, p. 22.

33. Calhoun, *op. cit.*, II, 55.

34. Andrew Combe, *A Treatise on the Physiological and Moral Management of Infancy.* (2d ed. Edinburgh, Maclachlan, Stewart & Co., 1841); see also *The Principles of Physiology Applied to the Preservation of Health* (New York, Harper & Bros., 1834).

35. "To Mothers and Nurses," *Parent's Magazine*, 1:245–46, July, 1841.

36. Sigourney, *Letters to Mothers*, pp. 78–79.

stated that there was "impiety as well as ignorance" [37] in imputing to Providence the national ills promoted by intemperance in eating and drinking and by indiscreet dressing. In another article she made a plea for more physical freedom for children, citing Dr. Combe's opinion that "not only the active sports, but the loud noise and shouting of children have a direct and important effect upon their health." [38]

Study of anatomy by mothers was urged by such writers as Catherine Beecher, Dr. William Alcott, and Mrs. Sigourney, whose flowery concept of the physical child is perhaps most significant in revealing the new approach to the child. She wrote of "the construction of the infant's frame; the little beating heart, sending life-blood through its thousand thread-like channels; the lungs, fastening . . . on the gift of the pure air; . . . the tender brain . . . all the mystery and beauty of this miniature temple." [39]

As a result of the scientific enlightenment of the public mind in matters of health, there was a reaction against child precocity, and also against poorly equipped school houses, with their health hazards. Dr. Humphrey wrote in 1840 of the dangers of "this eager poring over story books at so tender an age" which, he declared, "retards the growth, and robs the little cheek of its fulness and its color." [40] A family magazine deplored the fact that "common schools are generally kept in small, cold, and inconvenient buildings." [41]

The pseudo science of phrenology was, as we shall see in a later chapter,[42] of considerable importance in shaping health concepts as they applied to the child. It helped to focus attention on the laws which govern the human constitution,[43] and society's responsibility toward the young child in securing early adherence to these laws.

Social concepts with regard to child nature were of course as

37. Miss Sedgwick, "Was It Providence?" *Mother's Assistant*, 5:72, September, 1844.

38. C. Sedgwick, "A Plea for Children," *Ladies' Magazine*, 8:96, February, 1835.

39. Sigourney, *op. cit.*, pp. 27–28.

40. Humphrey, *op. cit.*, p. 76.

41. Theodore Sedgwick, "Causes of Poverty in the United States," *Family Magazine*, 5:213, November, 1837.

42. Cf. *post*, Chapter VI.

43. Cf. *post*, Appendix D.

varied as the different sections of the country. According to Calhoun, the social status of children was high, partly because of the small population of the country which placed a high valuation on childhood, partly because of the economic situation which made it possible for children to be financially independent at an early age, and partly because of the political importance in a new republic of each future citizen.[44] In New England, the latter emphasis seems to have been paramount, together with the religious emphasis on the high earthly destiny of man. In this connection it is interesting to note Calhoun's comment on the freedom of American children, ". . . in a democracy, the idea of 'superior' fades before the idea of equal sovereignty. All men are sovereigns. Personality is exalted; and the political status overflows and democratizes family institutions." [45] There can be no doubt that this concept was taking hold as the republic expanded and the secular goals of "life, liberty, and the pursuit of happiness" were substituted for the sterner aims of the old church-centered society.

With the growth of social consciousness and its stress on humanitarianism, poor children and children employed in factories were to come in for their share of public attention, but this activity did not reach its height until late in the century. In 1828, however, the establishment of infant schools for the poor was begun in New England, and these institutions influenced social concepts of the child. A notice of Bronson Alcott's *Observations on the Principles and Methods of Infant Instruction,* appearing in the *Ladies' Magazine* of 1830, includes the following extract, " 'Sympathy and imitation, the moral action of the teacher upon the children . . . form the common government of the school. . . . Harshness and restraint . . . will not be often required.' " [46] An editorial in the same volume commenting on the influence of the infant school said:

. . . it is not the benefit the children of the poor will derive, that makes . . . the importance of the subject. It is the inquiries and improvements which . . . will be . . . introduced into our systems of education. . . . In the nursery—that retired and scarce

44. Calhoun, *op. cit.,* II, 53.
45. *Loc. cit.*
46. Literary Notice in the *Ladies' Magazine,* 3:533, November, 1830, quoting from Amos Bronson Alcott *Observations on the Principles and Methods of Infant Instruction* (Boston, Carter & Hendee, 1830).

heeded place of instruction, but which, nevertheless, shapes more minds than all the public schools on earth—these experiments on the infant mind will operate with a power that must cause a great and rapid change.[47]

A later number of the *Ladies' Magazine* made the following appeal to the ladies of Boston: "Will you not remember, while sitting in your pleasant nurseries, surrounded by safe and happy children, of those poor little ones who have no nursery and no mother deserving the name? And will you not, with one accord come forward and afford your aid to their cause, and not rest till every section of the city has its Infant School?" This humanitarian appeal was reinforced by the argument that women know, better than men do "how much may be done towards forming the mental and especially the moral character, during the first four years of a child's life." [48]

It should be stated, at this point, that maternal associations, though preeminently religious in function, did for the rural communities some of the same things for the cause of childhood that the social institutions known as infant school societies did for the urban centers. They increased community speculation on the needs of young children and the means of physical, spiritual and intellectual nurture. This is interesting because infant schools, stemming from European naturalistic philosophies were part of a liberal movement in American education, whereas maternal associations, featuring the religious goals of evangelical protestantism, tended to stress conversion and the old time discipline. No attempt is made in this study to describe the activities of either organization, but the suggestion is made that both contributed to a broader definition of child nature by virtue of bringing together in their respective groups diverse opinions with regard to growth and development.[49]

In line with these developments is the common school controversy which centered around the methods of punishment to be used with children. Public sentiment was no doubt influenced by

47. "Infant Schools," *Ladies' Magazine*, 3:224, November, 1830.
48. "Infant Schools," *Ladies' Magazine*, 5:182, April, 1832.
49. Cf. "Maternal Associations," *Parent's Magazine*, 1:205–7, May, 1841; "Topics of Conversation at Maternal Meetings," *Parent's Magazine*, 1:283–87, August, 1841; and "Infant Schools," Art. 2, *American Annals of Education*, 3:296–304, July, 1833.

such discussion as that initiated by the *Seventh Annual Report* of Horace Mann with its ensuing rejoinders,[50] and by the forceful treatise published in 1847 by Lyman Cobb entitled *The Evil Tendencies of Corporal Punishment as a Means of Moral Discipline in Families and Schools.*[51] In both of these documents, which will receive further consideration in a later chapter,[52] the philosophy set forth heralded a fresh approach to child nature, an approach consistent with new stresses on individual freedom, dignity, and responsibility. Through such channels was the public mind informed of the nature and needs of young children. Many of the new ideas derived from European philosophies which were later to create the kindergarten with its recognition of the child as an active, social being.

Perhaps the best way to summarize the above trends, theories, and concepts with regard to child nature is to show the way in which they tended to elevate the status of the young child in the popular mind during the midcentury years. To the religious group, the young child was exceedingly important as a potential member of the church body and inheritor of the kingdom. To those of an economic or political turn, the young child was the future business man or citizen, equally capable of earning a million dollars or of aspiring to the presidency. To the socially minded, improvement of society was dependent upon the equal rights of every child in the new republic to an education and to legal protection. To those interested in the sciences, the child was significant as a growing being and participant in progress. As such, his welfare was of great importance. And finally, to the group as a whole, childhood, as distinct from the "miniature adulthood" of an earlier period, was a theme of new and vital interest.

Turning now to a consideration of the emergence of mothers as beings important to New England society, it is tempting to suggest that the growing emphasis of the midcentury period upon the rights, duties, and education of women was a logical outcome of the discovery that mothers were important as molders of childhood—that, in short, their status rose as a complement to the rising status of the child in society. For purposes of this study,

50. See especially Association of Masters of the Boston Public Schools, *Remarks on the Seventh Annual Report of the Honorable Horace Mann* (Boston, Charles C. Little & James Brown, 1844).

51. Lyman Cobb, *The Evil Tendencies of Corporal Punishment* . . . (New York, Mark H. Newman & Co., 1847).

52. Cf. *post*, Chapter VII.

such a logical deduction would be helpful, but one is obliged to admit, in viewing this chaotically active period in American history, that concepts with regard to women did not develop in consistent sequence during this time, nor can any set of concepts be attributed exclusively to a particular group of people, or period of years. As Groves points out in *The American Woman,* "Every influence, from whatever quarter, that operates upon the culture of a people may also act upon that special part . . . the sphere and status of women." [53]

Those students engaged in tracing the Woman's Rights movement from its origin might reasonably attribute female "emancipation" in the nineteenth century to industrial and economic causes, aided by the enlightened messages of the liberals, who strove to release woman from the confining duties of the fireside and to project her into public affairs. The social historian would undoubtedly point to the frontier woman whose courageous toil, immeasurably important to the success of pioneer enterprise, did much to lend dignity and prestige to the sex as a whole.[54] Those concerned with the history of education might, in defining woman's progress, give primary emphasis to the intellectual improvement of women attendant upon the rise of female education during the midcentury years. Those delving into medical and physiological research might place considerable weight upon the physical liberation of women, which was forwarded by scientific discoveries with respect to the close relation between current follies of fashion and diet, and the high mortality rate. And, finally, the literary scholar might, by searching, find the "new woman" emerging from European novels and other works which had considerable circulation in this country throughout the century.

It is obvious that all these approaches are important for an understanding of concepts of the period with respect to women as mothers. Whatever was thought, said, or written about mothers was in some way influenced by points of view with reference to these various angles of the woman question. Furthermore, as Branch points out, "There is no orderly progression to the feminine emancipation; all the phases seem coexistent." [55]

Taking all this into account, we may proceed to examine some

53. Ernest R. Groves, *The American Woman* (New York, Greenberg, 1937), p. 9. By permission of Emerson Books, Inc., publishers of the 2d ed. 1944.
54. Calhoun, *op. cit.,* II, 106–7.
55. Branch, *op cit.,* p. 218.

of the developments and concepts which elevated the status of
mothers in midcentury New England society.

In summarizing the so-called "liberal" agitation of the period,
Calhoun calls attention to the following developments:

. . . protest was made against the legal nonage of the wife,
against the husband's control of property, against the wrongs of
slave women. Women were urged not to let a drunkard beget children. It was recognized that the old "dainty notions" had made
women hot-house plants—half of them invalids. . . . It was denied that any portion of the species had a right to determine the
sphere of the rest; and suffrage was demanded as a means of self-
defense and education.[56]

This, in a nutshell, was the stand taken by supporters of the
woman militant. Needless to say, such doctrine was ill received
by conservative members of society. Even those who had read
and agreed, at least in part, with such writers [57] as Mary Wollstonecraft, Harriet Martineau, and Margaret Fuller Ossoli, dis-
creetly drew their skirts aside at the public activities of such innovators as Lucy Stone, Elizabeth Cady Stanton, and the Grimké
sisters. Frances Wright, radical lecturer on Woman's Rights,[58]
and Robert Owen, advocate of birth control and crusader against
existent marriage laws,[59] were "beyond the pale" of respectable
society. New England was not ready for a direct attack on the
woman question. A solution of the many problems raised by the
liberals was to come by intermediate steps.[60] And many of these
solutions were to come from that group of the socially minded
semi-orthodox referred to in this study as "domestic reformers."

Lydia Maria Child, who had established herself as a judicious
moralist in her *Mother's Book* in the 1830's, and subsequently
jeopardized her position by her connection with the Antislavery
movement, undertook, in the 'forties, a study into *The History and
Condition of Women of All Ages and Nations*.[61] This volume, one

56. Calhoun, *op. cit.*, pp. 121–22.
57. E.g., Sarah Hale gives full credit to these women in her *Woman's Record*
for their sincerity and their social consciousness, even while deploring some
of their views. Cf. Hale, *Woman's Record* (3d ed. New York, Harper & Bros.,
1870), pp. 780–81; 739–42; 665–70.
58. Branch, *op. cit.*, p. 208.
59. Calhoun, *op. cit.*, p. 123.
60. Branch, *op. cit.*, p. 208.
61. L. Maria Child, *Brief History of the Condition of Women*, 2 vols. in one
(5th ed. New York, C. S. Francis & Co., 1845).

of the first New England publications on the history of women, brought to view an important attitude with regard to the rights of women. This was, that seen in historical perspective, the lot of the American woman was far from deplorable. It was, in contrast to that of heathen women of an early period, really enviable. Thus, Mrs. Child declared, "perhaps there is no country in the world, where women, as wives, sisters, and daughters, have more influence, or more freedom." [62] She spoke derogatively of the "many silly things" being written in her time "concerning the equality of the sexes," while "that true and perfect companionship, which gives both man and woman complete freedom *in* their places, without a restless desire to go out of them, is as yet imperfectly understood." [63]

This point of view on the freedom of American women was supported by the observation of De Tocqueville on his visit to the states. Assuming the social inferiority of women, he nevertheless is quoted as saying that Americans "have done all they could to raise her morally and intellectually to the level of man . . . ," and, furthermore, " 'Altho the women of the United States are confined within the narrow circle of domestic life, and their situation is, in some respects, one of extreme dependence, I have nowhere seen women occupying a loftier position.' " [64] It was through this sort of statement that the question of "rights" for women began, in the minds of some, to resolve itself into one of "privileges." American women were to count their blessings and make use of those they had, before they could sensibly agitate for more.

Said Mrs. Hale in an editorial for the 1830 *Ladies' Magazine:* "In most countries, women have no privileges of mind—or at least but very few opportunities of acquiring any knowledge beyond the mere routine of domestic life. They are literally drudges. But our own beloved country furnishes not only the hope but the accomplishment of better things." [65] This editorial was one of many by Mrs. Hale which were to set the keynote for her crusade for female education, featured at first in the *Ladies' Magazine*

62. *Ibid.*, II, 265.

63. *Ibid.*, p. 211.

64. Calhoun, *op. cit.*, p. 111, citing Alexis de Tocqueville, *Democracy in America*, H. Reeve, translator (3d American ed. New York, George Adlard, 1839).

65. "Privileges of American Ladies," *Ladies' Magazine*, 3:40–41, January, 1830.

and later in the *Godey* books. For her group of followers, at least, "rights" became synonymous with opportunities for education. As for the to-do over the equality of the sexes, and the preeminence of the male in American society, these were seen as irrelevant to the task at hand. The question was not "whether the rose or the oak has the preeminence," but rather "for what ends were these different things designed." [66]

More direct and sober consideration was given to the legal condition of women in a book published in Salem, Massachusetts, in 1845, entitled *The Legal Rights, Liabilities, and Duties of Women*.[67] In this volume, attention was directed to the differences between the rights of a wife and of her husband. With respect to custody, it was pointed out that while a husband could use gentle restraint upon his wife in case of evil habits, the wife could exercise no such restraint upon an intemperate or idle husband. Inequalities of property and dower rights were deplored, but the writer stated that, in some of the states, "the free spirit which pervades the whole legal and social structure of the United States" [68] had caused an amelioration of American jurisprudence, and that laws were gradually being introduced into state legislatures which would remedy the condition in time.

Margaret Fuller Ossoli had cried out in indignation at the situation which existed with regard to factory women whose earnings could be turned over, by law, to the use of dissolute husbands.[69] Mansfield, while admitting this evil, saw as a solution not the rebellion of women, but education, which would enable them to think rightly—a three-way education so that, "as *mothers*," they might become "fit TEACHERS of infant men," secondly, to make them "fit teachers of AMERICAN men," and, finally, to render them "fit teachers of CHRISTIAN American men." [70] This became the essence of the "middle" position with regard to the condition of women in the midnineteenth century. Mothers were to raise up a new generation, educating it, and being themselves so well educated that a future period would see just laws and perfect harmony between the sexes. Women, far

66. "The Question," *Ladies' Magazine*, 7:476, October, 1834.

67. Edward D. Mansfield, *The Legal Rights, Liabilities, and Duties of Women* (Salem, John P. Jewett & Co., 1845).

68. *Ibid.*, p. 311.

69. Margaret Fuller Ossoli, *Woman in the Nineteenth Century*, in Margaret Fuller's "Works" (Boston, Roberts Brothers, 1874), III, 32.

70. Mansfield, *op. cit.*, p. 105.

from being oppressed, were beings possessed with the very clay of social improvement which they might mold to their choosing. Given this, why should they erect "liberty poles" and shout "freedom" from the forum? Was not their power rather a "calm, still, holy consciousness of mental and moral . . . elevation and strength which is born of knowledge . . . ?" [71]

It is most interesting to note, at this point, that the liberal and conservative groups were united on the woman question by the same force which drew them together in consideration of the child. This was education. The child, good or bad by original nature, was important to society because of his educability. And women, whether potential suffragists or guardians of the home and fireside, were the possessors of bodies and minds susceptible of improvements which were necessary to render them socially useful beings.

One can only conjecture as to why these facts should acquire such forcefulness in the minds of midnineteenth century reformers. Women and children had always been important to society, and education had been the pivotal center around which New England had rotated since colonial days. The renewed zest for learning and self-cultivation may, judging from Fish's study of this period, be attributed to the rise of the middle classes, and also to the all-pervasiveness of democratic ideas which conceived of man as susceptible of improvement in all walks of life.[72] Implicit always in the philosophy of the liberals from Mary Wollstonecraft's time to that of Margaret Fuller Ossoli was the ferment of the French Revolution with its emphasis upon freedom, independence, and self-realization.

But the conservative attack on the problem of female education was somewhat different. Women, it was declared, were not to be educated merely to develop their own faculties. This was dangerous Jacobinism, being spread in America by cheap European literature, and by the superficial education of fashionable boarding schools of the day. Women were to be educated to perform their special function in life and to help check evils of the period. In short, they had come to be looked upon as conservers of the

71. Miss S. C. Edgarton, "Female Culture," *Mother's Assistant*, 3:95, April, 1843.
72. Carl. R. Fish, *The Rise of the Common Man, 1830–50*, A. M. Schlesinger and D. R. Fox, editors, *A History of American Life*, Vol. VI (New York, Macmillan Company, 1929), pp. 7, 12ff.

status quo. Thus, Daniel Webster, staunch old Federalist and conservative, said in a speech printed in Griswold's *Prose Writers of
America:* "It is by the promulgation of sound morals in the community, and more especially by the training and instruction of the
young, that woman performs her part toward the preservation
of a free government. . . . Mothers are, indeed, the . . . effective teachers of the human race." [73]

Sarah Hale, Catherine Beecher, Almira Phelps, Emma Willard,
Lydia Child, and many other "active conservatives" carried this
message insistently to its logical conclusions. Their argument may
be expressed in the words of an article printed in the *Ladies'
Magazine.* If there are evils and ignorance in the world, it is because the mother, constituted by God as the "first teacher of every
human being," has been denied tools which "can enable her to discharge [her mission] . . . with discretion and effect." [74] And
further it is stated, "If half the effort had been directed to improve
the minds of females, which has been lavished on the other sex,
we should now have a very different state of society." [75] This
argument of the female crusaders pointed definitely to the need
for maternal education.

How, then, was woman to discharge her mission with discretion and effect? What was the new womanly ideal? How was
it to be achieved? Concepts developed thick and fast during this
period when reform was the byword. The domestic woman, or
the "keeper-at-home," was redefined in the light of her newly
recognized significance to society. It was granted that she was
subordinate to her husband, but her domestic tasks were seen by
some in a regal, almost a divine light. A reprint from the *Mother's
Journal* appeared in the 1841 *Parent's Magazine,* in which it was
stated that the mother or keeper-at-home is "not the less really
responsible, than is that youthful queen who now sways a sceptre
over four quarters of the earth." [76] In answer to Margaret Ossoli's charge that " 'the duties of a mother are low and neutraliz-
ing,' " another champion of the keeper-at-home claimed that

73. Daniel Webster, "Influence of Woman," in Rufus W. Griswold, editor,
Prose Writers of America (2d ed. Philadelphia, Carey & Hart, 1847), p. 185.
74. "The Mother," *Ladies' Magazine,* 7:568, December, 1834. *n.b.* It is very
likely that this article was written by Mrs. Hale herself, but there is no way
of establishing this as a fact, since the article is unsigned.
75. *Loc. cit.*
76. "For What Is a Mother Responsible?" *Parent's Magazine,* 1:221, June,
1841.

mothers feed the "fire of love and faith which will overcome the chilling, hardening influences of the world" [77] in training up their children to virtue and in leading them to eternal life. A contributor to the *Ladies' Magazine* saw woman's function in the rearing of her offspring and care of her household as "angelic and divine." Said she, "Inspiration springs up in her very paths—it follows her footsteps. A halo of glory encircles her. . . ." [78]

This enthronement of the mother was by no means limited to women sentimentalists who wrote for family magazines. Dr. William Alcott, interested chiefly in health and in good household management, saw fit to publish among numerous other home manuals and works for women a volume on the *Young Housekeeper*. He declared: ". . . Let me have the control of the nursery—let me direct the sweeping, the washing, the fire-building, the cooking, the conversation, etc., of the infant and the child—and I care comparatively little whether laws are made by one man, by a few men, or by many men." [79]

A class book for young ladies used in New England schools contained articles by Mrs. Sigourney and Catherine Beecher on the "Profession of Woman" and on "Maternal Influence" appealing to the mothers of future generations to look away from their selfish youthful pursuits to a contemplation of the duties and responsibilities which would confront them in the years to come. [80]

Those interested in prison reform found in their questioning of convicts that the only spiritual influence which could be exerted on the most depraved was that which wakened memories of their mothers, and of early home influences. In one eloquent account of such a case the prisoner was so aroused by this memory that he prayed again, was reformed, and acquitted. [81]

The interest of temperance reformers in the subject of the mother's importance to society will be commented on in Chapter III. Practical reformers, alarmed by intemperance in eating as well as in drinking, saw the household tasks of women in a new

77. Catherine Leicester, "Female Heroism," *Mother's Assistant*, 23:119, October, 1852.

78. "Principles and Influence of Taste," *Ladies' Magazine*, 3:83, February, 1830.

79. William A. Alcott, *The Young Housekeeper*, p. 33.

80. Ebenezer Bailey, *The Young Ladies Class Book* (21st ed. Boston, Gould, Kendall & Lincoln, 1839), pp. 201–3, pp. 263–65.

81. "A Mother's Prayers Are Not Easily Forgotten," *Parent's Magazine*, 1:146–47, January, 1841.

light. The *Ladies' Magazine* citing Dr. Caldwell on the gluttony of the times, called upon the mother as "the guardian of home," who can "regulate the habits of her household" and "form the habits of her children." [82]

By far the largest group interested in the woman in her home function was the religious group, both from the point of view of forwarding religious activity and of effecting moral reforms in family life. These concepts, too, will receive attention in later chapters. Significant to note here is the statement of the Reverend John S. C. Abbott:

It is maternal influence, after all, which must be the great agent, in the hand of God, in bringing back our guilty race to duty and happiness. Oh that mothers could feel this responsibility as they ought. . . . A new race of men would enter upon the busy scene of life, and cruelty and crime would pass away.[83]

Statements of this sort about women are so abundant in the literature of the period that there is seemingly no end to them.

To discharge her mission the mother had, in the first place, to recognize her own importance, and cease to regard the duties of the home and fireside as mean and degrading. She had, next, to educate herself in matters of household management, and in the duties of family government. For this purpose she had only to turn to the flood of advice given in household manuals,[84] cookbooks, etiquette books, medical books, and, finally, and most important, to texts on child care written for mothers. The womanly ideal was set forth repeatedly in current periodicals. Mrs. Hale wrote in 1834, "Read the Ladies' Magazine, during the year, and you will, we hope, be gratified with some charming pictures of the quiet, meek, christian beauty of character; and the affectionate, home-loving disposition, which will remind you of Eve when she tended her flowers—'herself the fairest flower.' " [85]

By skilful manipulation of this theme of the "home-loving" woman, domestic activity was occasionally portrayed as being compatible with intellectual, and even with literary activity. Proponents of the womanly ideal were eager to prove that Christian meekness and intellectual alertness and productiveness were not mutually exclusive. *The Mother's Assistant* of 1853 reported a

82. "The Good Dinner," *Ladies' Magazine*, 6:39–40, January, 1833.
83. John S. C. Abbott, *The Mother at Home*, p. 149.
84. Branch, *op. cit.*, pp. 220–23.
85. "Female Biography," *Ladies' Magazine*, 7:41, January, 1834.

"family conversation" in which a mother and daughter discussed the pros and cons of domesticity. The daughter complained "How is it to be expected that wit, imagination and intellect can condescend to keeping drawers in order, or to watching a clock so as not to be behind an appointment?" [86] The mother replied by pointing to the examples set by "really superior women" of intellect, Miss Edgeworth, Hannah More, Joanna Baillie, and Miss Mitford. "Let me tell you," said the mother, "that a fondness for domestic life, and the cultivation of the qualities which make home pleasant and beautiful, was, or is a characteristic of every one of them." [87]

In another volume of this same periodical a Massachusetts contributor praised American mothers such as Mrs. Hale and Mrs. Wells who had turned to " 'the toils and trials of authorship' " in order to use " 'the treasures of their own minds' " [88] to provide for their children. Authoresses of this high type were, because of their own home-loving qualities, exerting a definite effect upon the womanly ideal of the period, removing some of the stigma which had formerly been attached by conservatives to the intellectual woman, or "bluestocking." Gradually the concept of the "domestic woman" was expanding to make room for new activities and new aspirations. When it was seen that intellectual and literary as well as moral eminence were not incompatible with simple domestic interests, the way was made clear for a type of female emergence which was in line with the most acceptable social goals of the midcentury years.

Clearly, therefore, the social emergence of the mother as a free and responsible individual and participant in democratic progress, was paralleled, if not actually conditioned, by public recognition of the child as a being of social significance. The common cause of their mutual improvement was forwarded by domestic reform, a movement which will be recognized as this study proceeds in its forward looking and liberal as well as in its conservative aspects.

86. "Exactness, a Family Conversation," editorial, *Mother's Assistant*, 1853, p. 128.

87. *Ibid.*, pp. 128–29.

88. Mrs. J. S. Lunt, "Form and Principle," *Mother's Assistant*, 9:102, November, 1846.

CHAPTER III

DOMESTIC REFORM: THE CAUSE IN PRINT

VERY social cause of the midnineteenth century must be seen in its relation to the growing national consciousness of a young republic and to its most effective mouthpiece, the press. According to Goodrich, the book manufacture of the United States in 1820 was based on works which were of 30 per cent American and 70 per cent British origin. By 1856 such amazing progress had been made in publication of American writings that American works were estimated at 80 per cent, and British books at 20 per cent of the total book manufacture. In addition to this, the total amount of expenditure in the United States increased from $2,500,000 in 1820 to $16,000,000 in 1856.[1]

There were numerous reasons for the increase in American publications. The new printing presses facilitated speed of printing and made possible the publication of cheap books, newspapers, and periodicals for widespread consumption. The invention of the telegraph in 1836 helped to spread the contagion of "news consciousness." The penny press was begun and raised from humble beginnings in the hands of several able editors to elevated stature in the news world.[2] National prosperity and increased urbanization created for many, more leisure time for reading. New lamps were invented to shed their attractive glow on the family reading circle. Americans were highly conscious of the printed word. For the intellectuals, it was the vehicle for the flowering of culture; for the rising middle classes it was one means of attaining the much sought after "gentility"; and, finally, for the large group of American business men, and the quacks, commercial artists, and propagandists, it was useful for advertising purposes. As demands for printed matter increased at

1. Samuel G. Goodrich, *Recollections of a Lifetime* (New York and Auburn, Miller, Orton & Mulligan, 1856), II, 380–89.
2. *Ibid.*, p. 383.

all levels of society, American writers stepped forward to supply these demands.

Yet the "Americanism" which distinguished this era in literary history was not merely opportunistic. It was also vigorously constructive and in some cases reactionary. American writers had a great deal to say for the good of their country, and some reformers in their very saying of these things were rejecting European patterns of living and thinking.

This has important bearing on the subject of domestic reform. Those members of society who were concerned for the moral elevation of mankind viewed the increased output of the press with considerable alarm. They saw many cheap publications as organs of "drunkenness, licentiousness, falsehood" and were especially concerned at the "inundation from abroad." [3] Goodrich exclaimed "—we are alarmed at the influence of British literature, and its cheap, rapid diffusion among us, unless society will refuse to buy papers that deal out poison. . . . We are now in this current. Shall we yield to it, or shall we stem it? This is a question for mothers." [4] A Boston minister spoke of the younger generation who were growing up with notions "such as prevail in France, and amid the corruptions of the old world" because of their contact with Victor Hugo and Georges Sand, and with the "universally condemned" works of the English Fielding and Smollett. [5] A volume could be written on the reaction against Byron alone, who was likened to a deadly serpent [6] in his effect upon the morals of his readers.

It is interesting to observe the connection between this sort of sentiment and the "Americanism" noted by Fish as typical of the period 1830 to 1850. Of contact with Europe he said, "Relatively, . . . this was the period of least vital contact. . . . Fewer boys than before or since went abroad for their education.

". . . Americans were vitally conscious of their difference." [7] And this, at a time when the steamship had reduced the length

3. S. G. Goodrich, "Responsibility of Authors and Readers," *Mother's Assistant*, 1:34, February, 1841.

4. *Ibid.*, p. 35.

5. Reverend F. P. Tracy, "Cheap Publications," *Mother's Assistant*, 3:175, August, 1843.

6. Reverend A. A. Lipscomb, "Influence of Female Literature on Female Character," *Mother's Assistant*, 7:65, September, 1845.

7. From Carl R. Fish, *The Rise of the Common Man*, pp. 1–2. By permission of the Macmillan Company, publishers.

of the ocean voyage to twelve days! The explanation for this aloofness may be found, not alone in the economic expansion and pressing domestic affairs of a growing nation, but also in the new temper of the midcentury mind. Americans were reacting against the old dependence upon Europe. They were creating new patterns of their own and in so doing were confident that the world's future generations would regard them as perfect models. It is not surprising, therefore, that didactic works and school books constituted a very large proportion of the increased American book production. Goodrich wrote, in 1856, ". . . forty years ago we used English books adapted to our wants. Now . . . we produce annually more school-books than the whole continent of Europe!" [8] The midcentury period was definitely the era for teachers and moralists.

In this setting it was natural that the cause of domestic reform should flourish. New Englanders, conscious always of the importance of education, were keenly aware of the part played by the family in furthering this education. A searchlight was turned upon the American family and its members. Didactic books and periodicals were addressed to women, urging self-improvement, enlightenment in matters of domestic economy, medicine and physiology, dress reform, proper moral and religious attitudes toward problems encountered before and after marriage, and, in some cases, more daring attitudes involving emancipation and a new status for women. Instructive guidebooks for young ladies undertook in a steady flow of conventional advice to avert the dilemma of the giddy society matron mentioned in Chapter I.[9] Fathers of families, and young men were appealed to in a similar fashion, with additional stresses on the evils of intemperance and materialistic self-indulgence. The flood of didactic literature for children was such that it drew a protest from conservatives, who saw as a threat to the more solid nurture afforded by the Bible and primer, the "baby literature upon our book-seller's counters, . . . flying abroad, like the locusts, glittering in the sun, in their septennial transmigrations." [10]

Many sided as was this literary attack on the midnineteenth century family, it was on the whole unified in its goal, which was to create a new family ideal, a strong conservative pattern for

8. Goodrich, *Recollections of a Lifetime*, II, 389.

9. Cf. *ante*, p. 8.

10. Humphrey, *Domestic Education*, p. 103.

the American people, conventionally grounded in Christian morality and yet varied enough in its design to meet the many social
needs of an expanding culture. Domestic reform in its broader
sense comprised every activity which contributed to this goal.

The phase of domestic reform which stressed the home education of young children gathered momentum as the midcentury
years progressed. The importance of the maternal function was
increasingly apparent to those who tackled social and family problems. An educator wrote somewhat skeptically in 1836 of "the
general mass of well meant encomiums passed on the female sex,
and especially on the pre-eminent value of the maternal relation,
in the current of popular treatises on this subject which almost
daily issue from the press." [11] The 'forties saw a peak of popularity
for home literature designed to aid fathers and mothers in the
education of their children which was proclaimed to be indicative
of "an awakened interest . . . on this long neglected subject." [12]
And in 1857 a work entitled *Life at the Fireside* [13] went through
three editions, including as one of its chapters in the third edition, a prize magazine article entitled "The Era for Mothers." To
explain the persisting interest of the home theme during the "sentimental years" of the nineteenth century we must turn to the
group of writers who promoted domestic causes.

Perhaps the greatest impetus to domestic reform was given
by the large group of female writers who began to contribute to
the many small periodicals of the day. According to Miss Stearns,
"Every village had its local authoress." [14] An amusing cartoon
of the midcentury period shows a family scene in which the wife
sits, pen in hand, before a writing table while a distracted husband
tries vainly to quiet a crying baby.[15]

This feminine zeal for writing may be attributed to a number
of causes. Precedence for female production was to be found in
the works of English women, Mrs. Hannah More, Maria Edgeworth, Mrs. Anna Jameson, and Mrs. Felicia Hemans, whose pub-

11. John Hall, *On the Education of Children* (2d ed. Hartford, Canfield &
Robins, 1836), p. 41.
12. "The Abuse of Works on Education," *Parent's Magazine*, 2:145, March,
1842.
13. William M. Thayer, *Life at the Fireside* (Boston, Congregational
Board of Publications, 1857).
14. Bertha M. Stearns, "New England Magazines for Ladies," *The New
England Quarterly*, 3:629, October, 1930.
15. Branch, *The Sentimental Years*, p. 215.

lications, according to Harriet Martineau,[16] were widely read in America. There is evidence also that the works of French women such as Madame de Stael and Madame de Saussure received favorable notice.[17]

From the early decades of the nineteenth century, minor women writers received inspiration from the successes of their American sisters, whose names, too numerous to list here, are to be found in the works of Read, and of Hart.[18] The day of the woman writer had arrived, and numerous periodicals testified to this fact. Before 1830 there were in New England nearly a score of periodicals for women and in the 1830–60 period there were thirty some,[19] not including several family magazines and innumerable religious publications.

In addition to this stimulation, other causes must be noted which bear on the mainsprings of thought and action in the homes of the midcentury period. Released increasingly from the drudgery of farm chores, many women had more time to read, think, and write. Many of them were benefiting by the new provisions for female education and were intellectually aroused. Others, wrapped in the aura of romanticism produced by the reading of European novels and American fiction, were imaginatively stirred. And still others, active in religious, social, and educational activities, were morally inspired to take up their pens in behalf of the instruction of their countrymen. Of this latter category, many were influenced and financially aided by ministers who "felt the call of duty and took up the task of editing magazines for women as an effective method of keeping the world in order." [20]

It will be noted in examining the listed names and purposes of New England periodicals for ladies of the 1830–60 period as given by Miss Stearns that the literary rather than the domestic note prevailed, at first, in many of the smaller magazines.[21] Nevertheless, as the midcentury progressed, an increasing number of avowedly literary magazines began to encourage the contribution of didactic essays of the domestic variety. Thus, for example, the

16. Martineau, *Society in America*, III, 219.

17. Hale, *Woman's Record*, pp. 518, 886.

18. Thomas B. Read, *The Female Poets of America* (6th ed., revised Philadelphia, E. H. Butler & Co., 1855) ; John S. Hart, *The Female Prose Writers of America* (Philadelphia, E. H. Butler & Co., 1852).

19. Stearns, *op. cit.*, pp. 627–28.

20. *Ibid.*, p. 629.

21. *Ibid., passim.*

Ladies' Mirror of Boston, devoted to poetic elegance and belles lettres, encouraged local talent "by the offer of a prize of ten dollars for the best essay on 'Family Government.' " [22] The policy of the successful *Ladies' Repository* was modified after six years by the associate editorship, in 1839, of Miss Sarah Edgarton, who stated that she had been turned " 'from the more fascinating haunts of romance to the sterner and loftier poetry of woman's calling—to her duties, her influence, her mental and moral culture, her social ministry to the human heart.' " [23] Miss Edgarton might also have been impelled by a more pecuniary motive to contemplate the domestic realm of woman. Had not Sarah Hale's *Ladies' Magazine,* dedicated to this cause been the most successful ladies magazine in New England? Its amalgamation in 1837 with the Philadelphia *Godey's Lady's Book* had left a challenging gap to venturing lady editors. This, however, is irrelevant except as it indicates a trend—the growing acceptability to the public of moral and domestic subject matter. Since even the "fascinating haunts of romance" had, in the hands of female writers been given the moral tone of the age, it was a natural transition to the "home" type of literature. Indeed, with the growing tendency of the period to romanticize the mother, child, and family, literary ladies found ample opportunity in the domestic theme for the application of gilt.

The galaxy of female stars which shone most brightly in mid-century New England were those who were able to combine their literary talents with their zeal for social betterment. Of this group four stand out especially: Mrs. Lydia Child, Mrs. Lydia Sigourney, Miss Catherine M. Sedgwick, and Mrs. Sarah J. Hale. Mrs. Child, whose earliest publications dealt with historical fiction, turned her attention in subsequent works to domestic subject matter. In 1827 she edited the *Juvenile Miscellany,*[24] pioneer American periodical for children. Her *American Frugal Housewife,* the *Mother's Book,* and the *Girls' Own Book* were written between 1829 and 1831, and were followed by a series of five volumes for the *Ladies' Family Library* devoted to the history, condition, and biography of women.[25] In 1833 she published a

22. *Ibid.,* p. 631.

23. *Ibid.,* p. 634, citing Sarah Edgarton.

24. Algernon Tassin, "Books for Children," in Trent et al., *The Cambridge History of American Literature,* II, 399.

25. Hart, *op. cit.,* pp. 116–17.

work entitled *Good Wives,* which was praised as one of her best.[26] Although the publication in 1833 of her *Appeal in Favor of That Class of Americans Called Africans* turned many conservatives against her,[27] her writings were praised highly in the literary notices of the *Ladies' Magazine* for the "greater degree of enjoyment they throw around the domestic fireside," and for their important contribution to the "well-being of our country." [28]

Mrs. Lydia Sigourney, known at first for her historical writings in prose and in verse, produced during her prolific writing career the following works of domestic counsel: *Letters to Young Ladies; Letters to Mothers; How To Be Happy; The Girls Reading Book;* and *The Daily Counsellor.*[29] Mrs. Graves, discussing intellectual women of the period, said in 1841: "Mrs. Sigourney has laid aside the poet's lyre, whose tones struck so sweetly upon the ear, and has engaged heart and soul in the moral and intellectual elevation of her sex, proving that she can instruct as well as charm. Her 'Letters to Young Ladies,' and her 'Letters to Mothers,' are invaluable." [30]

Miss Catherine Sedgwick, best known in literary circles for her novels, was definitely drawn to moral and didactic works of a semi-fictional variety during the period when domestic reform was at its height. Chief among these were: *Home; The Poor Rich Man and the Rich Poor Man; Live and Let Live; The Morals of Manners;* and *A Love Token for Children.* The popularity of *Home* was so great that it ran through twelve editions in two years.[31] This work was in the nature of a story text on "the mutual duties of parents and children." [32] Her change of direction was lauded by Mrs. Graves, who rejoiced that Miss Sedgwick had "given up the pleasant trifles which formerly employed her pen" [33] to espouse a more practical and social cause.

Perhaps the outstanding crusader for domestic reform among literary ladies was Sarah Josepha Hale, well-known editor of

26. "Literary Notices," *Ladies' Magazine,* 6:237–39, May, 1833.

27. Martineau, *op. cit.,* III, 111–12.

28. "Literary Notices," *Ladies' Magazine,* 6:238, May, 1833.

29. Gordon S. Haight, *Mrs. Sigourney, the Sweet Singer of Hartford* (New Haven, Yale University Press, 1930), pp. 175–78.

30. Graves, *Woman in America,* pp. 187–88.

31. Sister Mary Michael Welsh, *Catherine Maria Sedgwick* (Washington, Catholic University of America, 1937), pp. 35–36.

32. *Ibid.,* p. 35.

33. Graves, *op. cit.,* p. 187.

the *Ladies' Magazine* [34] and later of *Godey's Lady's Book*. Her writing career, which began in 1827 with a novel, was given over entirely in subsequent years to the advancement of female education, of the public and domestic education of children, of household economy, of public health, and other civic and benevolent causes.[35] Most stupendous of her undertakings in book form was the publication of her *Woman's Record, or Sketches of All Distinguished Women from the Creation to A.D. 1868, Arranged in Four Eras with Selections from Authoresses of Each Era*. Her introductory remark on the import of this volume is significant:

If God designed woman as the preserver of infancy, the teacher of childhood, the inspirer or helper of man's moral nature in its efforts to reach after spiritual things; if examples of women are to be found in every age and nation, who, without any special preparation have won their way to eminence in all pursuits tending to advance moral goodness and religious faith, then the policy, as well as justice of providing liberally for feminine education, must be apparent to Christian men.[36]

This was the keynote to Mrs. Hale's crusade, which was carried on through the medium of her magazines, her editorials, and her numerous contributions to annuals, newspapers, and periodicals. In a sense, this was a crusade with two distinct purposes: one, to inform the world, and especially "Christian men" of the importance of females to society; and two, to instruct women through the homely avenues of their domestic interests how to be worthy of this high trust, and equipped to meet their responsibilities. Mrs. Hale, herself a widow and the successful mother of five children, was in an excellent position to make her appeals effective.

One further comment must be made about the writings of Sarah Hale. They exemplify in their philosophy the "middle position" regarding women and children which was implied above in Chapter II. A newspaper article written at the time of her death called attention to her emphasis on the *"via media"* of womanly influence "rather than direct responsibility, in public affairs." [37] Her acceptance of the new in combination with a firm grasp on

34. Cf. *post*, Bibliography.
35. Ruth E. Finley, *The Lady of Godey's* (Philadelphia and London, J. B. Lippincott Company, 1931), *passim*.
36. Hale, *op. cit.*, p. viii.
37. Cf. Newspaper article affixed to front matter of Yale University Library copy of *Woman's Record*, 1870 edition.

conservative values gave her domestic writings and those of innumerable contributors to her magazines a wide audience and favorable publicity.

To this group of New England women writers should be added two others: Mrs. Sarah Parton, the "Fanny Fern" [38] of *Fern Leaves* fame, whose works for adults and children alike were immensely popular in the 'fifties; and Louisa Tuthill, noted by Hart as a successful authoress of the period. Mrs. Parton, though a resident of New York, spent the greater part of her life in New England and was hailed as a faithful interpreter and friend of children "from the poor 'tormented baby,' on its nurse's knee . . . all the way up through the perils, difficulties, and exceeding bitter sorrows of childhood." [39] This literature, although not addressed specifically to domestic reform, was nevertheless instrumental in spreading far and wide sugar-coated tales which mirrored new social concepts of child nature.

Miss Louisa Tuthill, who published anonymous works of the religious variety as early as 1827, attracted attention in 1839 with her domestic volume *The Young Lady's Home,* followed by a series of didactic books for boys and girls. Especially to be noted is her publication for mothers entitled *The Nursery Book* which contains "counsels for young mothers respecting the duties of the nursery." [40]

Closely related in subject matter and in purpose to the productions of female writers of the midcentury were the publications of clergymen who espoused the cause of domestic reform. When Harriet Martineau visited the States in the 'thirties, she commented with some distaste upon the isolation of the clergy and the petty matters which claimed their attention, matters involving the guardianship of the "weak members of society; women and superstitious men." [41] The materialistic world of business, which tended to make the men of the nation less religious and increasingly indifferent to affairs of the church, had made religion the chief social preoccupation of many women who, freed from domestic labors, were desirous of justifying their existence by the furtherance of good works. Thus, clergymen and women

38. James Parton, Horace Greeley et al., *Eminent Women of the Age* (Hartford, S. M. Betts & Co., 1868), "Fanny Fern—Mrs. Parton," by Grace Greenwood, pp. 66–84.

39. *Ibid.,* p. 75.

40. Hart, *op. cit.,* p. 102.

41. Martineau, *op. cit.,* III, 290.

became closely associated. Whether or not this joining of forces was to have healthful consequences for the virility of the church, it was the means of much cooperative endeavor in the more enlightened communities of New England during this period of widespread reform. If ministers were separated from politics and business, they were also released from the old ruts of theological speculation and were turning their attention to immediate social problems.

When one considers that the American Tract Society issued 68,418,138 copies of books and tracts in this country between 1825 and 1843,[42] some estimate is gained of the immense output of religious agencies of the period. It would be impossible to give a complete picture of the connection between the clergy and the cause of domestic reform. But it is possible to select from the New England group a few names which stood out in the field of didactic letters, names familiar in the parent and child literature of the midcentury decades and sufficiently eminent to be listed in the *Dictionary of American Biography.*

The Abbott brothers of Massachusetts, active in female education, in religious work, and in literary endeavor during the midcentury years, have not even today sunk into total oblivion. Of these three men, the Reverend John S. C. Abbott was most directly concerned with domestic reform as related to the importance of mothers and young children to society. His publication, *The Mother at Home,* is said to have had "a very considerable vogue both in the United States and in Europe" [43] and this volume, published in the 'thirties, was followed by *The Child at Home.*[44] At the time these works appeared, Abbott was pastor of the Calvinist Church in Worcester, Massachusetts. His thinking reflected a strange intermingling of conservative orthodoxy and the emotionalism of evangelical protestantism. Observing the fact that "in nearly every instance, the early years of life, are entrusted to a mother's care," he concluded that "maternal influence, more than anything else, forms the future character." [45] Thus he declared, "This world's redeeming influence must come from a

42. Branch, *The Sentimental Years,* p. 323.

43. *D. A. B.,* I, 23.

44. O. A. Roorbach, *Bibliotheca Americana, 1820–1852* (New York, Peter Smith, 1939), p. 3.

45. John S. C. Abbott, *The Mother at Home,* p. 17. By permission of E. P. Dutton & Co., Inc., publishers; copyright, 1936.

mother's lips" and "The brightest rays of the millennial morn must come from the cradle." [46] In addition to numerous contributions to periodicals of the time, Abbott's historical publication in the 'fifties, of the *Life of Napoleon* deserves comment in the connection in which it is remembered today. Van Wyck Brooks quotes Emerson as saying of this work, " 'It seems to teach that Napoleon's great object was to establish in benighted Europe our New England system of Sunday schools.' " [47] This is reminiscent of an anecdote on Napoleon used by Daniel Webster during this period. Bonaparte, he said, "once asked Madame de Staël in what manner he could most promote the happiness of France," and her reply, "full of political wisdom," said Webster, was " 'Instruct the mothers of the French people.' " [48] This was obviously a useful anecdote to be used in a moral crusade, and Abbott, like Webster, no doubt made use of such tidbits even in his historical writings.

The Reverend Jacob Abbott, Congregational clergyman, educator, writer, and brother to John, was known in domestic circles not alone for his famous "Rollo" series, but also for a widely sold work entitled *The Young Christian*, which "went into many editions in America and the British Isles, and was translated into French and Dutch." [49] His total literary output was 180 volumes, together with numerous contributions to periodicals, most of which were inspired by his zeal for moral instruction of the younger generation. One small volume entitled *The Little Philosopher*,[50] or *The Infant School at Home*, deserves special notice in this study. Addressed to mothers, in 1830, it was designed to be used as a handbook in the intellectual instruction of young children. Jacob Abbott was profoundly interested in evolving a philosophy of child government which would combine the best features of conservative and liberal theories. Likening family government to the government of the United States, he appealed to parents to consider their part in restoring the country to balance. Yielding, he said, must be taught to the young, since government is like a "mighty engine" which "glides smoothly and pleasantly"

46. *Ibid.*, pp. 148–49.

47. Brooks, *The Flowering of New England*, p. 122. By permission of E. P. Dutton & Co., Inc., publishers; copyright, 1936.

48. Daniel Webster, "Influence of Woman," in Rufus W. Griswold, *The Prose Writers of America*, p. 185.

49. *D. A. B.*, I, 22.

50. Cf. *post*, Chapter V, p 103.

when yielded to, but when resisted "crushes you to atoms." [51] The proper yielding was to be taught to the young by parents, and the country thus restored to much needed balance. Previous to his career of preaching and writing, Jacob Abbott founded one of the pioneer female institutions in New England, the Mount Vernon School.[52] A work which appeared in 1871, entitled *Gentle Measures in the Training of the Young,* proved that he saw the cause of the young woman and the child as a joint one, and that his writings were based on practical experience in teaching and the ministry.

A third brother, Gorham Abbott, although not listed in the *Dictionary of American Biography,* should be noted here for his translation of a European text entitled *The Family at Home.*[53]

The Reverend Harvey Newcomb, Congregational clergyman, divided his career, like the Abbotts, between preaching, literary production, and female education, producing 178 volumes [54] and numerous articles during his busy lifetime. Of these we may note especially his *First Question Book,* published in 1837, which was used by mothers and teachers in the instruction of young children. His close interest in the concerns of parents may be seen by the titles of his contributions to periodicals: "Early Discipline"; [55] "Rewards and Punishments"; [56] and "Advantages of Maternal Associations." [57] Two other works addressed to the furthering of domestic reform were his *Young Lady's Guide* and *How To Be a Lady.*[58]

To this group of versatile clergy belong also the names of William M. Thayer, Massachusetts preacher, editor, and writer, and the Reverend Hubbard Winslow, teacher, clergyman, and writer. During the latter part of the midcentury period, Thayer took over the editorship of a periodical entitled *The Happy Home and Parlor Magazine* [59] and produced, in 1853, a volume for parents entitled *Life at the Fireside,* referred to above as containing his

51. Jacob Abbott, "On Moral Education," Lect. 2, *American Institute of Instruction,* 2:45–64, August, 1831.

52. *D. A. B.,* I, 21.

53. Roorbach, *op. cit.,* p. 1.

54. *D. A. B.,* XIII, 451.

55. *Parent's Magazine,* 2:271–72, August, 1842.

56. *Mother's Assistant,* 3:29–32, February, 1843.

57. *Mother's Assistant,* 3:197–200, September, 1843.

58. *D. A. B.,* XIII, 451.

59. This was published in Boston between 1854 and approximately 1861.

stirring article on "The Era for Mothers." A devotee of the temperance cause, his activities reached beyond the confines of church and schoolroom.

Winslow, a native of Vermont, succeeded Lyman Beecher as pastor of the Bowdoin Street Church in Boston and, popular as a preacher, was well received as a didactic writer and contributor to periodicals. Trinitarian and orthodox, his works were of the ultra-conservative variety which regarded all innovation as alarming. His texts for women, *Woman as She Should Be*,[60] and *The Ladies' Manual of Moral and Intellectual Culture*,[61] charged mothers with the task of emulating early models of pious womanhood, and enjoined upon them modest retirement, and the execution of religious duties. Childhood education he saw as tremendously important, but deplored new methods which "reduce all government to mere persuasion." [62]

The Reverend Daniel Wise, Methodist clergyman of New Hampshire, merits notice for his publication of a volume entitled *The Young Lady's Counsellor*,[63] which outlined "the sphere and duties of young women and the dangers that beset them." In the preface of this work, he proclaimed maternal influence as the "POWER BEHIND THE SCHOOL-ROOM AND THE CHURCH" which influences the infant mind "long before it can be made to feel the power of the teacher or the minister." [64] In discussing the true sphere of woman, he urged the young lady not to seek fame in "the highways of society, and jostle . . . for the offices and honors of public life," but to elevate herself by pursuing her important mission in the "peaceful sanctuaries of home." [65]

A type of literature which merged in purpose with publications of the American Tract Society and other organs of religious publication was that produced by Nehemiah Adams, Congrega-

60. Hubbard Winslow, *Woman as She Should Be*. (2d London ed. Boston, T. H. Carter, 1838).

61. Hubbard Winslow and Mrs. John Sandford, *The Lady's Manual of Moral and Intellectual Culture* (New York, Leavitt & Allen, 1854).

62. Hubbard Winslow, "On the Dangerous Tendency to Innovations and Extremes in Education," Lect. 7, *American Institute of Instruction*, 5:182, 1835.

63. Daniel Wise, *The Young Lady's Counsellor* (New York, Eaton & Mains, 1851).

64. *Ibid.*, p. 6.

65. *Ibid.*, p. 92.

tional clergyman of Salem, Massachusetts. His work *The Baptized Child,*[66] dedicated to the maternal association of his parish, went through five editions. It exhorted parents in their duties regarding church membership of children. He also wrote children's literature such as *Agnes and the Key of Her Little Coffin* and *Bertha and Her Baptism.*[67] This sort of literature, being narrow in its approach, falls into the category of sectarian teaching rather than domestic reform. Yet Adams undoubtedly exerted a more general influence as co-editor with Jacob Abbott and Hubbard Winslow of the *Religious Magazine* in Boston from 1837–40.[68]

Of most general service to the cause of domestic education were the somewhat obscure clergymen who edited, published, and contributed to periodicals of the day. It would be a hopeless task to attempt to trace and scan all the shortlived religious monthly and weekly printed sheets which carried domestic counsel into New England homes of the midcentury period, or to give credit to the ministers who fostered them. Several publications survive and stand out because of the quality of their contents and because of the alliance they represented between the strictly religious and the educational approach to domestic problems. The *Mother's Assistant and Young Ladies Friend,*[69] which carried on successfully from 1841 to 1863, had among its editors the Reverend C. Stone, and was made up almost entirely of contributions by well-known clergymen. The following titles selected from Vol. I, 1841,[70] are suggestive of the subject matter of these volumes: "Influence of Early Instruction" by the Reverend Hubbard Winslow; "Obedience of Children" by Reverend Jacob Abbott; "Maternal Decision" by the Reverend E. Otheman; "Rewards and Punishments" by Reverend A. B. Muzzey; and "Mother Does That" by Reverend Harvey Newcomb. In this group the Reverend A. B. Muzzey deserves further comment for his authorship of a text on home education entitled *The Fireside.*[71]

The *Parent's Magazine* [72] of Gilmanton, and later of Concord,

66. Nehemiah Adams, *The Baptized Child* (2d ed. Boston, William Peirce, 1836).

67. *D. A. B.*, I, 94.

68. *Ibid.*, XX, 396.

69. See Bibliography for variant titles.

70. Table of contents, *Mother's Assistant*, Vol. I, January, 1841.

71. Reverend A. B. Muzzey, *The Fireside* (Boston, Crosby, Nichols & Co., 1856).

72. See Bibliography for variant titles.

New Hampshire, was initiated by a Reverend I. Bird and his wife, and published by a Reverend J. Thompson. The first volume, published in 1841, stated as its purpose "to promote the early physical, intellectual, moral, and religious training of children" [73] stating that there was at that time no other such periodical in their section of New England. The second volume was given the new title *The Parent's Magazine and Young People's Friend,* with the following explanation printed in the prospectus: "Almost every family embraces in its bosom young persons and domestics who may be expected, in their turn, to become heads of families. And should persons qualify themselves for important duties *after* entry upon them, or *before?*" [74] Contributions to both these volumes were furnished, according to the original plan, "by clergymen and others in various parts of New England." [75]

Between the years 1854 and 1861, the *Happy Home and Parlor Magazine,* mentioned above in connection with the Reverend William Thayer, was published in Boston. Its first six volumes were edited by a Reverend A. R. Baker and their stated purpose was to address "all who endeavor to render home happy." [76] When Thayer took over the editorship in 1858, the *Happy Home* had amalgamated with *The Mother's Assistant* and Thayer had therefore a twofold purpose, to sustain the "elevation" of both magazines, and to make the combined effort more practical,[77] especially on the point of family discipline, which was a subject dear to his heart and of widespread interest during the 'fifties. He proceeded to include articles [78] with such titles as: "Teaching Children How to Deceive"; "Ways of Teaching Children to Be Selfish"; "The Juvenile Code Revised"; and "Letter to a Young Mother"; [79] with the result that the periodical became predominantly devoted to the problems of childhood education.

Horace Bushnell's work on *Christian Nurture* [80] must be seen in retrospect as the most important single contribution in print

73. Flyleaf, *Parent's Magazine,* Vol. I, September, 1840.

74. Prospectus of Vol. II, *Parent's Magazine,* Vol. I, No. 12, August, 1841.

75. *Loc. cit.*

76. Flyleaf, *Happy Home and Parlor Magazine,* Vol. II, 1855.

77. William M. Thayer, "Editor's Address," *Happy Home and Parlor Magazine,* 7:15, January, 1858.

78. *Ibid.,* table of contents, p. vi.

79. Mrs. Louisa C. Tuthill, "Letter to a Young Mother," *Happy Home and Parlor Magazine,* 7:363-66, 1858.

80. Cf. *ante,* p. 21.

to the cause of domestic education as it was related to religion. And yet, while it had profound results on theological thinking with regard to the moral basis of education and the Christian approach to child nurture, it was in some respects a departure from the teachings of the more orthodox of the clergymen mentioned in the above paragraphs. As has been stated previously, Bushnell was creating a new concept of the child and a new and milder system of instruction, whereas to many of the conservative clergy the "cause" of domestic education and of domestic reform was identified with a strong reaffirmation of the discipline and dogmatic religiosity of an earlier period. Here it should be stated, however, that so confused were the issues of the midcentury period and so blurred were the lines between the old and new ways of thinking, that it is not possible to separate the clergy into categories. Those who were writing and teaching, and especially those who were encouraging female authorship and the promotion of educational causes, were exposed to a stream of innovation which, whether or not they realized it, was modifying their orthodoxy. One therefore cannot make use of the term "conservative Congregationalist" or "orthodox clergyman" without qualification. As later chapters will show, there were many conflicting sub-issues in the domestic literature of the period which were overlooked by reformers united on the common ground of their faith in the application of Christian morality to daily life, and in the perfectibility of man.

It may be helpful at this point to consider two men who stood halfway between the religious and the educational approach to the cause of domestic education. The Reverend Heman Humphrey, Congregational clergyman and writer, was better known in his capacity as president of Amherst College for twenty-two years. His text on *Domestic Education* [81] was one of the most complete and comprehensive of the works designed to aid parents, and differed from those of other clergymen in its thorough examination into the principles of social, intellectual, and physical as well as of religious education. It is significant that out of sixteen chapters, only three were devoted entirely to religion. It is also significant that while statements may be quoted which classify Humphrey among the most reactionary of the conservatives, there are others which place him, paradoxically, among the "advance guard" of progressive thinkers and educators of the period.

81. Cf. *ante*, p. v.

For example, he held that man must be "regarded and treated as a fallen creature, as prone to evil and not to good, from the commencement of his being." [82] Rejecting mere moral suasion as a method, he recommended firm family government and checking of evil propensities, if need be by the rod,[83] and he urged that parents subdue the "self will" of their children.[84] On the other hand, he advocated physical freedom and healthful outdoor pursuits, since children were "born to run and laugh and breathe the fresh air and bound over the hills." [85] When discussing the development of the faculties, he advised parents to watch for their unfoldment, not to hasten it, since "Nature does these things infinitely safer and better than we can." [86]

Anticipating the later scientific approach to the child, he discussed "constitutional differences" and "education of the social affections," [87] devoting one chapter to a description of the social personalities of several individual children. Eminently practical, and in some ways reminiscent of Locke, Humphrey belongs definitely to the traditionalists, and yet he defies exclusive classification. He was one of the staunch advocates of the revival of the use of the New England Primer in the instruction of children, expressing dissatisfaction with the light weight fiction which was displacing the earlier, sterner fare. Of his introduction to the Worcester republication of the primer, Livermore wrote: "Undoubtedly, respect for the character and memory of the early New England Puritans, and a desire to have the children of the rising generation trained in the good old ways of their forefathers, was one of the chief moving causes of the re-issue in such quantities [of the primer], under the auspices of so distinguished an individual as President Humphrey. . . ." [88] A further clue to his espousal of domestic causes was his association with the temperance reform group,[89] which activity he definitely associated with the goals of childhood education.[90]

82. Humphrey, *op. cit.*, p. 140.
83. *Ibid.*, p. 58.
84. *Ibid.*, p. 25.
85. *Ibid.*, p. 64.
86. *Ibid.*, p. 71.
87. *Ibid.*, table of contents.
88. George Livermore, *The Origin, History and Character of the New England Primer* (New York, Charles Fred Heartman, 1915), p. 55.
89. *D. A. B.*, IX, 369.
90. Humphrey, *op. cit.*, pp. 207–8.

Samuel G. Goodrich, author and publisher was, like Heman
Humphrey, concerned with "fireside education" from more than
a religious angle. He held a unique position in the field of didactic
literature as a layman acceptable alike to the clergy and to the
proponents of new ideas in education. As the famous "Peter Parley" of story and textbook fame, he produced some 170 volumes,[91]
most of these being works for children which were read by millions during the midcentury period. His text for parents entitled
Fireside Education was a scholarly piece of work which, while it
stressed the priority of the home as seminary, and the parent as
teacher,[92] regarded the common school as "the great auxiliary of
the fireside," [93] and heartily endorsed the cause of popular education for the masses. While not explicit in the domestic counsels of
the clergy as a group, one senses in their religious literature a
note of alarm at the secularization of education, and a tendency
to make the family a sort of retreat or sanctuary *"without the
pale* of the world." [94] Goodrich, known to hosts of child readers,
helped to bridge this gap and to identify in a common cause the
goals of parents, of the clergy, of scientists, and educators.

Infancy, childhood, youth [he declared], all advancing to maturity
by the process of education, place the design of the Creator before
every parent and every member of society. Let parents, then, take
up and follow out this design; let the community at large engage
with providence in carrying to completion its benignant intentions
toward mankind. Let our legislators, those who have almost a
creative power over the society for whom they act—let these
coöperate in the great work of human improvement.[95]

Perhaps because of his large juvenile following, Goodrich could
appeal to the orthodox and progressives alike. His emphasis on
moral cultivation [96] established him as a conserver of the status
quo, while his emphasis on "gradual development," and the onward march of man as a "progressive being" [97] linked him definitely with embryo scientists of the pre-Darwinian period.

Among the group of educators proper who contributed to the

91. *D. A. B.,* VII, 403.
92. Samuel G. Goodrich, *Fireside Education* (New York, F. J. Huntington
& Co., 1838), p. 64.
93. *Ibid.,* p. v.
94. "Introductory Address," *Parent's Magazine,* 1:8, September, 1840.
95. Goodrich, *op. cit.,* p. 65.
96. *Ibid.,* pp. 171–273.
97. *Ibid.,* pp. 46–47.

domestic cause in print, the most outstanding names are those of
three women who saw as basic to social welfare the proper education of women as mothers, and of young children in the home.
These names stand apart from those of previously mentioned
female writers because of their professional status in the field of
education. Catherine Beecher, Emma Willard, and Almira Phelps,
all pioneers in female education were, despite their activities in
other sections of the country, primarily New Englanders, whose
early upbringing and teaching experience led them to take a stand
as "active conservatives" with regard to the woman question.

Catherine Beecher was of inestimable importance in domestic
reform, turning out during her busy career some two dozen books
in addition to numerous written addresses and magazine articles,[98]
of which the majority plead the cause of higher education for
women. An address entitled *Suggestions Respecting Improvements in Education,* printed in 1829, set the keynotes for her
later crusade. Daughter of the conservative Lyman Beecher, and
definitely opposed to woman suffrage, she held consistently to the
middle ground on the woman question. Thus, she wrote of woman's
sphere, "Though she may not teach from the portico nor thunder
from the forum, in her secret retirements she may form and send
forth the sages that shall govern and renovate the world." [99] This
was woman's true profession, she maintained, yet one for which
she was ill fitted.[100] She saw as the crying need for women, the
education which would fit them to execute their sacred mission.
If mothers were to care for the physical, intellectual, and moral
education of their children, they needed instruction in the *"principles* of that perfect and wonderful piece of mechanism," [101] committed to their care. From 1829 until late in the 'seventies Catherine Beecher's best efforts were directed toward instructing
American women in their duties and in attaching a new dignity
to the profession of housekeeping. Titles of her works [102] published during the 'forties and 'fifties are suggestive: *Treatise on
Domestic Economy* (1842) ; *The Duty of American Women to
Their Country* (1845) ; *The Evils Suffered by American Women*

98. Mae Elizabeth Harveson, *Catherine Esther Beecher, Pioneer Educator.*
Dissertation. (University of Pennsylvania, Philadelphia, 1932), chap. viii.

99. Catherine E. Beecher, *Suggestions Respecting Improvements in Education* (Hartford, Packard & Butler, 1829), p. 54.

100. *Ibid.,* p. 9.

101. *Ibid.,* p. 8.

102. Harveson, *op. cit.,* pp. 176–83.

and Children (1846) ; *True Remedy for the Wrongs of Women* (1851) ; and *Letters to the People on Health and Happiness* (1855). Of these volumes the *Treatise on Domestic Economy* bears most directly on the duties of women in the home. This work, declaring that "the mother forms the character of the future man" [103] gave practical instructions to the prospective wife and mother in matters of health, food, clothing, care of infants, and other household concerns, which today would be included under the heading of "Domestic Science."

Miss Beecher's efforts in behalf of children were extended beyond the home in her fight for teacher education. Women, she declared, should have first place in the schoolroom, and the teaching profession should reward them with respectable remuneration. The duty of American women to their country was to see and fill the great needs of untaught children, particularly in the west, where facilities for education were scarce.[104]

Emma Willard and her sister Almira Phelps, engaged as was Catherine Beecher in the teaching of young women, identified themselves in the same way with the cause of domestic reform. Miss Willard saw as the duty of the female sex the regulation of " 'the internal concerns of every family,' " stating that unless women were properly qualified for this they could not, with any " 'literary or ornamental attainments . . . be expected to make either good wives, good mothers, or good mistresses of families.' " [105]

Mrs. Phelps, writing for *Godey's Lady's Book* in 1839, asked:

Is not the character of the future men of our republic, to depend on the mothers we are now educating?

Physiologists tell us that the nursing infant imbibes with his mother's milk, her tastes and propensities. We do not suppose, indeed, that mind can be thus transfused from one soul to another; but we do think that the moral character of the future man may be influenced by the treatment he receives at the breast, and in the cradle; and that his physical condition may be seriously affected by the food which he imbibes from the maternal fount. . . .[106]

103. Beecher, *A Treatise on Domestic Economy*, p. 37.

104. Catherine E. Beecher, *The Duty of American Women to Their Country* (New York, Harper & Bros., 1845), *passim*.

105. "Mrs. Willard on Female Education," *Ladies' Magazine*, 7:169, April, 1834.

106. Almira H. Phelps, "Remarks on the Education of Girls," *Godey's Lady's Book*, 18:253, June, 1839.

Both Mrs. Willard and Mrs. Phelps stressed physical as well as intellectual and moral improvement of women.

Their outstanding contribution in print to the cause of domestic education was a translation of Madame Necker de Saussure's *Progressive Education,* which was published in Boston in 1835.[107] This work shows clearly from what source they derived their inspiration for the counseling of mothers, and their progressive ideas on method in the teaching of children. Mrs. Phelps, in particular, selected concepts of learning from those of Pestalozzi and Rousseau, incorporating them into her system of instruction, it is pointed out, "ten years before Mann made his famous Seventh Report to the Massachusetts State Board of Education." [108]

Following the advice of Madame de Saussure,[109] Mrs. Phelps kept a journal on the development of her own baby. This appeared in print as an appendix to the translation of *Progressive Education* under the title "Observations upon an Infant, during its First Year, by a Mother." [110] Anticipating the studies of Darwin, Compayre, Preyer and other pioneers in child study, this work was the first of its kind to be published by an American,[111] and was especially forward-looking in its stress on "the gradual development of the senses, the intellectual faculties, and the emotions." Mrs. Phelps regarded the study of this development as the joint task of the philosopher and the mother.[112]

Another domestic text which combined scientific ideas with conservative moral philosophy of the period was Mrs. Phelps' *Fireside Friend,* or *Female Student,* which appeared in 1836 as a revised edition of her *Lectures to Young Ladies* and had wide publicity, passing through six editions in the United States and three in London. This volume, addressed to young ladies, devoted one section to domestic habits, and moral and religious education, pointing out to its young readers that they would one day

107. Madame Necker de Saussure, *Progressive Education* translated from the French by Emma Willard and Almira Phelps (Boston, William D. Ticknor, 1835).

108. Emma L. Bolzau, *Almira Hart Lincoln Phelps* (Lancaster, Pa., Science Press Printing Company, 1936), p. 332.

109. De Saussure, *op. cit.,* p. 123.

110. Almira H. Phelps, "Observations upon an Infant," Appendix in De Saussure, *Progressive Education,* pp. 323–48.

111. Bolzau, *op. cit.,* pp. 346–47.

112. Phelps, *op. cit.,* p. 324.

"regard their own health and happiness, as but secondary to the well-being of those who will owe existence to them." [113]

Brief mention should be made of the two sisters Elizabeth and Mary Tyler Peabody for their contributions in print to the cause of childhood education. Elizabeth Peabody, teacher in Bronson Alcott's Temple School and later founder of the first American kindergarten, published her *Record of a School* in 1835. This volume, addressed to parents, gave circulation to Alcott's transcendental theories of child training.[114] A later publication of hers, the *Kindergarten Guide,* did not come out until 1863. This is of note chiefly for its inclusion of a series of letters by Mary Tyler Peabody, written some twenty years earlier, entitled *Moral Culture of Infancy.*[115] The latter, which sets forth an extremely enlightened view of child nature and growth, is significant because Mary Peabody became the second wife of Horace Mann and presumably contributed to his liberal philosophy of education.

Other well-known educators of the period who were concerned primarily with the cause of the child, rather than with domestic reform in general, are important for the interest in domestic education disseminated by their writings and editorial activities.

William Russell, editor of the *American Journal of Education* and a forerunner of Horace Mann, had, in the first volume of this liberal publication, stated it as his purpose to pay particular attention to *"domestic education,* or that which emanates from parental and family influence." He considered *"early and elementary education* more important than that of any other period or department." [116] Another statement from this prospectus of 1826 is significant; this was his reference to female education. "Whatever concerns the culture of the female mind," he said, "extends ultimately to the formation of all minds, at that early and susceptible period, when maternal influence is forming those impressions which eventually terminate in mental and moral habits." [117] In accordance with this early policy, initiated by Russell

113. Almira H. Phelps, *Female Student* (2d ed. New York, Leavitt, Lord & Co., Boston, Crocker & Brewster, 1836), p. 408.

114. Dorothy McCuskey, *Bronson Alcott, Teacher* (New York, Macmillan Company, 1940), p. 90.

115. Mrs. Horace Mann and Elizabeth P. Peabody, *Moral Culture of Infancy and Kindergarten Guide* (Boston, T. O. H. P. Burnham, 1863).

116. William Russell, "Prospectus," *American Journal of Education,* 1:3, January, 1826.

117. *Loc. cit.*

and carried out by Woodbridge when he took over the editorship in 1830,[118] the journal included accounts of the work of Pestalozzi, Wilderspin, and Fellenberg, articles on the government of young children and the education of females. It also publicized liberal works on education by Europeans such as George Combe and Madame Necker de Saussure.[119]

William C. Woodbridge, like Russell, a liberalizing force behind the movement of domestic education, stated in his initial editorial address that "no plans of improvement can be effectual which do not aim at purifying these fountains of maternal influence, whose clear or turbid waters may be perceived through the whole course of the stream . . . and give their hue to the broad river which is flowing into the ocean." [120] Woodbridge gave publicity to the infant school system, and focused attention on primary schools and Sabbath schools,[121] thus identifying the cause of fireside education with that of popular, growing agencies of childhood education.

Amos Bronson Alcott, transcendentalist educator, belongs in this liberal group as one of those who worked behind the scenes to lend important, though indirect, impetus to the cause of domestic reform. Alcott addressed two articles to mothers, both appearing in the *American Journal of Education*.[122] The first one, "Maternal Instruction," had been written in 1829 to call the attention of mothers to a pamphlet published in London entitled "Hints to Parents," the second part of which was described as being "In the spirit of Pestalozzi's Method." [123] "There is no relation more sacred than the *maternal*" [124] said Alcott, pointing out that "it was the great purpose of Pestalozzi, to inspire mothers with a just sense of their value in the scale of being." This article was followed several years later by a piece written for the *Ameri-*

118. Russell was editor 1826–29; W. C. Woodbridge, 1830–37; William A. Alcott, 1837–38. Title changed to *American Annals of Education and Instruction* in 1831.

119. See indices, Vols. 1826–38.

120. W. C. Woodbridge, "Editor's Address," *American Annals of Education* 1:329, August, 1830.

121. *Loc. cit.* See also *American Annals of Education*, 3:286, June, 1833.

122. "Maternal Instruction—Hints to Parents," Art. 6, *American Journal of Education*, 4:53–58, January, 1829. This article was not signed by Alcott, but is stated as being of his authorship in McCuskey, *Bronson Alcott, Teacher*, p. 36.

123. *Ibid.*, p. 53.

124. *Ibid.*, p. 54.

can Annals of Education expressing Alcott's own thoughts on "Maternal Influence." [125] In this, he hailed "a bright era in the history of man" to come when mothers might be "favored with opportunities and attainments for exerting a genial influence on infancy." He deplored the situation where "the maternal office is delegated to the nursery maid," and the mother's "best thoughts and freshest affections" [126] called off to other things. He stated that the child's propensities, affections and faculties, intellectual and spiritual, need the close ministrations of the mother.[127] A third article entitled *Observations on the Principles and Methods of Infant Instruction* [128] appeared as a pamphlet in 1830, in which he continued to establish his claims for the rights of infancy.

Bronson Alcott might have been considered one of the leading educators in domestic reform in his own day had it not been for the extremes into which his liberalism led him. His work, *Conversations with Children on the Gospels,* issued in 1836, was severely censured [129] for the innovations it proposed in the teaching of young children. This text, though grounded on the Scriptures, was very unorthodox in its approaches and open to questionable interpretation. Miss Elizabeth Peabody, his co-worker, joined in criticism of him but added, in defense of Alcott, that "Few persons will, perhaps, be able to understand and to sympathize with Mr. Alcott's entire course . . . or appreciate how much more is to be hoped than feared, from giving complete liberty to the yet undepraved and unsophisticated spirit." [130]

The Reverend T. H. Gallaudet, unlike Alcott, was generally acclaimed as one of the great educators of the period, and was best known for his labors in behalf of the education of the deaf. To the literature of childhood education he contributed a number of didactic books to be used by mothers and teachers on the early instruction of children. One work, entitled *The Child's Book on the Soul,*[131] attracted wide attention, passing through

125. Bronson Alcott, "Maternal Influence," *American Annals of Education,* 3:16–24, January, 1833.

126. *Ibid.,* pp. 17–18.

127. *Ibid.,* pp. 16–24.

128. Cf. *ante,* p. 26.

129. McCuskey, *op. cit.,* pp. 100–6.

130. Elizabeth P. Peabody, "Recorder's Preface," in Amos Bronson Alcott, *Conversations with Children on the Gospels* (Boston, James Munroe & Co., 1836), I, v.

131. T. H. Gallaudet, *Child's Book on the Soul* (Hartford, Cooke & Co., 1831). 2 Parts.

seven editions, and was commended as "deserving the attention, not only of parents, but of teachers in Infant and Sabbath Schools." [132] It is significant that this work, which had much the same purpose as Alcott's *Conversations . . .* succeeded where Alcott's failed. Gallaudet, very definitely influenced by the inductive methods of Pestalozzi, and new emphasis on sense perception in education, belonged in the front ranks of educational innovators. He employed these methods in his book on the soul, but, unlike Alcott, he did not tamper with the Gospel or lay himself open to attack by indulging in transcendental speculation. His religious orthodoxy is apparent in several of the titles of his other works for children, which were written for the purpose of moral instruction: *The Child's Book on Repentance; The Child's Book of Bible Stories;* and nine volumes of *Scripture Biography,* commencing with Adam and Joseph, and leaving off with Jonah.[133]

Horace Mann and Henry Barnard, engrossed as they were in the great task of improving popular education in Massachusetts and Connecticut, had small time to give to domestic reform as such, but Mann through the vehicle of his *Common School Journal* and his famous Annual Reports, and Barnard, through his *American Journal of Education,*[134] contributed to the joint cause of female education and early childhood education. Mann saw the furtherance of this cause as essential to the well-being of the country. Quoting Waterston in 1845, he wrote: " 'Here is the replenishing of the world; here is a new wave of existence. From these little children will be selected the judges and statesmen of the next half century. Thus are we the creators of a world's destiny; we are moulding the elements of coming society.' " [135] An innovator in methods of early instruction, Mann brought down a storm of controversy from conservatives by his advocacy of new and pleasant methods of learning the alphabet,[136] and by his plea for rule by love rather than by rod.[137] Here, again, Mann was criti-

132. "Recent Publications," *Spirit of the Pilgrims,* 5:122, February, 1832.

133. Heman Humphrey, *The Life and Labors of the Reverend T. H. Gallaudet* (New York, Robert Carter & Bros., 1857), pp. 280–81.

134. Barnard publicized such systems as that of Pestalozzi, e.g., in Barnard's *American Journal of Education,* 10:65–123, September, 1857.

135. Horace Mann, "Editor's Address," *Common School Journal,* 7:3, January, 1845.

136. Horace Mann, *Seventh Annual Report* (1844), in Massachusetts Board of Education, *Annual Reports,* pp. 91–99.

137. Association of Masters, *Remarks on the Seventh Annual Report of Horace Mann,* pp. 109–15.

cized for liberal ideas which, coming from the clergy or the conservative female writers of the period would have passed muster, particularly if disguised by the flowery moralization of the period. Mann, however, was outspoken. He was a Unitarian. He was an advocate of that questionable, pseudo science known as phrenology, and he was proposing a great many innovations [138] at one time, some of them seemingly un-American to critical contemporaries.

Henry Barnard said of "females" that their sphere was domestic.[139] He supported female education because he believed women should be enlightened companions of intelligent men.[140] He also believed women teachers were best fitted to mold the childhood and youth of the nation.[141]

So much, then, for the educators of the period. Two other groups were influential in focusing public attention upon the needs of women and children. These were the advocates of health, the proponents of the medical and physiological sciences, and the group which may be described as "social reformers" of the period.

Philadelphia rather than Boston was the center from which the earliest American texts on pediatrics were issued. The work of Dr. Dewees of that city *On the Physical and Medical Treatment of Children,* published in 1825, was referred to by New Englanders,[142] but American texts on this subject were generally rare during this period. There is evidence that the Scotch physician, Andrew Combe, brother of George Combe, the phrenologist, was an authority relied upon by Americans. His text on the *Physiological and Moral Management of Infancy* was recommended by the *Parent's Magazine* [143] of New Hampshire, and also used by Catherine Beecher.[144]

Nevertheless, despite the scarcity of authorized American texts on the subject, health was a byword in the literature of the mid-century and many popularized texts were to make their appearance to satisfy the clamorous demand for information. Health

138. B. A. Hinsdale, *Horace Mann* (Centennial ed. New York, Charles Scribner's Sons, 1937), pp. 189–92.

139. John S. Brubacher, editor, *Henry Barnard on Education* (New York and London, McGraw-Hill Book Company, Inc., 1931), p. 65.

140. *Ibid.,* p. 66.

141. *Ibid.,* p. 195.

142. See comment of William A. Alcott in his text *The Young Mother* (Boston, Light & Stearns, 1836), p. 30.

143. "To Mothers and Nurses," *Parent's Magazine,* 1:245, July, 1841.

144. Beecher, *A Treatise on Domestic Economy,* p. 214.

was the basis of the great movement toward dress reform for women and children. It gave rise to faddist groups who subsisted on vegetables and the products of wheat. Dr. Graham, the originator of graham bread, lectured at this time. As Fish pointed out "All Americans, stirred thereto eventually by their hastiness of diet, took a deep interest in their own interiors and bought generously and read persistently the many medical books arranged alphabetically by symptoms and drugs, which keen producers furnished to a ready market." [145]

The way in which this flood of advice came to women and children and the home was largely through the medium of the domestic reformer. Catherine Beecher, Emma Willard, and Almira Phelps all promoted the cause of health by advocating calisthenics for young women, proper diet, and clothing designed with regard for the human physiognomy. Sarah Hale, in her *Ladies' Magazine,* gave space, from time to time, to health topics. The specific contributions in print of these individuals will be considered more fully in a later chapter.

Phrenologists, speaking in behalf of the physical, intellectual, and moral culture of women and children stressed physical welfare. In the 1834 *Ladies' Magazine,* George Combe, visiting Scotch phrenologist of the day, is quoted on health: " 'For many years, the lives of children depend almost exclusively on the care of the mother. Young women, therefore, ought to be taught not only how to regulate their own habits so that they may preserve their health and vigor, but also how to treat children, both as physical and mental beings.' " [146] He goes on to explain that the study of phrenology will aid mothers in acquiring this knowledge.

Dr. Spurzheim, another European phrenologist, had seized upon the mother-child relationship to justify the spread of his science, writing, "the duty of *education* devolves particularly on the *mother;* but to be able to do her duty, she must have acquired notions herself." [147] Mrs. Hale called attention to this message also. Orson Squire Fowler, who popularized and publicized phrenology from his own publishing house in New York, deserves

145. From Carl R. Fish, *The Rise of the Common Man,* p. 210. By permission of the Macmillan Company, publishers.

146. "Books and Authors" reviewing George Combe's *Lectures on Popular Education, Ladies' Magazine,* 7:377, August, 1834.

147. Spurzheim, "Sentiment," *Ladies' Magazine,* 6:423, September, 1833.

mention here for two works, one entitled *Love and Parentage, Applied to the Improvement of Offspring* which, published in Boston as well as New York, reached its fortieth edition in 1844.[148] This work contained many of the so called principles of health advocated by phrenologists. The second work on *Education and Self-Improvement* will receive attention in Chapter V.[149]

The American name which stands out most vividly in the domestic health annals of New England is that of Dr. William Andrus Alcott,[150] cousin of Bronson Alcott. His interest in health was aroused by his early work with children as a schoolmaster in the poorly constructed, ill ventilated rural buildings of the period, and also by a trip south with his cousin Bronson.[151] William Alcott became a physician and author after attending medical school at Yale University, and produced throughout the midcentury period over a hundred volumes on medical and physical education and on general domestic reform. Worthy of especial note here are his texts entitled *The Young Mother, The Young Wife,* and *The Young Housekeeper,* all of which volumes contain practical advice on dress, food, and general health as well as on moral reform. His works on medical and physical education numbered some thirty-one volumes [152] and in each of these he attempted to popularize the laws of health for the general public.

Also noteworthy is a periodical which was edited by Alcott in the years 1835 and 1836 entitled *The Moral Reformer, and Teacher on the Human Constitution.* Through this organ Dr. Alcott proposed to show "not only the structure and laws of the human system, but the almost inseparable connection of health and morals," a connection which he declared was "too often overlooked or disregarded." [153] The philosophy of health implied in this statement will be considered in Chapter VI.

There were few social reforms of the midcentury which did not at some point come in contact with the cause of domestic education and family reform. Even the antislavery cause owed much of its strength to the New England reformers who drew attention

148. Branch, *The Sentimental Years,* p. 222.
149. Cf. *post,* p. 114.
150. *D. A. B.,* I, 142–43.
151. McCuskey, *op. cit.,* p. 16.
152. *D. A. B.,* I, 143.
153. William A. Alcott, "Editor's Address," *The Moral Reformer,* 1:5, January, 1835.

to women, children, convicts, and the insane as beings possessed
of rights which society had been too long in recognizing.[154] It was
only natural that the slave should eventually fall under this heading. A strong argument employed by conservatives who were opposed to slavery was that broken homes and faulty early education of many human beings are the inevitable results of the
slave trade. Gabriel suggests that Harriet Beecher Stowe's *Uncle
Tom's Cabin* owed much of its great success to the popular appeal
of the "broken home" theme.[155] Certainly it was effective propa-
ganda in many homes where the names of the Grimké sisters,
Mrs. Child, Mrs. Mott, and their daring co-workers, were taboo.
It is interesting to note that Barnes attributes the crippling of
Boston Abolitionism to the stand taken by William Lloyd Garrison
in regard to the clergy and the cause of women.[156] In opposing
the clergy he was alienating the support of many domestic reformers who had engaged with evangelical fervor in the antislavery cause. And to make this alienation complete, Garrison
pronounced the Grimké sisters to be "pioneers in the movement
to free humanity from the bonds of family, church, law, and government," [157] with the end result that he involved the Grimké
sisters in a controversy with the Congregational clergy and thus
retarded woman suffrage. Harriet Beecher Stowe was enthu-
siastically received because she kept the cause undefiled, and gave
to a home-loving American public little Eva and a stirring plot.

Lydia Maria Child, mentioned above for her contributions to
domestic literature,[158] represents, in a way, the stable or balanced representative of the antislavery movement, the idealistic
worker who, unlike Garrison, identified family solidarity and the
furtherance of religious goals with the cause of the negro.

These aspects of the thought behind the antislavery agitation
weighted much of the didactic literature of the midcentury period,
and therefore served to intensify public interest in the home and
its occupants.

Public sentiment in regard to crime was aroused by such statements as the following taken from the trial story of a Norwich

154. Ernest S. Bates, *An American Faith* (New York, W. W. Norton & Co.,
Inc., 1940), p. 431.
155. Gabriel, *The Course of American Democratic Thought*, p. 6.
156. Gilbert H. Barnes, *The Antislavery Impulse*, 1830–44 (New York
and London, D. Appleton–Century Company, Inc., 1933), p. 98.
157. *Ibid.*, p. 155.
158. Cf. *ante*, p. 43.

offender: "That germ, whose growth has been so bitter, was *insubordination,* from his childhood upwards. His whole course has been marked by self-will, breaking through all the common restraints of the family, of the school-room, of the counting-house, of social life, and of the law of God . . . let the parent tremble. . . ." [159]

Another number of the *Parent's Magazine* gives case studies of convicts, in each case presenting this sort of information: "His mother, although hopefully pious, never prayed with him in private. There was no maternal association in the place of their residence. . . . Reader, are you a parent? . . . *'Train up a child in the way he should go.'* . . ." [160]

As for the great temperance cause of the midnineteenth century, it is difficult to determine whether it took its impetus from the more general trend toward domestic reform, or whether domestic reformers were inspired by the social zeal of the temperance advocates. In any event their crusades were closely connected. There is scarcely a volume on domestic counsels for parents which does not mention the evils of alcohol and recommend the support of the temperance cause. Heman Humphrey [161] and Samuel Goodrich [162] were especially vehement in their warnings to parents. Family periodicals featured stories with titles such as "The Restored Family," and "The Emigrant's Daughter," [163] featuring the plot of the happy family reduced to misery and want by the drunkenness of the father. "The Restored Family," which won a fifteen dollar prize, showed the drunkard restored to health, the church, and prosperity by a religious child.[164]

There is some evidence of conservative resistance to the incessant temperance activity of the period. Thus we read: "Let children . . . be taught from their infancy that alcohol is a poison, and that it is very wrong to use intoxicating drinks, and there will be no need of so many temperance addresses, temperance

159. "End of Insubordination," *Parent's Magazine,* 2:105–6, January, 1842.

160. "An Interview with Convicts in the N. H. State Prison," *Parent's Magazine,* 1:236, June, 1841.

161. Humphrey, *Domestic Education,* pp. 207–8.

162. Goodrich, *op. cit.,* pp. 282–83.

163. Mrs. S. P. Clark, "The Emigrant's Daughter," *Mother's Assistant,* 9:39–43, August, 1846.

164. Mrs. M. O. Stevens, "The Restored Family," *Mother's Assistant,* 4:97–119, May, 1844.

societies, temperance papers, tracts and almanacs." [165] A contributor to the *Ladies' Magazine,* saw this cause, however, as peculiarly the business of mothers, declaring that while women continue "to use spirits in a variety of ways—in cooking, in medicine, in baths and lotions," while they consider it necessary, "intemperance will never be banished from our land." [166]

T. S. Arthur, the great temperance writer and author of the spectacularly successful play *Ten Nights in a Bar Room,* produced a text entitled *The Mother,*[167] which, like the semi-didactic novels of C. S. Sedgwick, endeavored to delineate the pitfalls of parenthood in sugar-coated form. This book was published in Boston and may therefore be considered pertinent to this study, although Arthur himself was a native of New York and Philadelphia. It is significant that he identified himself with the specific cause of fireside education and that he enlisted the help of mothers in removing intemperance by making a proper beginning in family government.

This chapter has attempted to show a cross section of that literary endeavor of the midnineteenth century which focused attention on the general cause of domestic reform. There is no real boundary to this cause in print and the data included here must be considered incomplete. It is also difficult to separate the various groups of "reformers" into categories. Educators, clergymen, women writers, advocates of temperance, and even abolitionists, were all working on a common ground when they sought to control society by reforming the family. It was inevitable that their ideas should interact and that each group should be modified by the ideas of the other groups. The effects of this interaction of thought will be seen in the chapters to follow.

165. "Bearing of Parental Fidelity on the Millennium," *Parent's Magazine,* 1:52–53, November, 1840.
166. "The Pledge," *Ladies' Magazine,* 7:134, March, 1834.
167. T. S. Arthur, *The Mother* (Boston, S. Colman, 1846).

PART TWO

CONCEPTS OF THE MOTHER'S ROLE
IN CHILDHOOD EDUCATION

CHAPTER IV

RELIGIOUS AND MORAL GUIDE

TO the conservative molders of midnineteenth century society there was no folly so blameworthy as infidelity. Catherine Sedgwick voiced the prevailing opinion on this subject when she quoted Paley on the title page of her novel, *Redwood,*

"Whilst the infidel mocks at the superstitions of the vulgar, insults over their credulous fears, their childish errors, their fantastic rites, it does not occur to him to observe, that the most preposterous device by which the weakest devotee ever believed he was securing the happiness of a future life, is more rational than unconcern about it." [1]

While "infidelity" admitted of a wide definition and exaggerated importance on the lips of ardent reformers, it was undoubtedly existent in the form of a growing indifference to religious dogma and a growing attachment to the pleasurable escapes and follies of a materialistic world. Organized religion had itself been partially responsible for this.

Unitarianism, before it had time to realize the implications of Channing's humanitarianism,[2] had been condemned by Lyman Beecher as the " 'icy system,' " [3] rejecting as it did the traditional creeds and myths of orthodox Christianity.[4] Consisting for the most part of negations,[5] it tended in its earlier stages to weaken religious ties, not only among the more rational of the intellectuals, but also among the rising middle classes of urban society, who found in the "fashionable religion" a sanction for personal freedom and liberalism.

This background is essential to an understanding of the midcentury's fervent "return to religion" which was the backbone

1. Catherine M. Sedgwick, *Redwood* (Revised ed. New York, George P. Putnam, 1850).
2. Parrington, *Main Currents in American Thought,* II, 332–38.
3. Brooks, *The Flowering of New England,* p. 64.
4. Bates, *An American Faith,* p. 402.
5. *Loc. cit.*

of the domestic reform movement. It also explains why so many of the clergymen reformers were Congregationalists during a period when Unitarianism was the leading religion in the urban centers of New England. Henry Barnard, in tracing the history of the churches, spoke of the loss of Congregationalist members to the Unitarian denomination from 1810 to 1830, but stated that ". . . soon after 1840 there was a spirit of greater activity and aggressive action roused in the Congregational churches." [6] Despite the eloquence of Channing's pleas for an aroused social conscience, Unitarianism, having won its victories in numbers had settled down into a complacent orthodoxy.[7] But complacency had small chance to grow in the turbulent 'thirties and 'forties. The Congregationalists, newly fortified, in part by the very liberalism which they opposed in theory, became a strongly vocal and active minority. And many of Channing's Unitarians became the inspired leaders of transcendentalism, "the religion of romanticism." [8] Quiescent orthodoxy and cold rationalism were alike repugnant to reformers of the period.

Most eloquent of the reactionaries were those who placed their hopes for the salvation of the country in the proper "nurture and admonition" of the rising generation. Laxness in family government and emphasis on intellectual culture at the expense of religious and moral culture were, they declared, responsible for the deplorable "atheism, licentiousness and intemperance" which had caused the downfall of the French government, but Americans might avert this catastrophe by stemming the tide of unbelief, by "seizing upon the infant mind, and training it up under moral and religious influence." [9]

The mother, therefore, was of supreme importance to the nation as guardian and guide of the days of infancy, and many definitions of her unique function were forthcoming. While some reformers were to stress the father's responsibility in family education,[10] popular sentiment granted to the mother the chief

6. Henry Barnard, "The Growth and Progress of Religious Denominations in the United States for the Past Hundred Years," Appendix, in *Educational Development*, republished from *First Century of National Existence* (Hartford, L. Stebbins, 1873), pp. 630–31.

7. Bates, *op. cit.*, pp. 402–3.

8. *Ibid.*, p. 404.

9. Mr. Welch, "Our Country," *Parent's Magazine*, 2:25, October, 1841.

10. Hall, *On the Education of Children*, pp. 45–46. See also Theodore Dwight, *The Father's Book* (Springfield, G. and C. Merriam, 1834).

influence over the emotions, the affections and the soul, through which channels the moral character of childhood was to be guided. "The mother holds the reins of the soul; the father sways the dominion of the intellect," [11] said Goodrich in 1838. "Companions, brothers and sisters, the father, . . ." another writer declared, "all perform their part, but the mother does the most" [12] since it is her feelings, passions, and expressions which the child imitates and absorbs. Religion, then, was to take root in the nursery, with the mother as the principal instrument "in restoring the race to its primitive purity." [13] This much was current sentiment among reformers of the midcentury. Even for those members of society who had rejected much of the religious dogma, this was translatable into terms of moral development. Endless generalizations could be made under the heading of maternal influence on human character.

The church made full use of this emphasis to further its own ends, whether these ends were to restore orthodox religious observances to the family circle or to promote religious activities beyond the walls of the home. The Reverend William Thayer, for example, in his prize essay, "The Era for Mothers," appealed to women to exert their influence in order to produce *"Citizens of enlarged benevolence," "Faithful and fearless ministers of the Gospel," "Missionaries of the Cross,"* in short, to form the rising generation to be ministers and reformers.[14]

Frequently sectarian beliefs in such practices as infant baptism [15] and early conversion [16] were enjoined upon mothers as essential stepping stones in the sanctification of their children. What if the mother or child should die before this important dedication was made? Questions such as these were raised to impress mothers with the urgency of their responsibility. In these arguments maternal influence was linked not only with the temporal usefulness, but also with the eternal salvation of the child.

11. Cf. illustration p. 150.
12. "The Responsibility of the Mother," *Parent's Magazine*, 1:156, March, 1841.
13. *Loc. cit.*
14. Thayer, "The Era for Mothers," *Mother's Assistant*, pp. 136–38, May, 1851.
15. "The Ground of Parental Obligation—No. 6," *Parent's Magazine*, 2:235–36, June, 1842.
16. "Bearing of Parental Fidelity on the Millennium," *Parent's Magazine*, 1:73, December, 1840.

Concepts of the mother's role in religious and moral guidance of childhood were, however, generally centered about the character of the mother and about the details of her program of religious instruction.

The power of maternal example is an ever recurring theme in the didactic literature of the period. "O, if Mothers did but realize," one writer declared, "how early, how imperceptibly they begin to impart their own spirit to the little ones whom God has given them, they would be more watchful never to exhibit before them a single unlovely or undesirable trait." [17] Under the Puritan regime, moral training of children had consisted in the enforcing of obedience to parental, largely paternal authority, and "line upon line" and "precept upon precept" were construed as adherence to the divine command as found in the printed word of the Bible, the catechism, and the primer. The child, as an originally sinful being, was responsible directly to God, and dependent for salvation upon repentance for his sins and ultimate conversion. Excluded from the fold of the "elect" until this conversion took place, which was frequently not until adolescence,[18] the period of early childhood was one to be lived through as quickly as possible, and the parent-child relationship was important chiefly in bringing about the subjugation of youthful, or evil spirits.

The nineteenth century experienced profound changes of thought with regard to the importance of this early training. These changes were brought about in part by pioneers in the study of the mind, who claimed that the unfoldment of the moral faculties begins, before intellectual development, in early childhood [19] and that impressions made in infancy lay the foundation for all future development.[20] They were brought about also by divines like Bushnell, who exalted children to a new position of importance in the church as beings susceptible from birth of positive spiritual nurture, and, finally, they were effected by the rediscovery of the Christian "way" of the New Testament. Just as Christ was proclaimed the guide or mediator [21] for men, the mother was seen as the guide or example for her children from infancy upward, pointing their way heavenward through the influence

17. Susan A. Tucker, "A Word with Mothers," prize essay, *Mother's Assistant*, 3:147, July, 1843.

18. Fleming, *Children and Puritanism*, pp. 172–74.

19. Humphrey, *Domestic Education*, p. 78.

20. Goodrich, *Fireside Education*, pp. 62–65.

21. Cf. *ante*, p. 19.

of the softer affections of love, kindliness, and benevolence.[22] While this parallel between maternal and Christlike influence seems somewhat farfetched, or extreme, it accounts for the occasional outbursts of midcentury extravaganza, which clothed the mother in an aura of divinity.[23] Mrs. Sigourney, writing of the mother's power as early guide declared, "If she fix her lever judiciously, though she may not, like Archimedes, aspire to move the earth, she may hope to raise one of the inhabitants of earth to heaven." [24]

To be adequate to this task, mothers were urged to reflect in their own behavior all that they wished their children to become.[25] "The expression of the countenance, the tone of the voice, the theme of conversation, and every movement of the body . . . have their influence on the imitative little beings. . . ." [26] said one writer. Women were, therefore, to let Christian feelings animate their hearts, and to reveal by every gesture and word a spirit of mildness, of benevolence, of gentle kindliness. Mrs. Child declared that mothers must never let children see or feel "the influence of bad passions, even in the most trifling things." [27] Catherine Beecher devoted a whole chapter, in her text *Domestic Economy* to "good temper" in the American housekeeper and mother.[28] Mrs. Sigourney declared, "The little child opens the door of its heart to the kind tone, the smiling brow, the eye looking above this world, to a brighter sun." [29] One notes especially the emphasis upon cheerfulness, and cheerfulness applied to religious manifestations. "Christians ought to be happy, and being so, should make it visible." [30] Domestic educators had made the important discovery that spiritual culture, to be effective, must have pleasant associations for children. Mothers were urged to maintain a serenity and peace of spirit which would demonstrate to children the efficacy of the Christian faith. Thus, mothers were addressed: ". . . if the cloud often hangs upon your brow,

22. Cf. poem, "Providence," *Mother's Assistant*, 1853, p. 116.

23. Cf. *ante*, p. 35.

24. Lydia Sigourney, "Maternal Influence," in Bailey, *Young Ladies Class Book*, p. 264.

25. "Example," *Mother's Assistant*, 3:13, January, 1843.

26. "Self-Discipline," *Parent's Magazine*, 2:257, July, 1842.

27. Lydia M. Child, *The Mother's Book* (Boston, Carter & Hendee, 1831), p. 9.

28. Beecher, *A Treatise on Domestic Economy*, chap. xiii, pp. 148–55.

29. Sigourney, *Letters to Mothers*, p. 194.

30. *Ibid.*, p. 195.

and words of complaint fall . . . from your lips, they will mistake the spirit you display for religion, and no wonder if they
do not love it." [31] This stress upon happiness is significant because it indicates among other things that the lot of the midcentury mother was frequently a hard one. A contributor to the
Mother's Assistant warned mothers that if cheeks were "frequently suffused with tears," children would be puzzled by the
statement that "to be good, is the way to be happy." [32] Confronted
with death and sickness, and burdened by household cares, women
must have found this requirement at times a difficult one.

Maternal attitudes toward death and suffering were regarded
as extremely important in their influence upon children. Mrs.
Child wrote, "Children should always hear death spoken of as a
blessed change; and if the selfishness of our nature will wring
some tears from us . . . they should be such tears as we shed for
a brief absence, not . . . utter separation." [33] The Reverend John
Abbott saw death scenes and periods of sickness as fit occasions
for impressing children with joys of a future world, and with
the providence of God's care.[34] To Mrs. Sigourney, the ideal mother
was the one who, bowing in submission to the divine will, could
bend over her dying child and praise the Lord for taking him to
that "glorious company" [35] in heaven. The poetry of the day carried this sentimentalizing of the death theme to a morbid extreme.[36] As will be noted later in this chapter, it had unhealthful
consequences when applied to religious instruction of children.
As a phase of maternal character, it is consistent with the religious pattern set for women by most of the domestic reformers.

Female piety was seen to be above all other traits in its influence upon the moral development of young children. A type
of "research" common to the midcentury period was that which
traced influences upon ministers, criminals, and monarchs to
their childhood origins. "Of every *ten* candidates for the ministry," said the Reverend S. I. Prime, "you will probably find

31 "Domestic Happiness," *Parent's Magazine*, 1:259, July, 1841.
32. Mrs. L. Pillsbury, "How to Train Your Children Aright," *Mother's Assistant*, 8:1, January, 1846.
33. Child, *op. cit.*, p. 76.
34. Abbott, *The Mother at Home*, pp. 115–16.
35. Sigourney, *op. cit.*, p. 240.
36. Bert Roller, *Children in American Poetry* (George Peabody College for Teachers, Nashville, Tennessee, 1930), pp. 48–49.

that *seven*, at least, are the sons of pious mothers." [37] Wardens in state prisons were quoted as quizzing hardened prisoners with regard to their early lives. In one case the prisoner recalled that his mother had been "a good pious woman" who prayed for him. Even the recollection of her piety was sufficient to cause his repentance.[38] The Reverend William Thayer, hinting at the fate of decadent Europe, quoted the statement of a French writer to the effect that out of sixty-nine French monarchs, three were reared by their mothers, and that these were the only three exemplary ones in the group.[39] The murderer, the thief, the atheist, the dissolute monarch, it was claimed, all were driven to their godless fates by the absence of early training in piety and virtue.

In addition to this somewhat negative "research" in the annals of pious or impious influence, there was considerable delving into the lives of great men in order to show how their characters were molded by virtuous and religious mothers. Attention was called, for example, to the character of the mothers of Washington,[40] of Dwight,[41] of Doddridge,[42] of Newton.[43] In each case, credit was given to maternal fidelity for the success attained by these leaders. Against their virtues were posed the vices and failings of the bad Lord Byron, whose pollution was attributed to the shortcomings of the mother.[44] Abbott declared that had Byron and Washington been exchanged in their cradles, "Washington might have been the licentious profligate, and Byron the exemplar of virtue and the benefactor of nations." [45]

The mother of Washington was eulogized in the *Ladies' Magazine* as one of the "glorious performers" behind the theatrical scenes of the American Revolution. Her piety was especially noted. Thus, we read, "She was in the habit of repairing every day to

37. Reverend S. I. Prime, "Mothers Can Do Great Things," *Mother's Assistant*, 3:227, October, 1843; cf. Thayer, *Life at the Fireside*, p. 265.

38. "A Mother's Prayers Are Not Easily Forgotten," *Parent's Magazine*, 1:146, January, 1841.

39. Thayer, *op. cit.*, pp. 265–66.

40. "The Mother of Washington," *Ladies' Magazine*, 4:385, September, 1831.

41. Literary Notice on *Incidents in the Life of President Dwight* . . . , *Ladies' Magazine*, 4:335, August, 1831.

42. Thayer, *op. cit.*, p. 55.

43. John S. C. Abbott, *The Mother at Home*, p. 18.

44. Thayer, *op. cit.*, p. 56; cf. Abbott, *op. cit.*, p. 15.

45. Abbott, *op. cit.*, p. 16.

a secluded spot, formed by rocks and trees near her dwelling, where . . . she communed with her Creator, in humiliation and prayer." [46] By this virtuous example, and by her genius and care of Washington, she laid the foundations of his excellent character in his early years.

In 1851 a volume entitled *Mothers of the Wise and Good* [47] went through four editions. Its preface, paying tribute among other writers to Mrs. Child, Mrs. Sigourney, John Abbott, and S. G. Goodrich for their attention to the subject of maternal character, stated as the plan of the volume to set forth "a series of delightful instances of the success of pious maternal influence." [48] Select essays at the end of the work have titles such as "The Mother's Charge," "Maternal Piety," "Power of Maternal Piety," "Early Religious Impressions," and "A Mother's Love." This volume epitomizes perhaps better than any other the sentiment of the midcentury with regard to maternal example.

It is interesting to note at this point that the appeals to history and reiterations on the importance of maternal piety held both threats and promises for midcentury mothers. The orthodox, retaining fast hold upon sin and depravity, could not only warn women of the consequences attendant upon their own impiety and liberalism, but could prescribe for them patterns of conformity with which to impress the rising generation, thus solving simultaneously the troublesome "woman question" and that of controlling the status quo through education of children. On the other hand, the romantics, the perfectionists, and especially the female crusaders for the improvement of the feminine mind, could stress the positive aspect of the picture. Thus we read in the *Ladies' Magazine:* "The mother may, in the unconscious child before her, behold some future Washington or Franklin, and the lessons of knowledge and virtue, with which she is enlightening the infant mind, may gladden and bless many hearts. . . ." [49] Carried a point further, this responsibility placed a premium on the enlightenment of the mother and scored a point for the improvement of female intellect. Was it not necessary for woman to

46. "The Mother of Washington," *Ladies' Magazine,* 4:390, September, 1831.

47. Jabez Burns, *Mothers of the Wise and Good* (4th ed. Boston, Gould & Lincoln, 1851).

48. *Ibid.,* p. iv.

49. "Religion Is the Strength of Woman," *Ladies' Magazine,* 7:226, May, 1834.

know something of political heroes and of political economy? Should she not examine into the "genius of her own government" in order to perceive its "superiority over the decaying governments of Europe?" This she should do, and could do, without stepping out of her peculiar sphere, *"without one sacrifice of feminine delicacy."* [50] Here was "the iron hand in the velvet glove," wielded effectively by Sarah Hale, Catherine Sedgwick, and other active conservatives. Agreeing with the clergy that the mother should be patterned on the traditional model, meek and mild, "born to perpetuate the reign of all good and gentle affections in the world, and to diffuse through all society a spirit of love, of forbearance, . . . to turn away wrath by soft answers," [51] they nevertheless refused to accept the shackling concepts which this model suggests, of submission to male domination, of emotionalism without the enlightenment of knowledge. Thus we read in the *Ladies' Magazine:* "Search the records of history, and see if it can be found that a great and wise man was ever descended from a weak and foolish mother." Mothers, it is stated, to be true models of Christian excellence, must have intellectual and moral advantages, and given these will exert them "to make men wiser, better, happier." [52]

So much, then, for the character of the mother. The repeated emphasis upon the importance of maternal example is significant chiefly as it reveals a shift from the authority-centered regime of the patriarchal family government to the more feminine culture of the midnineteenth century, which enthroned a benevolent god and made the diffusion of the softer Christian virtues a peculiar function of the mother.

Mothers were urged to begin early in training their children to religious observances. The *Parent's Magazine* for 1841 tells the story of a rural mother who confessed to her pastor that her older children had been brought up without the influence of a family altar, without morning and evening prayers. " 'O, that I had begun with my oldest children when they were *small,'* " she said, " 'That is the time to begin.' " [53] Within a decade she had come to realize the importance of early impressions in the re-

50. *Loc. cit.*
51. C. Sedgwick, "A Plea for Children," *Ladies' Magazine*, 8:93, February, 1835.
52. "The Mother," *Ladies' Magazine*, 7:569–70, November, 1834.
53. "The Time to Begin," *Parent's Magazine*, 1:163, March, 1841.

ligious education of her children. This emphasis upon early beginnings and upon the restoration of family observances of religion is typical of didactic literature of the period. Parents were
warned that good morals would degenerate in a family in which
prayer was not heard.[54] Thayer claimed that "family prayer
makes ineffaceable impressions upon childhood," [55] giving as one
example the words of an aging man, "My heart turns to the family altar where first I knelt by a mother's side." [56] In this instance,
Thayer referred to the altar at which the father officiated, surrounded by his family and servants. Mrs. Phelps referred likewise to the traditional form of family worship when she told of
having her baby present at family prayers. At these prayers, she
wrote,

Each person in turn read portions of the Scripture, and the baby
soon began an imitation of the reading. . . . When he grew weary
of confinement, by giving him something to hold in his hand, he
was quiet until the close of the exercises. . . . He did not indeed
comprehend the import of the scene . . . but they made their
impression upon his mind as well as his senses.[57]

The baby was at this time between nine and twelve months old.
This was the ideal set-up, with the family complete, the father in
charge, and the mother keeping her children in order, and ex-
posing them as early as possible to the religious atmosphere of
worship. But repeated reiterations of the importance of family
worship [58] are evidence of the weakening of this custom.

With the business of the world engrossing much of the father's
time,[59] prayer came to be regarded more and more as the function of the mother. Even Theodore Dwight, whose text, addressed
to fathers, was a protest against the feminization of domestic
education, wrote eloquently of the effects of maternal prayer upon
the young child. In addition to her participation in family wor-

54. Mrs. H. F. Hunt, "Domestic Education," *Mother's Assistant*, 10:51,
July, 1850.

55. Thayer, *op. cit.*, p. 178.

56. *Ibid.*, p. 180.

57. "A Mother's-Journal" (extracts from Phelps, *Observations upon an
Infant*), *Ladies Magazine*, 8:447, August, 1835.

58. "Family Worship," *Parent's Magazine*, 1:124, February, 1841; see also
Parent's Magazine, Vols. I and II, *passim*.

59. Reverend A. B. Muzzey, *The Fireside* (Boston, Crosby, Nichols & Co.,
1856), pp. 217–18; cf. Reverend S. R. Hall, "Causes of Indifference and
Neglect Among Parents . . . ," *Parent's Magazine*, 1:37–38, October, 1840.

ship he would have the mother retire to her closet at a certain hour each morning, for prayer and meditation. Speaking of an occasion when a little girl of two and a half years accompanied her mother to this place of devotion, he wrote, ". . . how intense and how tender may have been the exercises of this little girl's breast, when she realized for the first time that her mother not only spoke of God's goodness, but daily meditated on Him, loved Him . . . conversed with Him, and was becoming more loving and lovely by the exercise!" [60] The *Mother's Assistant* awarded a twenty-five dollar prize for an essay [61] which had as its heroine a mother who was forced by the death of her husband to fill his "patriarchal office" at the family altar, which duty, faithfully performed when her children were small, bore fruit in later years. Moral essayists were not quite ready to admit that the father's share of responsibility as religious preceptor could be shifted to the mother except by death, but it is significant that they put emphasis upon memories of maternal rather than paternal piety. Convicts [62] and sailors [63] lost in sin were represented as regenerated, not by recalling their father's voices at family prayer, but by the more appealing visions of faithful mothers struggling alone in their closets [64] or kneeling with them in affectionate prayer and pleading.

The object in all these anecdotes was to call attention to the importance of early religious impressions and to infuse with fresh meaning the observance of traditional customs which had grown perfunctory. Even table prayer, which, though universally practiced [65] in the majority of New England homes had lost much of its spirit, was seen in a new light as influential in child training. A contributor to the *Parent's Magazine* told of placing a baby, aged twelve months, at the family table while a blessing was craved. This model child was "apparently attentive" and with little hands folded on the table "was still during the exercise." [66]

60. Dwight, *op. cit.*, p. 50.
61. Reverend L. Matlack, "Truth Triumphant, or the Bible Vindicated," *Mother's Assistant*, 12:1–13, 25–37, January, 1848.
62. Cf. *ante*, p. 77.
63. "A Sailor's Mother," *Parent's Magazine*, 1:115–16, January, 1841.
64. The term "closet" was used to designate a small room in the household consecrated to prayer.
65. Calhoun, *Social History of the American Family*, I, 138.
66. "Family Scenes, No. 2," *Parent's Magazine*, 2:81, December, 1841.

Mothers were advised to take children to church at an early age,[67] since they might imbibe the spirit, if not the letter of the service. Heman Humphrey, although he did not recommend that infants be taken habitually to meeting, stated that the habit of attending public worship "cannot be formed too early." [68] In earlier New England days, small children had in some communities been taken to service as a matter of expediency, to enable the mother to attend church herself, but the midcentury emphasis was upon the child, and the benefit to be derived from exposure to divine influences. It should be stated that this new approach increased awareness of the limitations of childhood. Mrs. Child suggested that no unreasonable demands be placed upon small children on the Sabbath since they "cannot sit still and read all day," and that the walk to and from church be made pleasant and instructive.[69] It was granted, however, that "quiet toys" and a devotional atmosphere should distinguish the Sabbath from other days, even for children of two and three years of age.[70] The Sabbath school was of course growing in strength during this period and was regarded as an important auxiliary to home training,[71] but the literature of domestic education places chief emphasis upon maternal instruction of the youngest children.

Before turning to the specific steps to be employed by mothers in religious instruction of children, it is helpful to note some aspects of the controversy which arose in connection with Sabbath observance, since this controversy undoubtedly affected family attitudes toward traditional religious practices. With the midcentury stress upon the free individual, it was natural that liberals should again raise the time-honored question as to whether the Sabbath was made for man, or man for the Sabbath. The more conservative members of the clergy tended to cling to the latter view, emphasizing the solemn duties [72] of the day, the necessity for attendance upon morning and afternoon worship, and objecting to the sugar-coated literature which was supplanting

67. Child, *The Mother's Book*, p. 67; cf. Muzzey, *op. cit.*, p. 179.
68. Humphrey, *op. cit.*, p. 166.
69. Child, *op. cit.*, pp. 65, 67.
70. Humphrey, *op. cit.*, p. 164.
71. It is interesting to note that William A. Alcott wrote a volume entitled *The Sabbath School as It Should Be* (New York, Jonathan Leavitt, 1841), in which he discussed the Sabbath school as an aid to parents.
72. Humphrey, *op. cit.*, chap. ix; Thayer, *op. cit.*, chap. vi.

earlier catechisms and theological reading sacred to the Sabbath.[73]

At the opposite extreme were those who openly objected to the tenacious hold of the clergy upon the freedom of man, and who maintained stoutly that the Sabbath was made for man. It is interesting to note that William Lloyd Garrison was severely censured for his views on the Sabbath.[74] Harriet Martineau, regarded with respect for many of her theories, was on questionable ground when she struck out at the fear of Sabbath-breaking.[75] Catherine Sedgwick encountered opposition when she featured the family portrayed in *Home* as spending Sunday afternoon on the water, instead of in attendance at public worship. Advised by the editor to alter this chapter, she compromised,[76] taking a middle position which is significant. The family went for a walk instead of a sail and *looked at* the magnificent bay, that "they might feel the presence of the Deity in a temple not made with hands." Furthermore, they were careful not to be frivolous or to make "remarks upon the looks, dress, and gait of those they met." They returned home at one-thirty to a cold dinner, "prepared without encroaching on" the servant's Sabbath, and the afternoon was spent in instruction pleasantly given by the mother, who it should be stated, used methods which were far from orthodox. " 'Sometimes,' " said Willie, " 'she tells us Bible stories . . . and sometimes stories of real live children. . . .' " " 'And sometimes,' " continued Mary, " 'mother writes a little sermon on purpose for us, not a grown-up sermon. Then she teaches us a hymn; . . . and when she wants to read to herself, she sets us all down . . . to copy off some animal.' " Mrs. Barclay, the mother in question, defended this modified Sabbath by saying " 'We think clergymen would preach better and their people hear *more*, if there was but one sermon.' " And further, " 'We reverence it [the Sabbath] as one of the most important and dearest of all social institutions, and we are therefore . . . anxious that its effect on our children's minds should not be impaired.' " [77]

73. Humphrey, *op. cit.*, p. 101; Thayer, *op cit.*, chap. vii.

74. "The True History of the Late Division in the Antislavery Societies," from *Second Annual Report of the Massachusetts Abolition Society.* (Boston, David H. Ela, 1841), pp. 6–7.

75. Martineau, *Society in America*, III, 261–62.

76. *Ibid.*, p. 261, footnote.

77. Catherine M. Sedgwick, *Home* (New ed. Cambridge, John Wilson & Son, 1875), pp. 65–73.

The popularity of *Home* [78] testifies to the acceptability of Miss Sedgwick's moralizing. The Barclay family could on no counts be termed "infidels." If they strayed from established customs, they explained gently that it was the "spirit" that mattered, not the letter of the ancient law. Thus a common sense middle position was established, which, though morally airtight, was flexible enough to let in a host of new attitudes toward religious guidance. The Barclays, for example, walked out to worship God in nature, thus combining a healthful occupation with a pleasant expansion of the soul's faculties. At home, occupations were suited to the age levels of the children. Lessons were planned for, but they were pleasurable lessons. What mattered to domestic reformers in general was the mother's sincerity, her constant presence, and her attention to the spiritual needs of her children. To the mid-century public, indifference was the only real crime.

Returning, however, to the details of instruction: it was generally conceded that religious instruction, aside from the silent ministry of example and attendance at family and public worship, might be begun as soon as a child could understand simple language. A New Hampshire clergyman suggested that the mother begin as soon as her child's "eating, drinking and playing" became "more than instinctive acts" to point out to him the comforts and blessings of home as the gifts of God.[79] Muzzey and Abbott both recommended that little children be told of God's power to call forth wind and rain and to sustain the flowers with His sunshine.[80] Carried to an extreme this teaching involved fear-provoking statements such as "If God wished, he could make the wind blow with such fury as to beat in all the windows and destroy the house. But God will take care of you, . . . if you ask Him." [81] One mother instructed her small son to feel her pulse. She explained, " 'If it should stop beating, I should die,' " and " 'I can't keep it beating.' " " 'Who can?' " said the child. " 'God,' " was the reply. The child, in a deeply anxious state was then reassured that God would not stop his pulse if he prayed to Him for protection.[82] A less morbid approach is suggested by Mrs. Child, who stressed the more cheerful and childlike habit of giving thanks

78. Cf. *ante*, p. 44.

79. Reverend A. P. Peabody, "Common Scenes and Daily Events," *Mother's Assistant*, 5:32, August, 1844.

80. Muzzey, *op. cit.*, pp. 176–77; Abbott, *The Mother at Home*, p. 137.

81. Abbott, *ibid.*, p. 114.

82. "Leading Children to God," *Mother's Assistant*, 9:142, December, 1846.

to God for simple gifts. She described a little girl who had learned to pray as soon as she could lisp the words, offering up thanks for a sugar dog she had received.[83]

Waterston regarded love, faith, and spirituality as elements of character peculiarly native to childhood. "Certainly love," he declared, "dwells in the mind of a child." [84] Furthermore, since children never doubt unless driven to by disappointment and deception, faith is natural to them, and spirituality or susceptibility to religious influence follow naturally from a combination of love and faith in the unseen. This was the romantic approach to spiritual cultivation of children. The mother's function as guide was to seize every trivial occurrence of the child's day to strengthen these characteristics. Thus, if a child grasped a kitten roughly by the hair, he was immediately taught the lesson of love and the golden rule. Mrs. Sigourney tells of an instance in which a mother was so successful in teaching kindliness that when she described a bird who caught flies, her child "lisped, with a kind of horror upon his baby face, 'Oh! kill flies! Will God forgive it?' " [85] Faith and spirituality were to be preserved by the honesty and piety of parents in their dealings with children. "The infant heart," said one writer, "cannot be deceived in this serious concern." [86]

Over against this romantic approach to instruction which, it must be noted was not unmixed with orthodox "fear of the Lord," was the approach which regarded the task of religious education as not primarily one of unfoldment of innate goodness, but as the disciplines and straightening influences necessary to rescue children from the heritage of human depravity. To "check the wayward propensities of the child—to guard him against temptation—to inspire him with the fear and love of God," these things were regarded as important by Humphrey, as well as "to nurture up to their full maturity, all the moral faculties of the soul." [87] The mother, in addition to the teaching of positive virtues, was to keep the garden of her child's mind carefully weeded. Using the Bible as the family statute book,[88] she could thus refer the dis-

83. Child, *The Mother's Book*, p. 68.
84. R. C. Waterston, *Thoughts on Moral and Spiritual Culture* (Boston, Crocker & Ruggles, 1842), p. 64.
85. Sigourney, *Letters to Mothers*, p. 38.
86. Reverend P. C. Headly, "Did You Ever Take Me in Your Arms to Christ?" *Mother's Assistant*, 1853, p. 154.
87. Humphrey, *Domestic Education*, p. 13.
88. *Ibid.*, p. 174.

obedient child to the commandment "Honor thy father and thy
mother . . . ," and the "pilfering" child to the law "Thou shalt
not steal." Obedience to divine authority figured prominently in
this sort of instruction, and prohibitions were important to mold
child behavior to the pattern of conformity.

Abbott described the mother as the world's redeeming influence, and urged her to dwell upon the Savior in order to "awaken
contrition and melt the heart" [89] of her child. Even Mrs. Sigourney,
an exponent of sweetness and light, declared that the mother
must hasten to give religious instruction while there was yet in
the burial ground a shorter grave than that of her child.[90]

These emphases upon sin and repentance and especially upon
haste in instruction would seem to point to a belief in the necessity for conversion of children, and yet conversion is not referred
to directly as a goal of religious education except in periodical
literature,[91] and in accounts of precociously religious children
like the young Nathan Dickerman, whose brief and pious pil-
grimage on earth was described eloquently by Gorham Abbott [92]
for the benefit of spiritually ambitious mothers. John Abbott
warned mothers of a child who, on her death bed, reproached her
parents for not preparing her [93] to die. But he seemed to refer
rather to general spiritual culture than to the sort of preparation
generally thought of as preceding the emotional experience of
conversion. Thus he wrote, ". . . the period of your child's conversion may be at so early a stage of its existence, as to leave no
trace by which the time of the change can be remembered." This
change, he declared, might be manifested "by the tearful eye, and
the sad heart," but not by the deeper agonies felt by those who
have "grown old in sin." [94] To the ultra-religious, conversion was
still a literal experience, and there is reason to believe that the
older concepts prevailed in some sections,[95] particularly where

89. Abbott, *The Mother at Home*, p. 129.

90. Sigourney, *Letters to Mothers*, p. 34.

91. "The Conversion of My Little Daughter," *Mother's Assistant*, 4:74–81,
April, 1844; cf. Reverend P. C. Headly, *op. cit.*, pp. 153–54.

92. Gorham D. Abbott, *Memoir of Nathan Dickerman*, bound with John
S. C. Abbott, *The Mother at Home* and *The Child at Home* (New York,
American Tract Society, 1833).

93. Abbott, *The Mother at Home*, p. 109.

94. *Ibid.*, p. 141.

95. A. C. Curtis, "Extracts from the Report of the New Hampshire Maternal Association," *Parent's Magazine*, 1:82, December, 1840.

evangelical revivals were common. It is significant that reports
sent to periodicals from rural chapters of maternal associations
boast of the number of conversions effected among children in
their charge. For example, the Wayland Maternal Association
reported that eight children had "made a public profession of their
faith in Christ," and expressed hope for the conversion of all
their children.[96]

The function of the mother with regard to this literal conversion is described as that of helping children "to see and feel that
they are sinners, involved in guilt and ruin," [97] by instructing
them with regard to man's fall and redemption, and praying over
them, and with them, until they see the light. Details of this pro-
cedure, in all its long-drawn-out emotionalism, are seen in the
Dickerman account and in that of a contributor to the *Mother's
Assistant,* whose small child expressed a wish for a new heart,
and finally, after repeated prayer, was "adopted into the family
of Christ." [98]

To the progressive educators and thinkers of the midcentury,
this process was unnatural and unchildlike. Horace Bushnell did
much to modify the meaning of "conversion," making it almost
synonymous with day by day "nurture" of the soul.[99] Horace
Mann is said to have found fault with John Abbott for his emphasis upon sin and hell.[100] But it was difficult to break away from
the older concepts, even for those who hailed a new day for the
child.

A remnant of the old morbidity is seen in popular attitudes
toward death. Mrs. Child and Mrs. Sigourney both objected to
previous attitudes which had associated grief and fear with death,
and yet their antidotes for these were scarcely better. Mrs. Child
told of a mother who took her very young child to the bedside of
her dead aunt. The mother kissed the cheek of the corpse and said,
" 'We must not weep for dear Aunt Betsy. . . . She is living now
with the angels . . . and will rejoice when we are good.' " It is
not surprising that when the child in question died after two

96. "To the Editors of the Parent's Magazine," *Parent's Magazine,* 1:129–
30, February, 1841.

97. "Christian Education," *Parent's Magazine,* 1:200, May, 1841.

98. "The Conversion of My Little Daughter," *Mother's Assistant,* 4:77,
April, 1844.

99. Fleming, *Children and Puritanism,* chaps. xv, xvi.

100. Louise S. Boas, *Woman's Education Begins* (Norton, Mass., Wheaton
College Press, 1935), p. 111.

years she remarked, on her deathbed, " 'I shall see dear Aunt Betsy before you do, mother.' " [101] Mrs. Sigourney described an impressive funeral procession and the burial of an infant, commenting that the children who were present at this funeral would never forget the lesson learned there. Said she: "In order to give to those whom we instruct, cheering and consoling views of Death we must correct our own. We must make it the subject of daily contemplation, praying for divine grace, to consider it as . . . the end for which we were born, the summons to arise, and take upon us the nature of angels." [102] Seen in retrospect, this sentimental attachment to death is almost as unhealthful as the Calvinistic fear of hell. It is of a piece with the emotionalism which dictated that children be instructed in religious matters when they were ill, or melancholy, or subdued.[103] Yet the women writers who held this view of death were also among the chief dispellers of austerity in religion, and adult "forcing" of childhood. Even the progressive Waterston, whose emphasis upon moral and spiritual culture was largely positive, saw death and its lessons as a means of realizing the "stupendous destinies of a human soul." [104] Every child, he declared, is a "monitor pointing to the spiritual world," [105] and the mother must constantly realize that her living child may go at any time. Gallaudet, an innovator in many respects and one of the pioneers in inductive methods of teaching children, thought it necessary to include in his *Child's Book on the Soul* a scene in which the mother dwelt upon the lifeless qualities of a dead child. Her little son following this morbid object lesson with interest said, " 'Yes, mother . . . I touched his cheek, and it was cold as ice. I took hold of his little hand, but it was stiff. . . . He could not see, nor hear, nor move.' " [106] The purpose of this lesson was to teach the child that the soul was immortal!

Between the religiously orthodox, and exponents of new thoughts and methods on spiritual cultivation, it is difficult, therefore, to draw any definitive line. The midcentury period must at all times be recognized as one of ferment, of confused ideals and goals. The common meeting ground for domestic educators was

101. Child, *The Mother's Book*, p. 81.
102. Sigourney, *Letters to Mothers*, p. 232.
103. Abbott, *op. cit.*, p. 113.
104. Waterston, *Moral and Spiritual Culture*, p. 86.
105. *Ibid.*, p. 289.
106. Gallaudet, *Child's Book on the Soul*, Part I, p. 49.

the importance of the child, and the worth of his immortal soul, whether gauged in terms of moral, or precociously religious development.

Materials for daily religious instruction of young children were many and varied. Story material was at hand in the form of innumerable Sabbath school tracts and moral tales adapted to children of all ages. In place of the older formal catechisms were materials ranging from "diluted" catechisms and pictorial lessons for the youngest children, to sacred histories and sugarcoated literature of the Peter Parley, or Rollo book variety for older children.[107] To Humphrey, the substitution of this literature for the stern fare of religious instruction was a menace to the cultivation of piety.[108] His part in the republication of the *New England Primer* is indicative of his attitude.[109] For the smallest children he recommended bits of sacred history, hymns, and Dr. Watts' catechism,[110] and the Bible he regarded as a family oracle to be consulted at all times for children of all ages.

While Abbott makes no specific mention of materials of instruction, one infers from his reference to the Dickerman memoir that he would have children of five or six years of age familiar with hymns, and hymns with adult wording, as well as scriptural accounts of the Savior.[111]

Goodrich [112] and Muzzey [113] recommended reading of the "words of sacred truth," teaching of hymns and sacred verse. Said Muzzey, "When you speak of heavenly things, the child sits at your feet a willing listener." [114] The function of the mother is that of interpreter and illustrator to "awaken and develop" religious affections, and to "carry . . . thoughts forward . . . to the eternal home." [115]

Mrs. Sigourney and Mrs. Child, revealing a better understanding of the capacities of small children, gave more specific suggestions for the use of scriptural materials. Thus, Mrs. Sigourney

107. Tassin, "Books for Children," in Trent, et al. *Cambridge History of American Literature*, Vol. II.

108. Humphrey, *op. cit.*, pp. 101, 156.

109. Cf. *ante*, p. 54.

110. Humphrey, *op. cit.*, p. 158.

111. Abbott, *The Mother at Home* (1833 ed. bound with G. Abbott's *Memoir of Nathan Dickerman*), pp. 140–41.

112. Goodrich, *Fireside Education*, p. 144.

113. Muzzey, *op. cit.*, p. 184.

114. *Ibid.*, p. 174.

115. Goodrich, *op. cit.*, p. 144.

wrote: "Commence with simple stories, from the Scriptures, from
the varied annals of history, from your own observation of mankind. Let each illustrate some moral or religious truth, adapted
to convey instruction, reproof or encouragement. . . ." [116] The
youngest child, she said, might benefit by daily instruction "as
soon as it opens its bright eyes wider at the words 'shall mother
tell a story?' " [117] To daily periods of instruction she would add
an evening hymn and tender prayer. Mrs. Child expressed an
aversion for catechisms, declaring that religious teaching should
pervade daily life instead of being a "garment reserved only for
Sunday wear." [118] Among books selected for the instruction of
children four to five years of age were Mrs. Barbauld's *Lessons for
Children*, which were based on religious subject matter, and *Original Hymns for Infant Minds*,[119] by Jane Taylor. Mrs. Child
recommended, however, that the Bible be made precious to children. One feels that the chief difference between the conservative
approach of Humphrey and Abbott and the more progressive one
of the women educators lies in their attitudes toward the child.
The clergy tended to regard the child as a well into which scriptural truth must be poured. The educators, on the other hand,
regarded subject matter as a means of strengthening the child's
understanding and preserving its inherent spirituality.

Gallaudet's approach is of particular interest since it unites the
education of the intellect with that of the religious sentiments.
Gallaudet objected to the complexity of religious subject matter
for children. *"They who would teach children well,"* he declared,
"must first learn . . . from them." [120] His *Child's Book on the
Soul*, written with the object of teaching *"that a child has a soul,
distinct from the body, which will survive it, and live for ever,"* [121]
is set up on this principle of inductive reasoning, which, in making use of the testimony of the senses, and the simple reasoning
processes of young children, differs from the emotional approach
to religious truths employed alike by conservative churchmen and
the romantic progressives. Gallaudet's method, heralding the object lesson approach of a later period, places the mother in the

116. Sigourney, *op. cit.*, p. 91.
117. *Ibid.*, p. 92.
118. Child, *op. cit.*, p. 71.
119. *Ibid.*, p. 99.
120. Gallaudet, *op. cit.*, Part I, p. vii.
121. *Loc. cit.*

position of a daily questioner, illustrator, and counselor, who, in a series of carefully planned dialogues, leads her child from a contemplation and comparison of the properties of the common things about him, such as a pebble, a rose, a watch, and the like, to the meaning of life and of his own living body, to that of the soul and its eternal characteristics.

The final appeal of this volume is a traditional one, urging the child to worship God, to pray to Him, to read the Bible, and to keep the Sabbath. Thus the mother exclaims: "Oh! think, my son, of this wonderful soul which your heavenly father has given you! . . . Seek to know more of Him, and of what He wishes to have you do! Be careful not to displease Him! . . . Learn to read, and to understand, the Book which He has given to you! . . . Perhaps you may die soon! Get ready to die!" [122] Gallaudet, like Mrs. Sigourney and Mrs. Child, kept well within the bounds of orthodoxy in his resistance to older methods and materials of instruction, but his use of the mother as active interpreter was indicative of a significant change of focus in religious instruction. One has only to compare his text with that of the widely sold *First Question Book*,[123] a publication of the Massachusetts Sabbath School Society, to understand the difference between the "catechizing" method in which the parent or teacher served merely as questioner, and the newer method which made the questioner the prime mover of the understanding.

The moral education of young children, while brought about largely by the methods employed in religious education, was seen by domestic educators as an important end in itself, and one allied with the chief goals of social progress in the midnineteenth century. The *Ladies' Magazine* of 1830 featured an editorial entitled "The Worth of Money" in which an appeal was made to mothers to teach their children the "art of doing good," so that moral and mental excellence might take the place of a love of wealth and the "dominion of selfishness." To effect this change, mothers had "to aid, by . . . example as well as precepts the development of the noblest faculties of . . . children, the affections, reason, conscience," and to repress as much as possible "the selfishness of animal instinct,—of appetite." They were urged to begin early to

122. Gallaudet, *op. cit.*, Part II, pp. 107–8.
123. Harvey Newcomb, *First Question Book* (Revised ed. Boston, Massachusetts Sabbath School Society, 1837), Vol. I.

"open . . . little hearts only to the sweet impressions of love, which is benevolence." [124] Samuel Goodrich, agreeing with this approach to moral culture, obviously regarded the training of these "noble" faculties as all-important, devoting nearly a hundred pages of his text *Fireside Education* to a consideration of such qualities as Truth, Justice, Mercy, Forgiveness, Cheerfulness, Fidelity, Courage, Industry, Charity, and the like,[125] while he treated of the subject of Religion in a brief chapter of less than forty pages. He explained, however, that the two departments of culture were complementary, since true morality is a portion of religion. The moral law, he declared, is the second branch of the divine edict "LOVE THE LORD THY GOD WITH ALL THY HEART, AND THY NEIGHBOR AS THYSELF." [126] First in importance is the love of God, and piety, but next must come a love of mankind, and benevolence, which gives man a realization of his duties toward society. The Bible is the statute book of morality. Conscience is "sanctioned and enforced by revelation." [127] Thus religion and morality are inseparable.

Heman Humphrey, whose text on *Domestic Education* gave weight to religious education, conventionally described, nevertheless saw fit to include a chapter on the cultivation of the benevolent affections and of the conscience, as topics worthy of separate consideration.[128] He claimed that infants have a "moral instinct," standing in the place of reason,[129] which enables them, before the end of the second year, to distinguish between right and wrong. Though stating that the first duty of the mother must be to educate her child for heaven, he held that she might, while praying, and waiting for the blessing of spiritual rebirth, do much in the way of moral culture.[130] The mother's part is to convert "every little plaything into a teacher of self-denial and benevolence," and to mold the conscience by watching over "every budding emotion" and "every selfish outbreak." [131] Humphrey, like Goodrich, regarded the Bible as the "perfect rule or standard, of right

124. "The Worth of Money," *Ladies' Magazine*, 3:52, February, 1830.
125. Goodrich, *op. cit.*, table of contents.
126. *Ibid.*, p. 171.
127. *Ibid.*, p. 175.
128. Humphrey, *op. cit.*, chaps. xii, xiv.
129. *Ibid.*, p. 78.
130. *Ibid.*, p. 183.
131. *Ibid.*, p. 184.

and wrong." [132] Conscience, he declared, must be enlightened by the Bible, and religious goals viewed always as the ultimate ones. Yet midnineteenth century "morality" was to prove to be far more than the handmaiden of orthodox religion. In focusing attention on the temporal affairs of this world and upon human behavior in relation to current evils of the period, it provided a new social gospel acceptable alike to liberals and conservatives.

It is significant that "benevolence" was placed at the head of the list of moral virtues to be cultivated in the midcentury child. Implying an aristocracy of responsibility for those blessed with material wealth and superior education, it was an emphasis to which humanitarian reform owed much. While benevolence was generally thought of vaguely as any "kindly feelings towards others," [133] it was frequently associated with overt giving to the poor, to missionary societies and benevolent enterprises. An excerpt from the *Vermont Chronicle* printed in the *Parent's Magazine* advised parents to take their children with them to visit poor people and to let them give away something they value, thus learning the double lesson of unselfishness and benevolence. "If this whole generation of children," it stated, "were so taught to think and do, in a few years the world would be filled with light, love, and peace." [134] Another article suggested that little children be told "of the poor who are unfed: of the children who are pinched by the cold for the want of clothing . . . of the sufferings of the millions in slavery at home and abroad" [135] in order to take advantage of their tender sensibilities and render them eager to relieve distress. This was the very essence of the reform spirit of the midcentury period, brought down to the youngest members of the domestic circle. The *Ladies' Magazine* told of a child who asked for new embroidery on her little dress. Her mother, taking the occasion to deliver a sermon on vanity, and on the fruits of self-denial, persuaded her to spend the embroidery money on a frock for a poor child.[136] This is typical of many moral tales for the young in literature of the period. Dr. William Alcott wrote an article entitled "Lessons of Benevolence," in which he

132. *Ibid.*, p. 174.
133. *Ibid.*, p. 183.
134. "Stinginess," *Parent's Magazine*, 2:118, January, 1842.
135. "On Cultivating a Benevolent Spirit in Children," *Parent's Magazine*, 2:196, May, 1842.
136. "From a Mother's Diary," *Ladies' Magazine*, 4:129, January, 1831.

cited the case of the mother who, seeing but one choice strawberry on the vine, said to her tiny son, " 'Will you have that, . . . or will you give it to your little sister?' " The child after difficult deliberation gave it to his sister. "Benevolence . . . predominated," said Alcott.[137] By repetition of such incidents would this important faculty, he explained, be cultivated and strengthened.

Mrs. Hale deplored the fact that parents lived and preached the "heartless maxim" that " 'Time is Money.' " She exhorted, "Mothers, teach your children that *time is their opportunity for doing good.*" [138] It was difficult to impress this upon the success-minded populace of the prospering midcentury years. The common man was demonstrating daily that industrious application to the problems of the material world reaped financial success. Never before had this country held out more opportunity to the striving individual. Money was a reality to be dealt with, and to the emancipated middle classes was no longer regarded as "the root of all evil." Getting and spending were common topics of conversation in New England families of the period.[139]

Mrs. Sigourney, like Mrs. Hale, raised a protesting voice to mothers of families, expressing concern over the false sense of values accruing to the accumulation of wealth. The young child, she declared, is confused by frequent remarks from lips that he reveres, about "how much, such and such a person is worth." " 'Does *worth* mean *goodness?*' " inquires the child. " 'No. It means money,' " replies the worldly parent. The pious person who does good works may be dismissed with the derogatory remark that he is poor. "Alas," wrote Mrs. Sigourney, "that the forming mind should be left to undervalue those deeds and motives which . . . are the only true riches." [140]

Paradoxically enough, this idealistic protest was frequently linked with approbation of the principle of accumulation. The Reverend A. B. Muzzey wrote, "I would encourage a child to amass, that he might use, and use well, what he gains," and, further, ". . . every child, in whatever circumstances, should

137. William A. Alcott, "Lessons of Benevolence," *Mother's Assistant,* 4:30–31, February, 1844.

138. "The Worth of Money," *Ladies' Magazine,* 3:53, February, 1830.

139. Mrs. Graves elaborated on extravagant expenditure in her chapter on fashionable women. Cf. *Woman in America,* pp. 108–10; Mrs. Sigourney included a chapter on wealth in her *Letters to Mothers,* Letter XV.

140. Sigourney, *op. cit.,* pp. 169–70.

also be encouraged to save, not only for personal wants and uses, but for the express object of being able to give of his own to others." [141] Here was a sanction for wealth in the philanthropic disposal of it. Thayer's appeal to mothers [142] gives a clue to the clergy's approach to the problem. "Every benevolent enterprise of the present day is impeded in its course," he wrote, "for want of the requisite pecuniary aid." What society needs, therefore, is men, reared from childhood, "to embrace a world of sufferers, and who ever put less value upon the shining dollar in the pocket than upon a shining grace in the heart." [143] He does not say that society needs men who do not accumulate shining dollars!

Muzzey, despite his sanction of the accumulation of wealth, warned against "hoarding" and "the love of money," urging parents to inculcate in children a spirit of sacrifice and of self-denial.[144] This is most interesting in view of Max Weber's thesis on "The Protestant Ethic." [145] According to Weber, the asceticism of the Puritan faith survived as an essential ingredient of capitalism. This asceticism denied to the possessor of wealth a relaxation in the enjoyment of it, but accepted wealth as a necessary result of the activity and industry which "increase the glory of God." [146] When one reads Calhoun's account of the harassed lives of midcentury business men,[147] it is easy to believe that they were still under the domination of that philosophy which denied to them relaxation and easy enjoyment of their worldly goods. But—and here is the application of the "money philosophy" to this study: American women, not as a group engaged in getting money, were faced with the temptations involved in spending it. Reformers were alarmed at what Weber phrases "the enjoyment of wealth with the consequence of idleness and the temptations of the flesh." [148] Thus, they advised women as consumers to look, not after the flesh, but after the spirit, and women as mothers to cultivate in the rising generation the self-

141. Muzzey, *op. cit.*, p. 133.
142. Thayer, *op. cit.*, chap. xi.
143. *Ibid.*, p. 259.
144. Muzzey, *op. cit.*, p. 134.
145. Max Weber, *The Protestant Ethic* (London, George Allen & Unwin, Ltd., 1930).
146. *Ibid.*, p. 114.
147. Calhoun, *Social History of the American Family*, II, 131.
148. Weber, *op. cit.*, p. 157.

denying virtues of industry, frugality, economy, benevolence, and piety.[149] Benevolence was the new ingredient in this exhumed asceticism.

To understand the full import of the moral revolution of the midnineteenth century, and to account for the radiance in which the old and homely virtues were clothed, we must recognize what a powerful effect was produced on the mercantile mind of New England by the socializing of virtue which this new ingredient implied. Goodrich wrote: "A man may observe externally the rules of society, from a selfish regard to his own interests, and thus be called, in common phrase, a moral man; but the truly moral man is the one who feels the force of the great law—'LOVE THY NEIGHBOR AS THYSELF,' and who obeys it, because it is a good law, and because it comes from the great Lawgiver." [150]

There was an active, positive, outgoing emphasis in this new interpretation of the moral sentiment. Mrs. Hale attempted to define it thus: "By *moral sense,* I mean that feeling or sentiment, which not only distinguishes between right and wrong, but *inclines* to the *right*—an enlightened conscience. . . ." [151] A Massachusetts clergyman, lecturing in 1838, alluded to the powerful effect of this sentiment upon public affairs. "Conscience, moral principle, a conviction of right and duty, enters into and sways the mind of our community as it has never swayed community before." [152] "To appeal to a higher principle than patriotism, to think of legislating for the moral improvement of a country, or to be influenced at all by moral considerations in legislation, would, until recently have been regarded as visionary in the extreme." [153] This was the leaven of humanitarianism at work, the operation of the social virtues which helped to expand and enlighten the cramped and self-centered New England conscience. Yet this moral crusade must be recognized as more than the humanitarianism of the enlightenment making a tardy appearance in New England. It was, to the visionary reformer of this period, in-

149. Mrs. L. Pillsbury, "How to Train Your Children Aright," *Mother's Assistant,* 8:5, January, 1846; cf. "Formation of Habits," *Parent's Magazine,* 2:272–74, August, 1842.

150. Goodrich, *op. cit.,* p. 171.

151. Hale, *Woman's Record,* p. xlviii, footnote.

152. William P. Lunt, *Moral Education,* An address delivered before the teachers and pupils of the schools. (Quincy, John A. Green, 1838), p. 14.

153. *Ibid.,* p. 15.

extricable from the two other crusades which gave it being, that of democracy and of a newly invigorated Christianity.

The task which was urged upon American mothers in the moral and spiritual culture of their children was, therefore, regarded as part of a greater social task enjoined upon all responsible individuals of the times, the task of the spiritual nurture of a democratic society. In this mission, woman was given a conspicuous place, being described as "God's appointed agent of *morality*, the teacher and inspirer of those feelings and sentiments which are termed the virtues of humanity." [154]

154. Hale, *op. cit.*, p. xxxv.

CHAPTER V

MENTOR IN INTELLECTUAL CULTIVATION

AFTER visiting in a New England farmhouse during the 1830's, Harriet Martineau commented on the one way in which she and her friends had made their "kind hostess" uneasy, and this was by their neglect of "Charley's book-studies." [1] Charley was a six-year-old in Miss Martineau's party who had enjoyed the nineteenth century equivalent of a modern "progressive education." Miss Martineau, amused at the rural mother's reaction, explained that "Charley's little head was full of knowledge of other kinds," but that "the widow's children had all known more of the produce of the press at his age than he." [2] This throws an interesting sidelight on midcentury concepts with regard to the early intellectual cultivation of children. The newer point of view, represented by the visiting British party, was also that of enlightened Americans, who were beginning to conceive of child growth and its objectives in broader terms. The mental development of children, formerly thought of as the acquisition of the three R's followed by as rapid mastery as possible of the weightier "produce of the press," was coming to have a much wider definition involving the social, moral, and physical as well as the intellectual training of children. The drier system of book learning with its emphasis on memoriter drill and its unhappy forcing of the growth process was in sharp disfavor among advanced thinkers of the day.

Despite the infiltration of broader concepts of learning, however, the traditional approach of the farmhouse widow was to persist in many areas throughout the midcentury, and to exert a tenacious hold upon conservative New England minds. The storm of controversy aroused by Horace Mann's *Seventh Annual Report* indicates the amount of reluctance and fear with which the

1. Martineau, *Society in America*, I, 264.
2. *Loc. cit.*

older schoolmasters regarded innovations in education.[3] In the field of domestic education, it was small help to the cause of the "Charley" type of learning to have Miss Martineau as its champion, since even Sarah Hale looked upon her as "a sort of female Godwin," [4] too atheistic in her views to be followed safely. Bronson Alcott's views of early learning, as we have noted above, were not couched in cautious enough terms to satisfy conservers of New England tradition.[5] Ideas having to do with the destiny of the rising generation were scrutinized with care, and proponents of these ideas were frequently judged by their views of God, of Godwin, and of Byron; of the Antislavery Society, the French Revolution, and the "woman question"; of Unitarianism, transcendentalism, and Congregationalism. The path of the innovator was a precarious one.

Prophets of domestic education were faced, therefore, with the task of steering a middle course between the ultra conservative and ultra liberal points of view with regard to child culture. They had, on the one hand, to point out the dangers inherent in the old cut and dried approach to learning, and on the other, to warn against the godlessness or extravagant romanticism of the liberal position. In retrospect, this finding of a middle course seems a very bewildering task, in the face of the many conflicting and confused notions of human growth and learning current during the pre-Darwinian era. Fortunately, the midcentury reformer was confidently eclectic, able to take in his stride, phrenological concepts, fragments of Pestalozzianism, dawning concepts of scientific naturalism, and a resurgence of pietism. He knew what ideas to choose from all these to further his ends, and he had no time for hairsplitting. The young child was to benefit from this single-mindedness.

Upon one point most of the reformers were agreed, and this was that intellectual precocity was undesirable. Mrs. Sigourney wrote, "I once admired precocity, and viewed it as the breath of Deity, quickening to ripe and rare excellence. But I have since learned to fear it." [6] She saw as an evil the ambition to have children read at a very early age, not only because of the ill effects of this application upon their health, but because the in-

3. Hinsdale, *Horace Mann* . . . chap. viii.
4. Hale, *Woman's Record*, p. 740.
5. Cf. *ante*, p. 61.
6. Sigourney, *Letters to Mothers*, p. 147.

tellect of the infant is immature, and not ready to comprehend the ideas presented to it.[7] Goodrich deplored the "insane ambition" of a mother who forced to a premature development the mental faculties of her little boy, with the result that "while the boy's head grew rapidly, and at last became enormous, his limbs became shrunken, and almost useless."[8] Premature fruit, he declared, never ripens well.

Part of this distrust of precocity seems to have been occasioned by conservative reaction against the cold intellectuality of the eighteenth century. The nineteenth century, warmed by the flood-tide of humanitarianism, had come to the conclusion that the intellect "may be highly cultivated, while the moral nature lies dormant, or is palsied by disease."[9] Thus Humphrey commented: "How strange would it sound for anybody to deny, that Voltaire and Rousseau, that Hume and Gibbon were well educated men! And yet there must have been some great deficiency in their early training, or they must have been extremely unteachable on some most important points."[10] Without the superstructure of moral training and the "fear of the Lord, which is the beginning of wisdom," intellectual exertion could lead, they believed, only to a dangerous asymmetrical development, frequently eventuating in an early grave or in a state of moral degeneracy.

Hand in hand with this conservative argument went an affirmation of decidedly new and liberal attitudes toward child growth. Quoting Humphrey again:

. . . it is obvious how difficult a task it must be, to persuade parents to let their sprightly little darling alone, till the rain and the sunshine have opened the bud and prepared the way for mental culture. Had some older friend said to us, some four and twenty years ago, when we were arranging our lettered blocks, and showing our Reuben or Simeon, that h-a-t spells hat, "you are quite too early for the advantage and safety of your child, you had better leave the little fellow to his cob-houses and his antics till nature has had time to do her part," I dare say we should have gone on, without giving much heed to the advice, . . . But the common idea, that if you can teach an infant to read with considerable ease . . . in its third or fourth year, it is . . . so much clear gain, is extremely fallacious.[11]

7. *Loc. cit.*
8. Goodrich, *Fireside Education*, p. 81.
9. Waterston, *Moral and Spiritual Culture*, p. 4.
10. Humphrey, *Domestic Education*, pp. 11–12.
11. *Ibid.*, pp. 74–75.

By postponing the teaching of the alphabet two years longer, he further declared, a freshness and vigor of mind would result, not observable "after a precocious and hard tasked infancy." [12]

A contributor to the *Parent's Magazine* deplored:

the undue amount of intellectual exertion required . . . at the period when the human being ought . . . to be allowed to vegetate; the period at least, which ought to be chiefly devoted to cherish all the amiable moral feelings, and to strengthen the physical powers; the period at which the intellectual powers ought to be left to exert their own natural activity, without being excited and prematurely drawn forth. [13]

Goodrich stated quite simply that since the first three or four years of childhood "are occupied in educating the senses," which children can themselves perform with little aid, there is small use in teaching them the alphabet until they are six years old. [14]

Mrs. Child's first chapter in her *Mother's Book* is devoted to "the Bodily Senses," which she maintained would be early cultivated by presenting attractive objects to the child, "things of bright and beautiful colors . . . and sounds pleasant and soft to the ear." [15] A later chapter on the Intellect deals not with the A B C, as might be supposed, but with the cultivation of habits of thought, the association of words with objects, and the observation of the qualities of objects. [16]

These statements and approaches reveal much more than a rejection of precocity as a goal in education. They indicate a significant shift in emphasis from the world of words and ideas, to the world of things, from growth as a forcing process to growth as natural unfoldment. They definitely help to set the stage for the Pestalozzian system of object teaching and for later Darwinian concepts of evolutionary development. And yet, it will be seen in the course of this chapter, that the qualifications and reservations were many which restricted these new ideas in their practical application.

Perhaps the most important factor in the popular reaction against intellectual precocity was the growing recognition of health dangers inherent in the old system of learning. The 1834

12. *Loc. cit.*
13. "On Physical Education," *Parent's Magazine*, 2:217, June, 1842.
14. Goodrich, *op. cit.*, p. 292.
15. Child, *The Mother's Book*, p. 3.
16. *Ibid.*, p. 11.

Ladies' Magazine quoted Brigham as defining one of the causes of insanity the "predominance given to the nervous system, by too early cultivating the mind and exciting the feelings of children." [17] Reference has been made above to the public awakening regarding the hazards of poorly equipped school houses.[18] To this was added concern over the confinement of young children during the long school day. Horace Mann believed that "to make small children sit, both dumb and motionless, for three successive hours, with the exception of a brief recess and two short lessons," was "an infraction of every law which the Creator has impressed upon both body and mind." [19] In the appendix to his *Fourth Annual Report,* he cited the opinion of Dr. Woodward of the State Lunatic Asylum in Worcester, Massachusetts, that children under eight should enjoy long recess periods, and that children exhibiting alarming symptons of precocity should be taken immediately from their books and allowed to play in the open air.[20] These opinions cited by Mann in 1840 were still being quoted in 1859. The *Atlantic Monthly* magazine, referring to Mann and Woodward, and reiterating the perils of insanity inherent in precocity, stated that "the one thing about which doctors do *not* disagree is the destructive effect of premature or excessive mental labor." [21] Parents were implored to avert the blight and ruin of childhood which is caused by the "race of desperate ambition" begun in infancy.[22] Feebleness and disease were seen as no longer the visitations of Providence but the neglect of nature's laws of mental and physical health.

So much, then, for the midcentury trend away from precocity. To this study it is significant chiefly for two reasons. First, it helped to break up the patriarchal family pattern in which the father was responsible for the intellectual culture of children. His efforts in behalf of the youngest members of the family were seen to be actually damaging in their effects. The picture referred to above,[23] used by Goodrich in his text *Fireside Education* shows

17. "Causes of Insanity" (quotation from Amariah Brigham), *Ladies' Magazine,* 7:79, January, 1834.

18. Cf. *ante,* p. 25.

19. Horace Mann, *Fourth Annual Report* (1841), in Massachusetts Board of Education, *Annual Reports,* p. 26.

20. *Ibid.,* p. 100.

21. "Murder of the Innocents," *Atlantic Monthly,* 4:347, September, 1859.

22. *Ibid.,* p. 355.

23. Cf. *ante,* p. 3, also illustration p. 150.

an attempt to restore this family pattern, but it should be noted that the father is depicted as instructing an older child, while the younger ones are receiving their "cultivation of the heart" at the hands of the mother. Secondly, the reaction against precocity was accompanied by a demand for a substitute form of intellectual culture which, in its emphasis upon gradual and constant unfoldment of the mental powers from infancy upwards, was of necessity the function of the one most closely associated with the young child, the mother.

In defining this new type of rational education and the function of the mother with regard to it, it is helpful to turn to the preface of Jacob Abbott's text entitled *The Little Philosopher, or The Infant School at Home.*[24] This describes a scene in a family parlor where several children are playing on the floor. The mother enters, saying, "Come here, my little children; I have bought a new book, and am going to teach you *Philosophy,*"[25] whereupon the following conversation ensues:

William. What is Philosophy, mother?
Mother. It is the first thing which children learn.
William. Why, mother, the *first thing?* then it must be the a,b,c. Who would think that would be called such a name?
Mother. No, William; you learned a great many things long before you learned the a,b,c.
Ann. I am pretty sure the first thing that *I* studied, was my letters.
Mother. Look at baby there; what is he doing?
Ann. Oh! he is tearing the newspaper all to pieces; he will spoil it.
Mother. No matter if he does; but what do you think he is doing it for?
William. I don't know, unless it is for mischief.
Mother. No, William; it is not for mischief. A piece of paper is something new and curious to him; and he likes to shake it about to see how it will move; and to pull it, to see how strong it is, and how easily it will tear. In that way he is learning the nature of it. . . .
William. Why, mother, is this Philosophy?
Mother. Yes, William; and every child has a great deal of Philosophy to learn before it can walk or speak, and much more before it can read.[26]

24. Jacob Abbott, *The Little Philosopher* (Boston, Carter & Hendee, 1830).
25. *Ibid.,* p. v.
26. *Ibid.,* pp. v–vii.

The lessons on Philosophy which follow this illuminating preface have to do with such subjects as "Shape," "Colour," "Hardness and Softness," "Weight," and so forth, and progress to more intricate topics such as "The Weather," "Growth," "Motion," and the like. The mother's function in presenting this material is that of questioner and demonstrator. Instead of pouring information into the child's mind, she draws it out of him by appealing, not to memory alone, but to the familiar testimony of the senses and to dawning powers of reason and of association She says, for example, "Feel of your cheek, and tell me whether it is hard or soft. Is a cushion hard or soft? Why is it made soft?" [27]

This approach to mental cultivation, coming as it does from a conservative clergyman, shows the extent to which naturalistic methods were beginning to operate within the old Lockian framework. The concept of formal discipline prevailed but with a new emphasis upon things instead of abstract ideas, upon understanding of facts instead of memory and parrot-like repetition.

Gallaudet's methods of mental cultivation have been mentioned above in connection with his *Child's Book on the Soul*. He, like Abbott, felt that the newer type of intellectual cultivation could begin very early. In acquainting the child with his own spirit, the mother, he claimed, was producing the power of reflection, calling the consciousness into exercise, and forming habits of self-examination. It was her function to teach him to think for himself, and to employ his empirical knowledge to further his spiritual understanding.[28] The lessons given in his book as well as in Abbott's are adapted to use with a five-year-old child.

Turning to the concepts of women writers, we find the methods simplified according to the age and experience of the child. Mrs. Phelps observed the beginnings of intellectual activity in the year old infant. Thus, she wrote of her own child:

Perception is ever on the alert with him; if he hear the mewing of a cat, he looks after her that he may *perceive* her; if he hear a sound, he seeks to ascertain the cause of it. . . . *Memory* recalls to him the objects of his perceptions, aided by his reflections. He weeps to see his mother go out with her bonnet on. . . . Ask him where is papa, and he looks toward the place where he is accustomed to see him occupy. The faculty of *association* has connected the appellation, papa, with the person. . . . *Reason* has

27. *Ibid.*, p. 18.
28. Gallaudet, *Child's Book on the Soul*, Part I, p. vi.

taught him to avoid the hot stove; *curiosity* is constantly leading him to new observations, and *imagination* shows itself in his interest in pictures and images.[29]

The mother's function in regard to these manifestations was primarily that of intelligent observer. Mrs. Phelps recommended that mothers study the activities of their infants to learn from them, as well as to teach them. But her own record reveals the mother in the role of constant attendant, stepping in actively to multiply the experiences and thus exercise the faculties, of the child.[30] At one time she presented her boy with a box of wafers and suffered him to shake and pull at the box until he was able to open it. When "hundreds of bright round pieces fell about him in glorious confusion," she claimed that he "had conquered a difficulty and had made a discovery." "The same curiosity or love of knowledge," she wrote, "leads us on from one difficulty to another in science; and should we ever reach a point beyond which there could be no discoveries, like Alexander, we should weep that there was nothing more to be conquered." [31] The mother's duty was, therefore, to multiply opportunities for discoveries of this sort. Obviously Mrs. Phelps had come a long way from the Puritanical concepts of play as a sinful pastime and of knowledge as formal book learning.

Mrs. Child urged upon mothers the necessity of cultivating early habits of observation in little children, encouraging them to pay attention to surrounding objects, to name them at sight, and to inquire into "the why and wherefore of everything." [32] To trot a child up and down, or to amuse him by dragging his little cart or to repeat "pat a cake, pat a cake" was not enough for the mother to do, she declared, since "something ought to be mixed with these plays to give the child habits of thought." [33] And this something was information of the object lesson variety. "This ball is *round;* this little tea table is *square.* Now George knows what *round* and *square* mean." [34] We are apt to forget, said Mrs. Child, "that things long familiar to us are entirely unknown to an infant." [35] With the definition of instruction thus simplified, mid-

29. Phelps, "Observations upon an Infant," p. 348.
30. *Ibid., passim.*
31. *Ibid.,* pp. 341–42.
32. Child, *op. cit.,* p. 10.
33. *Ibid.,* p. 11.
34. *Loc. cit.*
35. *Ibid.,* p. 12.

century mothers had few excuses to offer for neglecting domestic education. Mrs. Child ridiculed women who complained that they were ill fitted to train their children's minds since they themselves lacked a proper education. ". . . If by education is meant book-learning, the excuse is indeed a poor one," she wrote, since learning is not necessary. "The mother, who has had no other advantages than are furnished by a public school in a remote country village, knows a great many more things than a child of three or four years can possibly know." [36] She can therefore arouse a spirit of inquiry which leads to a love of knowledge.

This admission that a mother could instruct the child's intellect without having intellectual attainments of her own might appear to be damaging to the arguments of those who were supporting female education. Mrs. Sigourney reconciles the two approaches to child training by stating that while "erudition is not demanded," no one has a stronger motive to the attainment of it than the mother who considers the future development of her children.[37] "Reading, orthography, and the definition of words, penmanship, arithmetic, and the expression of thought . . . she is surely capable of teaching," [38] and the admirable mother is the one who gives up the time-consuming social frivolities of the day [39] to keep pace with, and minister to, the intellectual, as well as the moral, social, and physical needs of her children.

This brings up the subject of domestic versus school instruction of young children. Mrs. Sigourney recommended that the mother who has it in her power to do so, conduct the child's education even beyond that of the ordinary preschool period. "Why," she argued, "expose it to the influence of evil example? . . . Why yield it to the excitement of promiscuous association, when it has a parent's house, where its innocence may be shielded, and its intellect aided to expand?" [40] Could not the mother, by devoting two or three hours a day, give to her child a greater proportion of time than could the teacher of a school? She spoke of an aged and intelligent man who, having learned to read from maternal instruction, "gave it as one reason why knowledge was pleasant to his soul, that its rudiments entered there with the association

36. *Ibid.*, pp. 10–11.
37. Sigourney, *op. cit.*, p. 104.
38. *Ibid.*, pp. 104–5.
39. *Ibid.*, pp. 110–11.
40. *Ibid.*, p. 103.

of gentle tones, patient explanations, and tender caresses." [41]

The new type of intellectual cultivation could not thrive in the crowded schoolroom where children's bodies were cramped and their mental faculties stimulated by artificial means only. Dr. William Alcott declared that one hour well spent in the *"family school"* might "do more towards teaching the young what they ought to know, than is now done by our whole array of processes and instruments of instruction," from those of the college to those of "the smallest and humblest collection of mere infants." [42] While Alcott strove to restore the post of family instructor to the father, another contributor to the *Mother's Assistant* described in a similar article the ways in which the mother might supply this office. Little children, he said, ask questions like " 'How do flies walk on the wall?' " and " 'What makes it rain today?' " By informing them in simple language of the causes behind these phenomena, the mother could "gratify the thirst for knowledge manifested by her child." If perchance she heard questions she could not answer, "they would induce her to read, as opportunity offered." No school could be found, he believed, like "the schoolhouse at home, with the tender mother as the mistress." [43]

Here, as in other midcentury trends of thought, one is puzzled by the mingling of conservatism and progressivism. It is entirely possible, for example, that advocates of fireside education were reacting conservatively against the mass movement in popular education. Undoubtedly the stress on the cultivation of the moral feelings and of the heart was partially conservative, an attempt to control the unruly upsurgence of crude American individualism. The mother at home as schoolmistress was seen as less of a menace to the status quo than the socially conscious, lyceum-attending, intellectual woman of the day. And children safe at home under the simple and limited tutelage of the mother were protected from the influences of evil associates [44] and ultra democratic ideas. Didactic juvenile literature reveals ideal children of the period as well dressed, superior little prudes and snobs

41. *Ibid.*, p. 102.

42. William A. Alcott, "There Is No School Like the Family School," *Mother's Assistant*, 3:2, January, 1843.

43. Charles Holden, "The Family School," *Mother's Assistant*, 3:248, November, 1843.

44. Muzzey refers to the "vast influence" which the neighborhood has in forming the characters of children, hinting at the danger of "noisy, profane, vulgar or untruthful" associates; *The Fireside*, p. 170.

definitely aware of class distinctions, and carefully protected from the influences of the streets.[45] Aristocratic New Englanders were still too close to their English origins to be willing to pattern their progeny on the common school mold, though they admitted at the same time that the well-being of the country depended upon the proper education of the masses.

The "family school" movement had much more behind it, however, than the cautious instincts of the reactionary conservator. In admitting new concepts of learning it effectually ushered within the narrow walls of the home the broader horizons of the world of objects and of nature. A prize-winning essay which appeared in 1844 extolled the virtues of an English mother, Mrs. Robinson, who withdrew all three of her young children from school, believing that her own "vigilant study" [46] of their dispositions, and the expedients contrived by her maternal instinct for their control, would promote an education far superior to the "tasked lessons" given in the sedentary confinement of the schoolroom.[47] In place of these lessons, she provided a pictorial primer for the eldest, a boy of seven, and in place of formal teaching she "contrived to give an air of recreation to his hours of study" with the result that he taught himself how to read within a year. All three children were turned out into the world of nature where they cultivated their own garden plots and ran freely in the forest. Mrs. Robinson believed that "if children learn at all from books before the period of infancy has passed, it should be in some form of amusement and at the domestic hearth." [48] The most significant statement in this account is one concerned with the function of the educator: ". . . the word educate is from *educo,* to draw out; and not as is generally supposed, to 'fill up.' " [49]

This essay, together with many others of the period, was proclaiming new principles of learning, and bringing about conditions for the effectual emancipation of mothers and children from the fetters of tradition. Thus, the "family school" was an institution which could be supported by groups having fundamentally different philosophies.

Before defining further the duties of the mother with regard

45. Jacob Abbott, *The Rollo Code of Morals* (Boston, Crocker & Brewster, 1841), pp. 95–100.
46. Stevens, "The Restored Family," *Mother's Assistant,* 4:99, May, 1844.
47. *Ibid.,* p. 101.
48. *Ibid.,* p. 102.
49. *Ibid.,* p. 99.

to intellectual cultivation of children, it is necessary to examine into the new pseudo science of the mind which was exerting a powerful influence upon midcentury educators and reformers. Phrenology,[50] the theory that the mind consists of some thirty or forty localized independent faculties correlated with the prominences of the skull, was widely publicized in the United States by the lectures of Spurzheim in 1832, and by the writings of George Combe, popular Scotch phrenologist [51] in the late 'thirties.

This system labeled the propensities or passions located in the lower and posterior portion of the brain as "amativeness, philoprogenitiveness, continuity, adhesiveness or friendship, combativeness, destructiveness, etc." [52] The sentiments situated at the superior portion of the cranium were listed as "self-esteem, love of approbation, cautiousness, firmness, benevolence, etc." The intellectual faculties, situated in the anterior portion of the brain, were "individuality, form, space or size, weight or resistance, color, locality, etc." [53] To these were added also the reflective faculties of comparison and causality.[54] The size of each prominence indicated the degree of intensity of the faculty.

This theory, incredible as it seems to the twentieth century reader, was of serious importance to many well educated Americans of the midnineteenth century, while it became a true vogue with the half educated middle classes. Skull readings were given in professional offices set up for the purpose,[55] and these readings were consulted not only to determine the shortcomings and potentialities of the persons involved, but were also used to predict suitable vocations, and to determine prospects for future compatibility of couples contemplating matrimony.

Horace Mann is reported to have said that if a young man had but one dollar to his name he should spend it "in learning from a Phrenological examination what occupation he should pursue." [56] Sarah Hale publicized the crusades of Spurzheim and of Combe in her *Ladies' Magazine*.[57] Daniel Webster and Henry Ward

50. "Phrenology," *New International Encyclopaedia*, XVIII, 568–69.
51. Cf. *ante*, p. 64.
52. "Phrenology," *New International Encyclopaedia*, XVIII, 568.
53. *Loc. cit.*
54. "Phrenology," *Encyclopaedia Britannica*, XXI, 537.
55. Branch, *op. cit.*, p. 280.
56. *Ibid.*, p. 284.
57. See *Ladies' Magazine*, 5:474, October, 1832; and 7:376–79, August, 1834.

Beecher were believers.[58] Heman Humphrey betrayed at least an acquaintance with phrenology in his volume on *Domestic Education*.[59] Samuel Goodrich quoted George Combe in his text *Fireside Education*.[60] The popularity of Orson Squire Fowler's *Love and Parentage, Applied to the Improvement of Offspring*, a text based on phrenological concepts, has been mentioned above.[61]

The significance of this bump-reading craze for the mothers of young children may best be seen by examining the editorial comments of Sarah Hale. In 1832 an article appeared entitled "What Good Will Phrenology Do the Ladies?" In this Mrs. Hale declared that if phrenology, as a science, was ever to be made effective "in moulding the character of mankind, so as essentially to affect their condition, improvement and happiness," it should be understood by women "because the principles must be acted upon in the education of 'young beings' from their birth." [62] Two years later, in reviewing a publication of George Combe's, she pursued the same theme, quoting the following passage from Combe:

"If we should ask any mother, who has not studied mental philosophy, to write out a catalogue of the desires, emotions, and intellectual powers which she conceives her children to be endowed with;—to describe the particular objects of each faculty; its proper sphere of action; the abuses into which it is most prone to fall; and also the best method of directing each to its legitimate objects, . . . we know well she could not execute such a task." [63]

Combe had said further that mothers experiencing this "darkness" subsequently studied phrenology and were gratified with the light which it shed upon their practical duties.[64]

Phrenology's emphasis upon the study of the mind [65] coincided well with the arguments which had been advanced for the cause of female education. In 1829 Catherine Beecher had asked of young women, "Have you been taught the powers and faculties

58. Branch, *op. cit.*, p. 278.

59. Humphrey, *op. cit.*, pp. 128–29.

60. Goodrich, *op. cit.*, p. 93.

61. Cf. *ante*, p. 65.

62. Sarah J. Hale, "What Good Will Phrenology Do the Ladies?" *Ladies' Magazine*, 5:474, October, 1832.

63. "Books and Authors" reviewing George Combe's *Lectures on Popular Education, Ladies' Magazine*, 7:378, August, 1834.

64. *Loc. cit.*

65. "American Institute of Instruction," *Ladies' Magazine*, 6:422, September, 1833.

of the human mind, and the laws by which it is regulated? Have you studied how to direct its several faculties; how to restore those that are overgrown, and strengthen and mature those that are deficient?" [66] A popular address, "The Influence of Woman on Society," delivered at a Social Lyceum in Boston, had included a statement with regard to the intellectual cultivation of children that "the mother must perfectly understand the laws of mind." [67] Mrs. Phelps' purpose in writing her "Observations upon an Infant" was to set down notes on the progressive development of her child's senses and other native faculties [68] as an aid to herself and to other mothers.

Thus, on the surface, at least, phrenologists were at one with progressive educators in their insistence upon objective study of the mind, and upon the importance of early guidance in the development of the human faculties. To the popular mind, there was little difference between the aims of the phrenologists and those of the physiologists and scientists who were slowly evolving the tested body of facts which was to eventuate in an American science of psychology.[69] It is as if the twentieth century were to compare the work of a newspaper columnist of the trouble-clinic variety with that of a highly trained psychiatrist. Phrenology was just accurate enough in its general presuppositions to gain a wide circle of converts.[70]

Beneath the surface, however, were disagreements which involved fundamentally different approaches in education. Mrs. Phelps objected to the phrenologist's preoccupation with the skull of the subject under observation. Thus, she wrote: "The educator ought to know the predominant faculties in the mind of his pupil; but there is, in my opinion, a surer way to ascertain this than by examining his cranium; and this is by observing his actions. If he is quarrelsome and contentious, this disposition ought to be

66. Catherine E. Beecher, *Suggestions Respecting Improvements in Education* (Hartford, Packer & Butler, 1829), pp. 8–9.

67. John A. Bolles, "The Influence of Women on Society," *Ladies' Magazine*, 4:259, May, 1831.

68. Phelps, *op. cit.*, p. 325.

69. Edwin G. Boring, *A History of Experimental Psychology* (New York and London, copyright, 1929, D. Appleton–Century Company, Inc.) Page 55 states that "the theory of Gall and Spurzheim is . . . an instance of a theory which is essentially wrong, but just enough right to further scientific thought."

70. *Ibid.*, pp. 54–55.

checked, whether the organ of *combativeness* be prominent or
not." [71] A similar objection is voiced in the 1833 *North American
Review:*

. . . the object and end of education being to strengthen, or
weaken, . . . particular faculties or propensities, and it being
admitted on all hands, that we can so operate upon them; it seems
to us a most barren question, whether the organ is, or is not developed. . . . If we make our children religious and benevolent,
by proper instruction and discipline, . . . the organs may shrink
or swell at their own pleasure or that of the phrenologists, it matters not to us.[72]

Carried to its logical conclusions the phrenologist's preoccupation with the physical characteristics of the brain led to a somewhat fatalistic or materialistic philosophy, which denied to the
educator the power to "mould" the mind beyond certain physical
limits. Andrew Combe, brother to George, who wrote the well-
received *Treatise on the Physiological and Moral Management of
Infancy* declared: ". . . we can no more add a new feeling or
a new power, by education or other means, than we can cause ap-
ples to grow on one branch of a fig-tree and plums on another." [73]
Compare this with the statement addressed by the American,
Humphrey, to parents: "You have nothing to do in giving it [the
child] new faculties, or in supplying any which may be wanting." [74] The sober realism of these statements gave pause to those
who were, in the flush of midcentury optimism, granting to parents the power to form their offspring along perfectionistic, mil-
lennialistic patterns.

It is hardly likely that the full implication of this realism penetrated to the popular mind; nevertheless, it is interesting to note
the way in which it found expression in an article published in
the 1833 *Ladies' Magazine* entitled "A Chapter from the Book of
Marriage." [75] This tells of a fat sullen boy who, accompanied
by his mother, boarded a stagecoach. The narrator, a passenger
on the coach, observed when the boy removed his cap that "the
forehead at the base was wide, and came out rather full between

71. Phelps, *Female Student*, p. 402.
72. "Phrenology," Art. 3, *North American Review*, 37:73, July, 1833.
73. Andrew Combe, *On the Management of Infancy*, p. 379.
74. Humphrey, *op. cit.*, p. 71.
75. "A Chapter from 'The Book of Marriage,'" *Ladies' Magazine*, 6:262, June, 1833.

the eyes, or, as the phrenologist would say, *individuality* was strongly marked, and *eventuality* was not wholly wanting—but above that there was not room for a thimble-full of brains in front." He noted further that "the animal faculties seemed in full development" whereas the "human sentiments were dwarfed, and cribbed in the smallest possible space." [76] Instead of calling attention to the shortcomings of the mother's educational efforts and implying her responsibility for the expression of her child's lower faculties, the writer of this sketch stated that "the lady was the picture of maternal thoughtfulness and softness," pious and "willing to *do* as well as *pray*" [77] for her child. She was doing all in her power to aid the boy by taking him to the country where he could engage in activities suited to his low capacity. She had, however, made the mistake of marrying a cousin and thus endowing her offspring with these undesirable hereditary tendencies.[78] The note of fatalism is obvious in this sketch. The mother is granted only a limited power in shaping the course of her son. Her initial mistake, made by marriage, was not possible of rectification, but neither was she morally condemned on that account.

This is at once different from the religious approach which held out hope of regeneration and salvation through the joint prayer and efforts of the mother and child, and from the perfectionistic hope of the era which believed all things possible to the morally inspired educator. Spurzheim had commented on the dangerous impression, current among midcentury thinkers, "that faculties are to be in some sort *formed,* instead of being *cultivated*—that the mind and character of each pupil is to be cast in some prescribed mould instead of being merely developed according to his individual capacity and destination." [79] The earlier phrenologists set limits to the efficacy of the parent or educator, limits which neither religious faith nor educational zeal could transcend.

It was inevitable that so important a change of base should cause a reaction among those who were granting regenerative powers to mothers. The materialism of phrenology struck at the very roots of the midcentury faith in the promise of gentle nur-

76. *Ibid.*, p. 262.
77. *Ibid.*, p. 264.
78. *Ibid.*, p. 265.
79. "Review of Spurzheim on Education," Art. 3, *American Annals of Education and Instruction*, 3:124, March, 1833.

ture for the rising generation. Furthermore, the charge of "atheism" was brought against the new science. Mrs. Phelps called attention to the fact that if an accident to the skull can damage the organs of veneration and conscientiousness, then hope of the salvation of the soul is jeopardized! [80]

Phrenology might have gone down under these charges, at least for the majorities who could not delve deeply into the convincing treatises of George and Andrew Combe, had it not been for that ingenious fanatic who popularized the cause for the American public, Orson Squire Fowler, the Dale Carnegie of the midcentury period. Benefiting from the constructive educational philosophy set forth in Combe's *Constitution of Man*,[81] and aware of the strong emotional climate in the realm of childhood education, Fowler published in 1844 a treatise entitled *Education and Self-Improvement, Founded on Physiology and Phrenology*, which went through two editions and was sold in the leading cities of the northeastern United States. In the preface of this work, addressed to parents and teachers, he said: "Too long . . . have Phrenologists been content with *knowing* themselves by this science. It is now high time for them to *apply* it to their own mental cultivation, and to the intellectual and moral improvement of mankind, especially of the rising generation." "IMPROVEMENT," he declared, "is the leading characteristic of the nineteenth century." [82] Fowler, like other reformers of his period, was finding a middle ground in the improvability of the human race, a safe common cause which could temporarily disregard both the implications of fatalistic materialism, and the debatable question of the perfectibility of man. For, if these exponents of the new science had doubts regarding the educability of the criminal, they had great hopes for the plastic infant whose faculties were rightly directed.

Out-trumpeting the most eloquent religious enthusiasts, Fowler addressed women thus: ". . . ye mothers, pause and consider! Stop short! for ye are spoiling God's works, whereas ye were placed here to burnish them. . . . O mothers! mothers! your

80. Phelps, *Female Student*, p. 402.

81. George Combe, *The Constitution of Man* (Boston, William D. Ticknor, 1838), chap. iv.

82. Orson Squire Fowler, *Education and Self-Improvement* (2d. ed. New York, O. S. and L. N. Fowler, 1844), I, 3–4.

race is imploring salvation at your hands! Ye *can* bestow it, and ye *must* . . . first LEARN your duty, and then DO it." [83]

By examining what Fowler proposed that mothers should do with regard to intellectual cultivation of children, we come finally to the significance of phrenology for this investigation and its contribution to the growing science of mind study.

After obtaining knowledge of her child's development with respect to his intellectual organs, the mother was advised to proceed to the improvement of the separate faculties. Since "Individuality" is one of the first intellectual organs developed, "education should be *begun* and *continued*" by showing children "*things*, and how *to do* things." [84] Reading, Fowler stated, is not interesting to the very young child and therefore weakens his intellectual organs instead of strengthening or enlarging them. Observation should come first; books and papers afterward.[85] Mothers should begin with the infant of three months:

. . . Place a variety of *objects* before it; [we read], take it into rooms and places which it has not yet seen. . . . At six months, take hold of the things shown it, and call them by name. . . . At one and two years old, take it out of doors much, . . . show it flowers, trees, leaves, . . . animals, etc., . . . and when it asks you . . . "Ma, *what* is that?" instead of chiding it with an "Oh, dear, you pother me to death with your everlasting questions, do hush up," take pains to explain it all. . . .

As they become three and four years old, take them to the Museum: . . . and then take them into the laboratory of nature, ...[86]

To the mother who complained that she had no time for these excursions, Fowler said scornfully, "Then you should not have time to *marry*." [87]

Eventuality, the faculty of "*memory* of things seen and knowledge acquired," was next in importance for early intellectual development. Fowler objected to the practice of sending children to school from three years of age, to " 'set on a bench and say

83. *Ibid.*, p. 200.

84. Orson Squire Fowler, *Fowler on Memory* (New York, O. S. and L. N. Fowler, 1842), p. 18. This is bound with Fowler, *Education and Self Improvement* (1844).

85. *Ibid.*, p. 21.

86. *Ibid.*, pp. 22–23.

87. *Ibid.*, p. 23.

A.' " [88] Rote learning, he believed, does more harm than good. It is of no interest to young children to know the shape of A, but "only tell them a *story,* or just show and explain passing *things* to them, and they are instantly electrified with interest." [89] This interest excites memory and thus enlarges the organ of eventuality. If recollections are pleasurable, the exercise of the faculties is greatly facilitated.[90] The first reasoning power comes, said Fowler, from simple lessons in the laws of nature, and this reasoning should be of the inductive variety which begins with present facts.[91]

To develop the organs of "Comparison" and "Causality," mothers were urged to attend carefully to the questions of children instead of turning them off with the admonition that children should be seen and not heard. New facts are needed to increase the powers of comparison, and as for the causes and laws of things, these must be constantly explained "from three years old and upward" in response to a child's "Ma, what *makes* this? Pa, what is that *for?"* [92]

With regard to language, phrenology dictated, said Fowler, that children should "talk all they please." The expression of ideas "increases their flow, and quickens the action of the mind." To the parent who objected to the incessant clamoring of children, Fowler replied that he had no more right to keep his children still than "to stop their breathing and eating." [93] Only the full unrestrained use of the tongue could develop adequately the language faculty. Mothers should refrain, he said, from talking baby talk since children "over two years old, understand, . . . most that is said to them," [94] and should have the correct example to imitate. He anticipated twentieth century methods in suggesting that foreign languages should be "talked" to children rather than read to them or learned from books.[95]

Of the remaining intellectual faculties, of form, weight, calculation, time, tune, locality, order, size, and color, Fowler made

88. *Ibid.,* pp. 25–26.
89. *Loc. cit.*
90. *Ibid.,* p. 35.
91. *Ibid.,* p. 38.
92. *Ibid.,* p. 43.
93. *Ibid.,* p. 53.
94. *Ibid.,* p. 55.
95. *Ibid.,* p. 56.

the following comments, significant for a new philosophy of education:

. . . Form is the proper organ for spelling and reading; and therefore children should be taught to read and spell by the *looks* of words, not by *rote*.[96]

Instead of holding or bracing up a child, so that it *cannot* roll over or fall, let it . . . roll into some uncomfortable position, so as to teach it to steady itself, and sit up, creep, etc., early.[97]

At two years old, teach them to count your fingers, and other things. . . . I verily believe that if every arithmetic in christendom were destroyed and no more printed, the rising generation would learn to cast accounts *better* than they now do.[98]

The only means of cultivating it [the faculty of time] is, to EXERCISE it. . . .[99]

Let all young children sing themselves, and . . . instead of waiting till they have taken *lessons* in music, . . . strike up the cheerful lays when about the house. . . .[100]

. . . when your child is two years old, it will know the house in which it has lived from other houses. . . . Beginning with the rooms in your house, teach it which way is east, west, north, and south. . . .[101]

. . . give them breakfast . . . at stated times; have them take their naps regularly . . . and so have a *time* for every thing. . . .[102]

Let children be shown pictures . . . and let those pictures be *painted* to life.[103]

In setting forth the above details for the guidance of mothers, Fowler was not entirely original. His predecessors, George and Andrew Combe, had laid down the principles underlying this guidance, and some of the details.[104] But Fowler was an American and a showman. He had his own publishing house. He had published one pot-boiler which had capitalized on the most sensa-

96. *Ibid.*, p. 59.
97. *Ibid.*, p. 61.
98. *Ibid.*, p. 62.
99. *Ibid.*, p. 65.
100. *Ibid.*, p. 71.
101. *Ibid.*, p. 75.
102. *Ibid.*, p. 92.
103. *Ibid.*, p. 96.
104. Andrew Combe, *A Treatise on the Physiological and Moral Management of Infancy*, pp. 369–80; George Combe, *Lectures on Popular Education* (1st American ed. Boston, Marsh, Capen & Lyon, 1834), *passim*.

tional aspect of phrenological teaching, that having to do with marriage and parentage.[105] His text on *Education and Self-Improvement* came out after the publications of Mrs. Child, Mrs. Sigourney, John Abbott, Samuel Goodrich, and Heman Humphrey, addressed to parents. It is possible therefore that he reaped the benefit of their cumulative knowledge of domestic education, which he used to further the cause of phrenology. That he had read Mrs. Sigourney at least, is likely from his technique used in admonishing mothers [106] of their duties with regard to home education. It seems probable also that he was influenced by Humphrey,[107] and by Horace Mann's ideas of suitable methods in teaching the young.[108]

What he lacked in originality Fowler made up for in timeliness and concreteness. He told mothers what to do and when to do it, and he couched his teaching in compelling, bombastic, popularized language, calculated to inspire the masses. He attempted to answer objections to phrenology in a volume entitled *Religion Natural and Revealed*,[109] of which there were ten editions in four years. In this work, as Branch has noted, he pointed out that both phrenology and the Bible "enjoined sentiments of justice, penitence, and forgiveness; inculcated hopes of immortality; demanded filial piety, moral purity, connubial love, patience, hospitality, and the rest of the moral virtues" while both "interdicted profanity, murder, and kindred vices." He interpreted original sin in terms of " 'the Phrenological doctrine of hereditary descent.' " [110]

So much, then, for the influence of phrenology upon the science of the mind, and its ramifications for the patterning of human behavior. Parent educators of the midnineteenth century would probably have objected to the inclusion of Fowler within their ranks, although they might have admitted the contributions of George and Andrew Combe to a philosophy of education.

Returning to the mother and young child in the home, we may

105. Cf. *ante*, p. 65.
106. Cf. *Fowler on Memory*, p. 23, and Sigourney, *Letters to Mothers*, pp. 107–13.
107. Cf. *Fowler on Memory*, p. 26, and Humphrey, *Domestic Education*, pp. 81–83.
108. Cf. *Fowler on Memory*, pp. 17–26, and *Horace Mann, Second Annual Report* (1839), pp. 47–54.
109. Branch, *The Sentimental Years*, pp. 284–85.
110. *Ibid.*, p. 285.

conclude that the many new concepts of learning, regardless of their sources, had definite effects upon maternal attitudes toward the cultivation of the child mind. They associated intellectual cultivation with the simple every day observations and other sensory experiences of infancy. They placed a premium upon pleasurable learning. They evoked "natural laws" of growth which called for the moderate, uniform development of all the faculties, excluding, on the one hand, disuse or neglect, and on the other, premature forcing of the powers of childhood. They called attention to the correlation between physical and mental well-being. And, finally, they suggested a common meeting ground upon which the empiricist or environmentalist might meet with the nativist or perfectionist to achieve common ends in the improvement of the rising generation.

CHAPTER VI

GUARDIAN OF THE TEMPLE OF THE IMMORTAL SOUL

O F all the reforms of the midnineteenth century, the most timely was that which directed the attention of busy Americans to the evils suffered by their own mistreated physical frames and interiors. These evils, of diet, of dress, of posture, and of employment, were accelerated at first only in those sectors of urban society given over to the "fashionable follies" of the period. As communication increased, however, and American patterns of social life were diffused throughout society by the press and travel, the sufferings of the "genteel" became the lot of the rising middle classes, who assumed many of the bad and few of the good habits of their social superiors.

Mention was made in Chapter I [1] of the devastating effects of these evils upon the American family, the high mortality rate of infants and of young children, the early decline and short life span of men and women living in urban areas. It is important to this study to understand the concept of womanhood which prolonged this state of affairs, and caused European visitors to this country to comment on the "apathy" existent in the states on "the subject of health." [2] This was the concept which put a premium upon languor, delicacy, and frailty. Before the various health crusaders joined forces to create a new ideal of vigorous womanhood, it was fashionable to be sickly, and "genteel" to go into a decline. The verse and fiction of the period gave support to this notion. A young ladies' class book of the 'thirties contained a poem by Percival, the first verse of which begins with the lines:

> There is a sweetness in woman's decay,
> When the light of beauty is fading away,

and ends with:

1. Cf. *ante*, pp. 5–7.
2. Martineau, *Society in America*, III, 156.

> When all, that was bright and fair, is fled,
> But the loveliness lingering round the dead.[3]

One of the popular novels of the period gave a central place in the plot to bedside scenes in darkened rooms where the mother of the heroine lingered in this world just long enough to launch her child safely on the sea of life.[4] The ailing mother was accepted as a matter of course. The following verses are extracted from a contribution to the *Parent's Magazine:*

> I must not tease my mother;
> And when she likes to read
> Or has a headache, I will step
> Quite silently indeed.
> I will not choose a noisy play,
> Nor trifling troubles tell
> But sit down quiet by her side
> And try to make her well.[5]

This concept was of direct consequence in the care and treatment of young children. The ignorance which valued delicacy in women made possible either a laissez-faire policy in the physical management of offspring, or, in the education of daughters, a definite repetition of the pattern followed by the mother. Infants and young children in fashionable, or would-be fashionable homes were frequently turned over to the care of ignorant hirelings who knew little or nothing of health principles, and who relied instead upon patent medicines or "old wives tales" when their charges were ailing. Daughters were additionally doomed when mothers chose to bestow attention upon them, since this attention, when given, was directed to the curtailment of natural child activity in accordance with the dictates of fashion. Thus a contributor to the *Ladies' Magazine* wrote:

I have heard of one mother . . . who forbade her child the active sports . . . which are so conducive to health—for fear her foot should be rendered less delicate in size and form! . . . and I have even heard of mothers, who *dread* the appearance of robust health

3. J. G. Percival, "Consumption," in Bailey, *Young Ladies Class Book,* p. 58.

4. Susan Warner, *The Wide Wide World* (New York, George P. Putnam, 1851), chaps. i through vi.

5. "My Mother," *Parent's Magazine,* 1:168, March, 1841.

in their children—to whose diseased fancy there is a charm in a pale cheek and an attenuated form! [6]

Superimposed upon these views were frequently those of the religious fanatic, who viewed death as a blessed release, or those of the romanticist, who regarded childhood as a period for fond indulgence. In either case there was complete ignorance of the laws of health.

While the spectacle of the ailing and fashionable mother and child was to persist far into the nineteenth century, there were many forces at work to dispel the ignorance which gave sanction to it. Public recognition of the importance of health began to dawn early in the midcentury years. By 1859 a contributor to the *Atlantic Monthly* was able to comment humorously on the pendulum swing in the other direction, toward extreme health consciousness. Thus, he addressed adult Americans:

I hear of you from all directions, walking up hills in the mornings and down hills in the afternoons . . . blistering your hands upon gymnastic bars, . . . shaking up and down on hard-trotting horses, and making the most startling innovations in respect to eating, sleeping, and bathing. Like all our countrymen, you are plunging from one extreme to the other. Undoubtedly, you will soon make yourself sick again; but your present extreme is the safer of the two. [7]

National health, said this writer, in more solemn vein, "must be amended, or the American race fails." [8]

Between the pendulum swing from apathy to aroused national consciousness of health lies the story of a domestic revolution which was in its way fully as important for the mother's role in education as any of the factors considered thus far in this study.

To understand the urgency with which reformers attacked time-honored maternal duties such as those concerned with food, clothing, and shelter of young children, it is necessary to examine briefly into the deeper causes of this domestic revolution.

European visitors to America were commenting, some in derogatory fashion, on the manners and customs, health and intelligence,

6. "A Supplement to a Plea for Children," *Ladies' Magazine*, 8:603, November, 1835.

7. "The Murder of the Innocents," *Atlantic Monthly*, 4:345, September, 1859.

8. *Ibid.*, p. 355.

of the American people.[9] Thus, a contributor to the *Ladies' Magazine* in 1835 remarked, ". . . the whole train of British tourists arraign us for misdemeanor, because American manners are not English." At one time, this would have spurred Americans on to a closer imitation of European models, but a "new declaration of independence"[10] was the order of the day. "It is really amusing to see John Bull," it is stated, "afflicted with diseases and approaching decay, set himself up as a model for our young, healthy, vigorous nation; and take us to task, because, forsooth, we do not imitate his bed-ridden habits. . . ."[11] This country was beginning to take pride in its newness and strength, which set it apart from the decaying elegance of the European cultures. The concept grew of a distinct and separate destiny for America, one which would make its people "the most vigorous and powerful race of human beings, both in mind and body, that the world has ever known."[12]

In this roseate picture there was no place for the decadent, weak, and inactive woman or the pale, precocious child. A new vogue of robustness and health began to make itself known. Sarah Hale quoted a Philadelphia commentator in 1834 on the change in the appearance of the fashionable misses who promenaded the city streets. His observation was: "To one rosy cheek girl that used to grace our public walks five years since, there are at least three at present."[13]

It should be noted that reformers who contributed to this health "vogue" were not necessarily motivated by a turning away from Europe. Goodrich, for example, even though he was strongly nationalistic,[14] advised American women to emulate their British sisters who, he declared, "take an airing almost every day, and usually walk several miles."[15] Catherine Beecher called attention to the fact that English women, even in the wealthier classes, "are able to walk six and eight miles, without oppressive fa-

9. Calhoun, *Social History of the American Family*, II, 22–25.

10. "American Manners," *Ladies' Magazine*, 8:507, September, 1835.

11. *Ibid.*, p. 508.

12. Amariah Brigham, *Remarks on the Influence of Mental Cultivation and Mental Excitement upon Health* (Boston, Marsh, Capen & Lyon, 1833), p. viii.

13. Mathew Carey, "Fashion," *Ladies' Magazine*, 7:149, April, 1834.

14. Goodrich, *Fireside Education*, pp. 225–27.

15. *Ibid.*, p. 289.

tigue." [16] For these molders of American manners, Americanism meant a rejection of false and artificial modes, not those wholesome patterns representative of the best British tradition. Hand in hand with the proud and somewhat narrow nationalism of the midcentury period went a keen spirit of self-criticism, which enabled New England moralists, especially, to turn European criticisms to valuable account in highlighting social evils of the day. And when this criticism bore on matters of the household and of health, many New England women, long noted for their good management, began to be cognizant of those ingredients in their own educations which had contributed to their health and efficiency.[17]

Closely related to this "manifest destiny" approach to national health was the approach which vested physical habits with moral significance. As recognition increased of the relation between fashionable dress, overeating, overdrinking, late hours, and the "debility" of the physical constitution, healthful habits and manners were seen as moral obligations. Articles on fashion,[18] on beauty,[19] on eating,[20] and on temperance [21] struck moral and religious overtones. This emphasis was more than a revival of Puritan simplicity, for it was permeated with the warnings of phrenologists and physicians. Thus, for example, overeating was identified with overdevelopment of the faculty of "alimentiveness," or the "lowest animal propensity," capable of leading captive man's "noble reflective faculties." [22] Not only physical debility but moral degeneracy was viewed by some as the result of this form of indulgence.[23] Carried to an extreme, this overweighting of the moral significance of eating produced faddists such as the Grahamites, and the vegetarians who engaged in social experiments such as Fruitlands.[24] Cornelius Mathews was not unfair, said Branch, when he scoffed, " 'The fiend Infidelity is to be put out of the way by nothing less than spare diet and a course of

16. Catherine Beecher, *A Treatise on Domestic Economy*, p. 45.

17. Graves, *Woman in America*, p. 34.

18. "Fashion," *Ladies' Magazine*, 3:311–15, July, 1830; cf. "The Toilet," *Mother's Assistant*, July, 1851, p. 188.

19. "Beauty," *Ladies' Magazine*, 3:31–35, January, 1830.

20. "The Good Dinner," *Ladies' Magazine*, 6:38–40, January, 1833.

21. Reverend E. N. Kirk, "Temperance," *Parent's Magazine*, 1:21–22, September, 1840.

22. "The Good Dinner," *Ladies' Magazine*, 6:39, January, 1833.

23. Cf. *post*, Appendix F.

24. Branch, *The Sentimental Years*, p. 358.

vegetables.' " [25] The "cold water" crusades, the tirades against tea drinking, the dress reforms of the midcentury period, all combined a fervent moral zeal with a new physiological self-consciousness which veered at its outer edges toward transcendental pantheism.[26]

We come finally to a consideration of the third and most important factor in the heightening of American interest in physical welfare, and this was the merging, in the popular mind of the mental and physical man. Mention has been made above [27] of the way in which man's body came to be accepted as a channel for spiritual growth rather than condemned as a base hindrance to his progress. The deism of the eighteenth century had focused attention on man, but man dwindled to a thin stature by the cold blast of reason. The nineteenth century inflated this dwindled man and bathed him in the warm light of divinity. The body as the "casket" or "temple" of the immortal spirit took on significance, especially for those imbued with the idea of progress and of the perfectibility of man. Added to this religious emphasis was that of medical men and students of the mind, who preached of the close interaction between mind and body. For example, Dr. William Alcott wrote ". . . if anything in the body is wrong, it affects either our thoughts or our feelings, or both." [28] When phrenologists helped to establish the brain as the instrument by which the mind operates, and correlated mental action with the prominences on the skull, body and soul were irrevocably linked. The effect of this is seen upon the thinking of Goodrich, who declared that while the body is material and the mere instrument of the soul, "every portion of it is penetrated by nerves, which carry home to the brain, the seat of the soul, a constant succession of sensations." Mental distress, said he, is promoted by a diseased state of the body, "the soul itself being thrown off its balance by the irregular action of the body upon it." [29]

We have noted above [30] that Mrs. Sigourney confused the mind and the soul of the babe. It is startling to carry this to its logical conclusions. If the soul is the mind, and the mind resides in the

25. *Ibid.,* pp. 261–62.
26. *Ibid.,* pp. 257–64.
27. Cf. *ante,* p. 20.
28. William A. Alcott, *The House I Live In* (Boston, Light & Stearns, 1837), p. v.
29. Goodrich, *op. cit.,* pp. 276–77.
30. Cf. *ante,* p. 20.

brain, and the brain is shaped by the skull, then man is considerably lower than the angels and the cries of "materialism" and "atheism" [31] directed against the phrenologists were justified. But the midnineteenth century prophets, phrenologists included, did not reason in this way. They moved triumphantly in the opposite direction, taking the brain, the skull, the senses, and the organs of the human frame up the scale of values toward the transcendental realm of spirit. Thus, Henry Ward Beecher declared:

Our life on earth begins in the body, and depends for vigor upon the fulness and power of our physical nature. An acorn at first sprouts from the soil, and spreads its young leaves upon the surface of the ground. Every year its top grows away from it towards heaven; yet the top neither forgets nor scorns the earth-buried root.

Man's physical nature, he believed, is never to be "crucified or exterminated" but "trained, guided, [and] restrained," so that the passions may become "the harnessed steeds which bear the chariot of the sun." [32]

The moralization and the glorification of the physical man were obviously related to the domestic concerns of the home and fireside. They exalted the humble role of the housewife to a new position of importance. The most trifling duties of the mother were vested with significance and redefined in the light of their moral consequences. Her mission as guardian of the "miniature temple, where the ethereal spirit is a lodger," [33] was solemnly enjoined upon her. New knowledge and new skills were demanded of her, but more especially a new kind of physical education was required for her and for her children.

Physical education, as it was redefined in the midcentury decades was, accordingly, considered more pervasive in the growth process, more basic to intellectual and moral development, than it had been prior to that time. It meant a "sound mind in a sound body." It meant calisthenics for women, and fresh air and activity for children. But it also meant much more than that. Goodrich attempted to express the scope of physical education when he

31. Cf. *ante*, p. 114.

32. Henry Ward Beecher, *Life Thoughts*, Edna Dean Proctor, editor (Boston, Phillips, Sampson & Co., 1858), pp. 75–76; cf. Sigourney, *Letters to Mothers*, pp. 27–28, and Humphrey, *op. cit.*, p. 61, for the concept of the body as a dwelling place of the immortal spirit.

33. Sigourney, *op. cit.*, p. 28.

contrasted the physiological powers of the human infant with those of young animals. Young animals, he said, frequently come to perfection in their physical powers a few months after their birth, whereas man must acquire his every act by "a process of teaching and training." [34] In speech alone, "the tongue, the ear, the lungs, all the oral mechanism, consisting of a thousand nerves, muscles and fibres . . . each and all must be taught of experience, each and all must receive line upon line and precept upon precept." [35]

Henry Ward Beecher's concept of the harnessing of physical nature was consistent with this broader definition of physical education popularized during the midcentury years. The phrenologists listed those faculties located in the posterior part of the brain as the "selfish propensities." [36] These were frequently thought of as constituting man's "lower" or "animal" nature. They included not only "Alimentiveness," or the love of food, drink and so forth, but other propensities such as "Combativeness," "Destructiveness," and "Acquisitiveness," [37] which were as much a part of man's physical nature as his animal appetites, and which were closely related to organic health. Before these "faculties" were allocated in the brain and analyzed by the phrenologists, they had been regarded merely as base passions to be stamped out, rather than educated. But when it was admitted that these faculties were not all "bad" [38] but capable of redirection, a broader field was opened to the physical educator.

Thus, it might be said that the new type of physical education embraced not only the cultivation of the healthy frame, the education of the senses, nerves, muscles, and so forth to perform their special functions, but also the guidance or redirection of certain native appetites and propensities.

What, then, was the maternal role with regard to this set of duties? The uniqueness of her function was a matter of agreement among domestic reformers. Catherine Beecher defined it as the *"profession"* of a woman "to guard the health and form the physical habits of the young." [39] Dr. Alcott declared that mothers

34. Goodrich, *op. cit.*, p. 31.
35. *Ibid.*, p. 30.
36. Branch, *op. cit.*, p. 283.
37. *Loc. cit.*
38. George Combe, *Constitution of Man*, p. 97.
39. Catherine Beecher, *Suggestions Respecting Improvements in Education*, p. 8.

alone "operate on our whole nature." "Other educators," said he, "as the world now is, seldom reach the physical man." [40] Emma Willard called attention to the words of a prize essay, that mothers make society what it is, " 'for the physical and moral tendencies are generally communicated or excited before the child passes from the sphere of the mother's influence.' " [41] Dr. Spurzheim, the popular phrenologist, was quoted as saying that the welfare of the world depended more upon the physical education of women than upon that of men.[42] Likewise Dewees, conservative Philadelphia doctor, whose treatise on children went into many editions, maintained that much depended upon the mother either to ensure "a vigorous constitution" or to prevent "a feeble frame." [43]

In order to be fitted for her duties with respect to this important field, the mother's first task was seen as that of acquiring knowledge of the laws of physical well-being. This demand was given a strong impetus by the proponents of female education. As early as 1829 Catherine Beecher was insisting that the mother must know "at least some of the *general principles* of that perfect and wonderful piece of mechanism committed to her preservation and care." [44] How else, she asked, were those evils to be eradicated which were "operating to destroy the health and life of the young?" [45] Her text *A Treatise on Domestic Economy* was later dedicated to American mothers. In its preface, Miss Beecher declared that for over ten years she had been striving vainly "to induce various medical gentlemen . . . to prepare a short and popular work on Physiology and Hygiene, for the use of female Schools." [46] In the absence of such a text she felt justified in using health knowledge as she saw fit. She did not advocate that mothers should "undertake the minute and extensive investigation requisite for a physician," but she designated knowledge of the human frame and of "the laws of health" [47] as essential for

40. William Alcott, *The Young Housekeeper*, p. 25.
41. Emma Willard, *A Treatise on the Motive Powers Which Produce the Circulation of the Blood* (New York and London, Wiley & Putnam, 1846), p. 170, citing a prize essay from the *Educator*.
42. Graves, *op. cit.*, p. 46, citing Spurzheim.
43. William P. Dewees, *A Treatise on the Physical and Medical Treatment of Children* (4th ed. Philadelphia, Carey & Lea, 1832), p. xi.
44. Catherine Beecher, *Suggestions Respecting Improvements in Education*, p. 8.
45. *Loc. cit.*
46. Beecher, *op. cit.*, p. 8.
47. *Ibid.*, p. 69.

every woman in a position of household and educational responsibility.

Emma Willard, in the appendix to her treatise on the circulation of the blood, quoted a statement which made health knowledge a " 'two-fold necessity' " in female education, " 'to enable women . . . to protect their own health . . . and to enable them, as mothers, to do all that enlightened reflectiveness can for the happiness of the beings entrusted to them.' " [48]

Almira Phelps made knowledge of physiology one of the central features of the senior class program at her Patapsco Institute.[49] She likewise revealed in her "Observations upon an Infant" her views on the necessity of correct medical guidance and information for the young mother.[50]

While the educators of young women laid the foundations for practical health knowledge, and good physical development of prospective mothers, phrenologists were attacking maternal ignorance from a much broader base. This was done by calling attention to all the laws of man's being, and to the universal "natural" laws in which they were grounded. George Combe's *Constitution of Man*,[51] which appealed so widely to midcentury thinkers, had divided natural laws into three classes, "Physical, Organic, and Moral," [52] each set of laws operating independently of the other. The first two classes deserve our notice here. Physical laws were defined as those which operate regardless of moral considerations. Thus, it was declared, the law of gravity applies equally to the heathen and to the Christian. The benevolent missionary may sink in an unsound ship, whereas the "greatest monsters of iniquity" might have a successful voyage in a seaworthy craft.[53] Organic laws were likewise defined as operating independently. The man who has inherited a good physical constitution and who obeys "the rules of temperance and exercise, will enjoy robust health, although he may cheat, lie, blaspheme, and destroy his fellow men." [54] It therefore behooved the mothers of men to acquaint themselves with these laws, and to cease imputing the ills of society to Providence, or to irreligious behavior.

48. Willard, *op. cit.*, p. 170.
49. Bolzau, *Almira Hart Lincoln Phelps*, p. 147.
50. Phelps, "Observations upon an Infant," p. 328.
51. Cf. *ante*, p. 114.
52. George Combe, *op. cit.*, p. 21.
53. *Loc. cit.*
54. *Ibid.*, p. 22.

But it has just been noted above that the American tendency was to break down the barriers between organic and moral considerations. The Americanized or later versions of phrenology kept all that Combe had presented on the importance of the knowledge of natural laws, but took more particular cognizance of the close link between moral goodness and physical soundness and health. Thus Fowler wrote:

> . . . *virtue, moral* perfection, *holiness, goodness*—depend considerably more upon the *health,* and are *produced* by it—by a sound and vigorous *physiology*—than most good people suppose; while depravity, sinfulness, . . . and all the vices that degrade man . . . , are *caused* by—are the *legitimate, necessary products* of *physical derangement*—more than of all other causes combined.[55]

By making this important connection between obedience to "natural laws" and a state of moral goodness, phrenologists had found not only a logical ground of compromise with the religiously inclined, but a powerful weapon with which to combat maternal ignorance. Said they, mothers must learn causes and effects in nature, not just to ensure the physical well-being of their offspring, but to understand all the conditions of life, health, and happiness, for which the Almighty had given them breath. To avail themselves of this information, the study of physiology was therefore not enough. Phrenology must be added. The two together, Fowler declared, evolve "all the *elementary principles*" of man's nature, "thereby embodying all the laws of his being, all the conditions of his happiness, and all the causes of his sufferings." [56]

The third, and perhaps most important, group who prescribed a course of physical education for mothers were of course the physiologists and medical men of the midcentury. While New England was not the seat of the greatest medical activity of the period, it did much to apply the cut and dried findings of practical doctors to the reforms of the period. Catherine Beecher cited the names of Dr. Combe,[57] Dr. Bell,[58] and Dr. Eberle [59] as among

55. Fowler, *Education and Self-Improvement,* p. 48.
56. *Ibid.,* p. 27.
57. Andrew Combe, M. D.
58. John Bell, M. D.
59. John Eberle, M. D.

"the most approved writers" [60] on medical care of children. None of these were New Englanders. Dr. Combe was the brother of George Combe, the phrenologist, and was quoted most frequently by those interested in the instruction of mothers.[61] The titles of his volumes [62] explains his emphasis, which was upon the laws of the human constitution, and the necessity for knowledge which would ensure the adaptation of infant treatment to these laws.[63]

In addition to the approach of the technical treatise, there were two popular approaches to maternal instruction. One was the lyceum or lecture, and the other was the instructive manual. The former was publicized by the *Ladies' Magazine* during the 'thirties.[64] Attention was called to a series of lectures on physical education given at the Boston Athenaeum by a Dr. William Grigg. These lectures were addressed to "a large and attentive audience . . . of the fair and fashionable." [65] Dr. Grigg described the purpose of his lectures as follows:

"The first object will be to make you acquainted with the general principles of anatomy . . . in order that you may understand the . . . principles which should be kept in view in a correct system of education. The course will consist of six lectures—the two first of which will be on Anatomy, the next on Fashion, and the rest on the injuries it has produced, and the means of remedying the difficulties." [66]

This approach, aiming directly at reforming social evils, combined the appeals of the female educators and phrenologists with the technical information of physiologists and medical men.

The other popular approach to female instruction was what may be termed, for want of a better name, the "domestic manual" or "guidebook" approach to health matters. At least three women concerned with fireside education and reforms wrote cookbooks, or manuals giving instructions to women. Mrs. Hale wrote a *Cook's Book.*[67] Catherine Beecher, in addition to her volume *Do-*

60. Catherine Beecher, *op. cit.*, p. 214.
61. e.g., Andrew Combe, M. D., "Frequency of Nursing," *Mother's Assistant*, 3:11–13, January, 1843; and "To Mothers and Nurses," *Parent's Magazine*, 1:245, July, 1841.
62. Cf. *ante*, p. 24n.
63. Andrew Combe, *op. cit.*, p. 7.
64. "Dr. Grigg's Lecture," *Ladies' Magazine*, 4:514–18, November, 1831.
65. *Ibid.*, p. 514.
66. *Ibid.*, p. 516.
67. Roorbach, *Bibliotheca Americana, 1820–1852*, p. 129.

mestic Economy, wrote a *Housekeeper's Receipt Book.*[68] Mrs. Child published the popular *American Frugal Housewife.*[69] These volumes were all strictly utilitarian, dealing with food and household management, but the assumption underlying them was that one important road to physical well-being was through proper knowledge of the affairs of the kitchen.

Greatest of the guidebook exponents was Dr. William Alcott, who combined all the approaches given above with that of the moralist and religionist. His many manuals for household use were themselves designed to serve as texts, but he considered these as merely supplementary to a more thorough course of study for women. Cookbooks, such as the *American Frugal Housewife* he considered valuable, but, he wrote, "something more philosophical will still be necessary." [70] The mother must have "a profound knowledge of domestic chemistry, as well as of the intimate structure and laws of life, or animal and vegetable anatomy and physiology." [71] To gain this knowledge, Alcott prescribed the following course to be read by both parents:

I would say—begin with Paley's Theology. Then take up and read Combe's Constitution of Man, rejecting, if you choose, the phrenological part, . . . Next to Combe's work, I should recommend the study of Lawrence's Lectures on Physiology, Zoology, and the Natural History of Man. Combe's Principles of Physiology may now be advantageously studied; and afterwards some of the more complete and scientific works on physiology. By this time, and not in my opinion before, . . . we are prepared to study books on health, such as Johnson's Economy of Health, Willich's Lectures on Diet and Regimen, Dunglison's Elements of Hygiene etc.

Nor is it much sooner that the young wife can with entire safety, study the nature or cure of disease, either infantile or adult.[72]

Fortunately, Alcott's own practical texts, *The Young Wife, The Young Mother,* and *The House I Live In,* furnished readable alternatives for those mothers who were unable to follow this heavy course of reading. Alcott did not advocate that the young wife invade the doctor's realm. Only after such an ambitious

68. *Ibid.,* p. 48.
69. Cf. *ante,* p. 10.
70. William A. Alcott, *The Young Wife* (Boston, George W. Light, 1837), p. 190.
71. *Loc. cit.*
72. *Ibid.,* p. 314.

course of study as the one outlined above did he grant that she might "look over such a work as Buchan's Domestic Medicine." [73]

This leads us to another consideration involved in prescribing a course of study for mothers. This was the emphasis upon correct information in health matters. Medical quacks and charlatans flourished during the midcentury years, and many well meaning adults who believed they were acting in the cause of physical welfare were actually contributing to sickness and death by the application of false medical remedies. Thus, warnings appeared in the press. One writer declared:

Correct knowledge . . . would lead to a corresponding correct action. The credulity of the affectionate but misguided mother, is too often practised upon by the artful empyric, in the exhibition of "Universal Panaceas," "Soothing Syrups for Children" etc., which are at best of doubtful efficacy, and often prove highly injurious. [74]

Another contributor to the *Parent's Magazine* spoke of fatalities caused by the use of opiates present in soothing syrups or " 'fit drops,' " which had been "pompously advertised and highly recommended to mothers." [75] A double urgency was given to these warnings by statistics quoted from the *London Medical Gazette* which revealed the large number of child deaths in England and Wales from narcotic and anodyne drugs. [76]

Thus far, we have seen that the mother's first duty was to be properly informed. This was considered possible for every mother and supremely essential to intelligent action in the physical education of her children.

Given this many-sided knowledge, then, the mother was to put it to first hand use, not just by instructing her servants but by administering, herself, to the physical needs of her children. Emphasis was placed particularly on the crucial importance of the early months of the infant's existence. Mrs. Sigourney, in speaking of the mother's role during this "halcyon period" wrote, "She has it in her power so immediately to hush its moanings, to soothe its sorrows, to alleviate its sicknesses, that she is to it, as a tutelary spirit." [77] The mother who jeopardized her own health by attend-

73. *Ibid.*, p. 315.
74. "Teething," *Parent's Magazine*, 2:167, March, 1842.
75. "Caution to Parents," *Parent's Magazine*, 1:204, May, 1841.
76. *Loc. cit.*
77. Sigourney, *Letters to Mothers*, p. 30.

ance on the fashionable evening party, and by intemperance in dress and food, was urged to forego these indulgences and devote herself closely to her nursery duties. "During this first sacred year, trust not your treasure too much to the charge of hirelings." [78]

Mrs. Child, also, specified that the mother should "take the entire care of her own child." [79]

This close physical relationship between mother and child was deemed essential for a number of reasons. One of these was the prevalent belief that characteristics both moral and physical were transmitted in the nursing process. We have noted above Mrs. Phelps' statement from the physiologists of the period "that the nursing infant imbibes with his mother's milk her taste and propensities." [80] She carried this even farther by saying that "not only is the bodily health of an infant, in a great degree dependent on that of the mother but . . . that with the nourishment he imbibes from her, is conveyed into his soul some portion of the moral qualities whether good or evil, which predominate in her character." [81] By the same token, the infant in the care of a nurse was regarded as susceptible to the influences, good or bad, emanating from that individual. While granting that a sound, healthy, cheerful, and conscientious nurse might occasionally serve in the mother's stead to supply milk and care, when the mother was too delicate to do so, Dr. Combe warned mothers against the dire results of improper selection. He spoke of "all the vices to which nurses are liable." [82] These vices were threefold. They involved physical shortcomings such as slovenliness and poor health. Secondly, they included the changes induced in the quality of the milk by the nurse's diet, with special emphasis on the dangerous effects of alcoholic stimulants. And finally and most significantly, they had to do with the passions, or lack of mental and emotional stability of the nurse. Combe quoted Eberle as saying that " 'violent anger and habitual sourness of temper, are peculiarly apt to give a pernicious quality to the milk.' " [83]

78. *Ibid.*, p. 32.
79. Child, *op. cit.*, p. 4.
80. Cf. *ante*, p. 57.
81. Phelps, "Remarks on the Education of Girls," *Godey's Lady's Book*, 18:253, June, 1839.
82. Andrew Combe, *On the . . . Management of Infancy*, p. 232.
83. *Ibid.*, p. 226.

The entire system of the child was endangered by exposure to such influences.

This view of the importance of physical relationships in infancy goes back to attitudes current in the midcentury period with regard to the influence of the mother on her offspring during pregnancy. While Combe and other accepted medical authorities of the day attempted to dispel earlier superstitions, which attributed deformities and imperfections of the infant to the imagination of the mother, they retained and strengthened the emphasis upon the health of the mother, and upon those predispositions to nervousness or to disease which inhere in the close traffic between mother and infant in the prenatal period.[84] Another whole area involved in the consideration of this relationship is that having to do with the transmission of hereditary characteristics, an emphasis greatly promoted by the phrenologists.[85] It is not the purpose of this study, however, to carry physical education back to its prenatal origins. Suffice it to say here that such considerations gave weight to the belief that no one could take the place of the mother. It is significant that Combe advocated, in cases of strict necessity, a nurse resembling the mother in all respects, "a duplicate of the mother." [86]

It is interesting to note the way in which two important domestic educators of the period viewed this exclusive office of the mother. William Alcott carried the concept to an extreme, insisting that the mother, in order to be the true guardian of household health, must herself superintend every minutest detail of the nursery and kitchen. He advocated that domestics be dispensed with entirely.[87] Proper attention could be given by the mother to food, drink, clothing, and so forth, to the physical education of herself and those about her,[88] Alcott said, by proper management of cookery and economy, by the healthful simplification of the menu, and by devoting less of her "precious and invaluable time" to fashion.[89]

84. *Ibid.*, chap. v; cf. Dewees, *A Treatise on the Physical and Medical Treatment of Children*, chap. iii.

85. See especially, Orson Squire Fowler, *Hereditary Descent* (New York, Fowlers & Wells, 1854).

86. Andrew Combe, *op. cit.*, p. 221.

87. Alcott, *The Young Wife*, p. 153.

88. *Ibid.*, p. 174.

89. *Ibid.*, p. 173.

Mrs. Sigourney, on the other hand, while insisting upon the mother's devotion to child care, considered that her powers as educator were diminished by everlasting attention to the harassing details of household management. She painted a vivid picture of the run-down, fatigued mother so engrossed in "the mysteries of culinary science, and all the complicated duties of housekeeping," [90] that her health was seriously impaired. Mrs. Sigourney advocated aid for the mother in the shape of an "efficient person, in the nurse's department." [91] This was not to relieve the mother of responsibility, but to enable her to "give herself more exclusively to their highest and best interests." [92] The would-be fashionable mother, she believed, sacrificed the interests of her children to the preparation of elaborate food and clothing.

Essentially, however, Dr. Alcott and Mrs. Sigourney agreed on the importance of a close mother-child relationship and upon the need for simplification of the machinery concerned with the essentials for living.

We come then, finally, to a consideration of these more tangible "essentials of living" and to the mother's duties with respect to their fulfilment.

If dyspepsia was the besetting malady of adult Americans, a variety of ailments was the portion of infants and young children because of ignorance of correct feeding and dosing. The errors committed by mothers and nurses were of commission more often than of omission. It was William Alcott's belief that nearly every child in the arms of its mother was overfed.[93] This was also Dr. Combe's opinion.[94] This overfeeding resulted from the attitude which dictated that "a little of this or a little of that" [95] was good for an infant, and that food or "remedies" should be proffered every time a child cried.[96] An article of Combe's, which appeared in 1843,[97] stated that the mother should follow the example of the lower animals, who "rather repel, than encourage, the first en-

90. Sigourney, *op. cit.*, p. 87.

91. *Ibid.*, p. 84.

92. *Ibid.*, p. 87.

93. Alcott, *The Young Mother*, p. 122.

94. Andrew Combe, *The Physiology of Digestion* (1st American ed. Boston, Marsh, Capen & Lyon, 1836), pp. 241–42.

95. "Hints to Young Mothers," *Ladies' Magazine*, 7:52, February, 1834.

96. Beecher, *A Treatise on Domestic Economy*, p. 215.

97. Andrew Combe, "Frequency of Nursing," *Mother's Assistant*, 3:12, January, 1843.

treaties of their young, and yield to them only when appetite is clearly and actively indicated," with the result that "indigestion and bowel complaints are as rare as they are common among mankind." The *Ladies Almanac* of 1856 called attention to the over-indulgence of infants during dentition by mothers prone to "too anxious an interference" with natural symptoms. This article states further, "It is our opinion, indeed, that, if they were left somewhat more to themselves and nature, we should hear much less than we do of the sufferings of children whilst cutting their teeth." [98]

As we have noted above, the same was true of medicines. The tendency was for mothers to administer laxatives, calomel, and syrups containing opiates to very young infants without consulting a physician. Even Almira Phelps, who boasted in her "Observations upon an Infant" that her child required no medicine during his first month, admitted to the use, during that month, of "a little magnesia," "catnip tea" and "once . . . three or four drops of laudanum." [99] Catherine Beecher declared that medical men were most emphatic in their opinion "that it requires the utmost skill and judgment to ascertain what would be proper medicines, and the proper quantity to be given." [100] She quoted Dr. Combe as saying that mothers who use medicine constantly in a nursery may be sure that there is something essentially wrong in their treatment of children.

The change of attitude toward infant feeding is portrayed in a prose piece of the period entitled "Cousin Helen's Baby." This deals in a humorous vein with the plight of a young mother, who, not able yet to get up to care for her new infant, was suffered to listen to the following conversation between neighborhood visitors and "Mrs. Bagley," the ignorant hireling in charge of her baby:

"I hope you've given the little thing some physic, Mrs. Bagley."

"La, yes," . . . "I always gives *caster ile* the first thing—nothing better, you know."

"And then, I suppose, you feed it some, till its mother has milk sufficient?"

"The little darling don't suffer, I can tell you," . . . "I take the top of the milk and sweeten it up well, and it has as much as it can

---

98. "Hints to Young Mothers on the Physical Management of Children," *Ladies Almanac*, 1856, p. 80.

99. Phelps, "Observations upon an Infant," p. 327.

100. Beecher, *op. cit.*, p. 215.

take. Mrs. Wadsworth talked about leaving things to *nater,* but I tell her I guess *nater* would leave her if *I* didn't stick by."

"I hope, in all conscience, you won't get any of these new-fangled notions into your head, . . . Why our minister's wife is half crazy with her book larning about babies. She washes hers all over in cold water every morning, and e'en almost starves it, too; for no matter if it cries ever so hard, she won't feed it till the time comes, as she calls it, and that's once in three hours." [101]

When the baby in question began to use his lungs powerfully, to the distress of those present, another visitor remarked, "Babies didn't use to cry so when I was young; and I never thought, when I had a baby, that I could do without a decanter of gin. There's nothing like it for the cholic. . . ." [102]

This conversation finally terminated with recommendations for the use of "soot tea," "catnip and sage," and other remedies to stop the crying, after which Mrs. Bagley acted on her own initiative, and administered nicotinized water, which so seriously affected the infant that the family physician had great trouble, when he arrived, to bring about a recovery of the child. The piece ended with the comment, "It was a sad lesson to a young mother." [103]

This sketch is, of course, a caricature, but allowing for exaggeration, it portrays conditions which are mirrored in the medical literature and guidebooks of the day. Catherine Beecher felt it necessary to quote Dr. Combe, for example, not only that medical doses are dangerous when not given on a doctor's advice, but also that a child should never be given " '*bread,* or *cake,* or *meat,* before the teeth appear.' " [104] Miss Porter's sketch is most significant, however, in its statement about the minister's wife, portraying the new role of the mother bringing to bear her "book-larning" on the problems of the day and no longer satisfied with old wives' tales.

For infants, then, the proper food was declared to be that "which the God of Nature has provided for it in the bosom of its mother." [105] Various other simple formulas were supplied for

101. Ann E. Porter, "Cousin Helen's Baby," in Hart, *Female Prose Writers of America,* p. 348.

102. *Ibid.,* p. 349.

103. *Ibid.,* p. 352.

104. Beecher, *op. cit.,* p. 216.

105. "Hints to Young Mothers," *Ladies' Magazine,* 7:52, February, 1834.

the child "brought up by hand," [106] but the mother was considered unfortunate who was unable, for any reason, to nurse her own infant.

For children old enough to take solid food, diets and regimens were scrutinized from a number of angles. One was the reaction against the self-indulgence which prompted fashionable women to be "eternally munching cake and confectionery" and to suffer their children to "gorge themselves on hot bread, preserves, cake and pastry, *ad libitum*." Robust, beautiful English children, said Fanny Fern, have nothing but "the plainest puddings, the stalest bread, and the most unmitigated roast and boiled meat. . . ." [107] A contributor to the *Parent's Magazine* told of a little boy who refused, at the breakfast table, to drink his coffee until he had pie. Having had pie, he asked for cake, and so forth, "his fond parent yielding to him all the while, to the destruction of her comfort and the ruin of the child." [108] In this approach to the feeding problem, concern for the child's health was mingled with concern for his moral welfare. Unlimited indulgence or pampering was considered to be fatal to the development of essential traits, such as self-denial and self-control,[109] and overeating, or eating between meals, was regarded as weakening to the stomach, which should be afforded time for rest.[110]

Humphrey devoted an entire chapter in his volume *Domestic Education* to "*Restraining and governing children's appetites and passions:*—Food-Drink-Anger-Revenge-Envy." [111] His approach was therefore that of controlling or educating the "lower nature" of the child. He complained of the mother who allows "present gratification" of her children "to overrule all the teachings of nature and experience" so that her children lose their relish "for every kind of nutrimental diet." [112] He recommended that the mother take pains to preserve the natural appetite of her child for "plain nutritive food, simply prepared, without gravies or

106. Beecher, *op. cit.*, p. 216.

107. Fanny Fern (Mrs. Sarah P. Parton), *Fresh Leaves* (New York, Mason Brothers, 1857), pp. 108–9.

108. "Family Scenes, No. 1," *Parent's Magazine*, 2:13, September, 1841.

109. Alcott, *The Young Mother*, p. 207; cf. Beecher, *op. cit.*, p. 224.

110. Catherine Beecher and Harriet B. Stowe, *The American Woman's Home* (New York, J. B. Ford & Co., 1869), p. 129; Alcott, *op. cit.*, p. 192,

111. Humphrey, *op. cit.*, pp. 190–99.

112. *Ibid.*, p. 192.

condiments," [113] and thus to assist him "in forming a habit of self-denial." [114] Under this sort of educational influence the child might become the master of his appetites and grow, not only in health, but in self-control. It seems possible that Humphrey may have derived some of his authority for this point of view from the detailed advice given to young mothers by Dr. Alcott. The latter being himself a vegetarian and, in general, opposed to the use of "animal foods," [115] placed great emphasis upon the virtue residing in "good wheat bread" [116] and a spare, frugal diet which avoids meats and the "overstimulating food and drink" by which "the bulk of mankind benumb their sense of taste." [117] Alcott made a definite connection between depravity of taste in food and moral depravity.[118]

Humphrey and Alcott both sang the praises of "cold water, fresh and sparkling" as second in goodness only to the "pure fountain of the maternal bosom." [119] Love of strong drink, from tea or coffee, up the scale to intoxicating liquors, could be traced only "to some indulgence, or to some indiscretion, on the part of parents." [120] It was this emphasis which gave such a strong impetus to the "cold water crusade" in temperance reform.[121]

These comments on the eating and drinking of young children are typical of many others of the period in their major emphases. They are important to this study not so much for their explicit as for their implicit advice to mothers. Certain principles of physical education are reiterated throughout this material, and these principles dictate an active role for the mother from her child's infancy upward. Briefly, they are as follows: 1. Follow nature. In an advanced state of civilization, there is departure from nature with resulting corruption. 2. Be moderate. Excess of anything is bad. 3. Be simple. Elaboration is contrary to nature. 4. Cultivate a spirit of self-denial and restraint. By so doing the animal appetites can be controlled and man's moral nature thereby elevated. And, finally, 5. Seek to determine the law of man's

113. *Ibid.*, p. 191.
114. *Ibid.*, p. 192.
115. Alcott, *The Young Housekeeper*, chap. xiii.
116. Alcott, *The Young Mother*, pp. 167–70.
117. *Ibid.*, p. 168.
118. Cf. *post*, Appendix F.
119. Humphrey, *op. cit.*, p. 193.
120. *Ibid.*, p. 194.
121. Branch, *op. cit.*, p. 245.

physical being. Supplement information with reliable testimony of authority.

That these principles, as applied to eating, were recognized as a part of childhood education is indicated by a statement set forth in the *Ladies' Magazine* of 1834:

When we shall have learned that a sound mind and a sound body usually accompany each other, and our practice shall harmonize with our principles, the due preparation of our food will be deemed as important a point in the education of a child as it now is in the education of a puppy or a pig. . . . Then will cookery, as a means, indirectly, of forming human character, be deemed worthy of attention and study. Then will that which has a bearing on the prospects of the individual, for eternity as well as time, become a matter of consequence in the work of education. . . .[122]

Many of the principles involved in the feeding of infants and young children applied also to the clothing of them. At the same time that women were being urged to release themselves from the whalebones and stays so hampering to their own natural growth, they were also instructed to begin correctly in the physical education of their infants. Attention was turned to the unnatural practice of binding infants too tightly and restraining their movements by unsuitable clothing. This reform was given a particularly strong impetus by physiologists who traced many ailments to "a compression of the infantile organs." [123] Sickness and fits, crying and restlessness, were attributed to this cause by one writer who claimed that freedom of motion was absolutely necessary "and most of all in that period of life when the animal organs . . . are about to take form." [124]

American medical treatises of the early nineteenth century reveal by their injunctions against the swaddling of babes [125] that the practice was still countenanced in unenlightened regions. According to Dr. Alcott, two-thirds of the nurses in the country wrapped infants too tightly.[126] A manual for nurses and mothers published in Hartford, Connecticut, during the 'thirties was care-

122. W. A. A., "Should Females Be Employed in Cookery," *Ladies' Magazine*, 7:483–84, November, 1834.

123. "Physical Education of Women," *Ladies' Magazine*, 4:33, January, 1831.

124. *Ibid.*, p. 32.

125. Dewees, *op. cit.*, pp. ix–x.

126. Alcott, *The Young Mother*, p. 49.

ful to point out that the belly band of the infant should be fastened loosely to allow for natural growth and freedom.[127] In an article addressed to mothers, in 1841, we read of clothing, "If the dress of the infant be not loose, the delicate muscles are confined and compressed, which retards their growth and makes the child puny and feeble." [128] In the caricaturized sketch of "Cousin Helen's Baby" given above, we find Mrs. Bagley, the nurse, using pins and tight clothing instead of the new "strings and loops." "What kind er shape suppose your baby'll be, if I don't pin it up snug and tight now?" [129] she asked the mother.

The idea of restraint, or hindrance of natural growth and activity, was raised by Humphrey in regard to the practice of creeping. He defined it as the natural and inalienable right of childhood to creep, and recommended that clothing of infants be loose enough to allow for this. "When a mother asks me," he wrote, "who is to wash so many slips and bibs for my favorite young creeper, I am brought to a dead stand . . . but *helps* or no *helps,* I would still let him creep on to his heart's content." [130] He suggested, furthermore, that such great figures as Washington and Franklin probably enjoyed the untrammeled freedom of creeping in their infancy.[131]

Injunctions against restrictive clothing were even more severe when applied to children beyond the creeping age. The *Family Magazine* of 1837, citing a Dr. Faust on suitable clothing for children between the ages of three and eight, commented: "At present, children are frequently muffled up with their caps, hats, bonnets, cravats, pelisses, frills, muffles, gloves, ribands, and other paraphernalia, as if they were to be reared like plants in hot-beds; so that the shape and beautiful proportions which nature has given them can scarcely be distinguished." [132]

The principle of simplicity was applied to children's clothing not only for health reasons but also as a reaction against the spirit of display and extravagance. Goodrich complained of parents who "from a frivolous vanity, dress their children in an elaborate manner," thus "tarnishing the youthful spirit with the same

127. Richard S. Kissam, M. D., *The Nurse's Manual and Young Mother's Guide* (Hartford, Cooke & Co., 1834), pp. 28–30.
128. "Management of Infants," *Parent's Magazine*, 2:4, September, 1841.
129. Porter, *op. cit.*, p. 348.
130. Humphrey, *Domestic Education*, p. 63; cf. Alcott, *op. cit.*, p. 222.
131. *Loc. cit.*
132. Dick, "Clothing of Children," *The Family Magazine*, 4:462, 1837.

paltry vice which sways themselves." [133] An article entitled "Childhood," included in the *Young Ladies Class Book*, spoke with distaste of the "modern practice of dressing little girls in exact accordance with the prevailing fashion" and causing them to ape "the graces and courtesies of maturer life," as if there would not be time enough "from thirteen to seventy" for "ornamenting or disfiguring the person at the fiat of French milliners." "Oh," said this observer, "leave children as they are, to relieve, by their 'wild freshness' our elegant insipidity; leave their 'hair loosely flowing, robes as free,' to refresh the eyes that love simplicity." [134] It would be illuminating to trace this attitude through the fashion plates of the day. The *Godey's Lady's Book*, for example, shows children dressed as miniature adults in fashion plates as late as 1843,[135] but reveals the new trend toward loose-fitting and simple garments during the 'fifties. Thus, two figures of dresses for infants were accompanied by the comment "SIMPLICITY is, in all cases, the best general rule in dressing little children; and infants, particularly, should be spared all unnecessary ornament. . . .

"Caps are not now in vogue, fortunately for the poor little things, who would otherwise be made uncomfortable by them." [136] The dresses shown in these plates demonstrated the new simplicity by making the neckline higher and the waist line looser. One model eliminated the waist line altogether.

The moral approach to clothing, with its emphasis upon unselfishness and self-denial, varied from mild reaction against "silly pride" and vanity in matters of dress to a severe condemnation of mothers who keep the world "degradingly ignorant" by "instilling . . . into the very heart's core, the love of self and sensuality." [137] The *Ladies' Magazine* pursued, in general, a skilful middle-of-the-road course which ridiculed woman's slavery to fashion while appealing to her nationalistic pride and independence. Thus, we read: ". . . there are objects more worthy to call forth the energies of rational beings than the tie of a cravat, or the trimming of a bonnet. And when the moral and intellectual beauty of character is displayed, we hope that the 'foreign aid of ornament' will be found less necessary. . . ." [138]

133. Goodrich, *op. cit.*, p. 81.
134. "Childhood" in Bailey, *Young Ladies Class Book*, p. 243.
135. Branch, *op. cit.*, illustration opposite p. 292.
136. "Dresses for Infants," *Godey's Lady's Book*, 40:142, February, 1850.
137. "Boarding Schools," *Ladies' Magazine*, 4:146, April, 1831.
138. "The Mode," *Ladies' Magazine*, 4:196, May, 1831.

A short piece entitled "Children's Dresses" warned mothers against indulging in the purchase of expensive dresses for their children. This affirmed that even if parents can afford such clothing they should recollect "that it will do their little ones no good" and it will set a bad pattern of "ruinous extravagance." [139]

The judicious mother was the one who, combining "grace, delicacy and neatness" in her own dress, gently discouraged in her children all desire for expensive ornament. Mention has been made in Chapter IV [140] of the mother who argued that the price of embroidery on her child's dress might be used toward the purchase of a new frock for a poor child. In giving this sort of guidance to her daughter, she was cultivating three desirable virtues, self-denial, a spirit of benevolence, and a regard for simplicity, or good taste in clothing. It is easy to see, in this sort of example, the workings of the new doctrine of the "physical man." This wise mother was not only guarding the "casket" of her child's soul but was using its adornment as a means of cultivating the soul's virtues. Reformers of this period were concerned not only with what was worn as covering for the body, but the spirit in which it was worn.

The mother's guardianship of her child's body was not considered complete when his food, drink, and clothing were properly attended to. Pressure was put upon her to extend her vigilance to the many other details of nursery management, to the temperature and air of the sleeping department, to suitable bed coverings, to the number of hours of rest required by infants and growing children, and to their habits of posture while sleeping and waking. Dr. Alcott found it necessary to warn mothers that the small infant who sleeps in a bed with an adult is in danger of injury or suffocation.[141] The most obvious facts about ventilation were discussed. Mrs. Sigourney, lending dignity to this sort of information, wrote, "Let us educate a race who shall have room to breathe." [142]

It was as if reformers had discovered for the first time that every infant has an inalienable right to fresh air, and to a space designed especially for him. The concept of the suitable nursery or playroom of the midcentury house changed almost overnight

139. Mrs. Rantoul, "Children's Dresses," *Ladies' Magazine*, 6:463, October, 1833.

140. Cf. *ante*, p. 93.

141. Alcott, *op. cit.*, pp. 259–60.

142. Sigourney, *op. cit.*, p. 78.

from the darkest, most unsavory department of the household, to that of a cheerful, clean, and well-ventilated room, adapted in every way to the needs of the growing beings housed there.[143] The housekeeping duties once viewed as drudgery, unsuitable for the genteel lady, were thus given new importance. Alcott saw this role as even above that of the minister, saying: "He may watch, and labor, and pray for the soul; but the house-keeper . . . presides over, and moulds, and shapes. She forms the 'house' the soul 'lives in'; and, in this way, almost entirely directs the motions and tendencies of the soul itself." [144]

Final and most important of maternal duties in the physical education of young children were those concerned with the ways in which children should employ their time. With the widespread investigation of the evils of the common school, came new standards with regard to this important subject. Conviction grew that little children must not be confined at one employment for hours at a time; that they must not sit on hard benches without backs "and raised so high that the feet . . . cannot possibly touch the floor." [145] Social indignation was likewise roused by the child labor abuses. "How many crooked spines, emaciated bodies, decaying lungs, as well as scrofulas, fevers, and consumptions," said Alcott, "are either induced or accelerated by these unnatural employments!" [146]

Most reprehensible of all mortals was the mother who suffered any of these physical evils to befall her child through neglect or desire to get him out of the way. The good mother was advised to live with her children, to rise with them early in the morning, to walk abroad with them, to find for them "sports and gambols" [147] and "well contrived amusements, conducted as much as possible in the open air," [148] or lessons "from the flower, the plant, the tree, . . . the bird, the beast, . . ." [149] Dr. Alcott saw it as the mother's task "to promote cheerfulness and health and love and happiness" [150] by these active employments. He sought to make a place in the business-like adult world of the period for the child

143. Alcott, *op. cit.*, pp. 33–36.
144. Alcott, *The Young Housekeeper*, p. 37.
145. Alcott, *The Young Mother*, p. 327.
146. *Ibid.*, p. 329.
147. *Ibid.*, p. 235.
148. *Ibid.*, p. 237.
149. *Loc. cit.*
150. *Loc. cit.*

as something more than "a mere cypher in creation," [151] a being of more consequence than the "pet" to be fed, caressed, and displayed from time to time but thrust aside, for the most part, to make room for adult activities.[152]

There were a number of reasons for recommending that the mother take her child "abroad" or beyond the narrow confines of the nursery to enjoy active employments, and in these reasons we may discover a fair cross section or summary of the various philosophies of physical education held by domestic reformers of the period.

We will recall that Humphrey advised active employments out-of-doors because children were born "to run and laugh and breathe the fresh air and bound over the hills," as well as to "work and study and sit up perpendicularly by their grand-mother's rocking-chairs." [153] Yet he also appealed to the Lockian philosophy of hardening the constitution. One purpose of this rugged activity was to check natural or depraved tendencies toward softness and comfort and ease.[154] Early rising, spare diet, cold water, and rigorous outdoor employments were all symbols to Humphrey, essential for rearing bodies and minds impervious to the weak temptations of the flesh. He quoted one authority as saying " 'Who would think of planting the royal oak in a green house, or of rearing the cedar of Lebanon in a lady's flower pot?' " [155] Implied in this attitude of Humphrey's was a spirit of asceticism, which in reality pervaded many of the physical reforms of the midcentury period. It was of a piece with the lingering morbidity and "sense of sin" which we have noted coloring the concepts of some of the progressives otherwise liberal in matters of moral and spiritual development.

Horace Bushnell, aware, like Humphrey, of the evils to which flesh is heir, believed in the importance of subjecting the body to a rigorous discipline to conquer its "appetites, passions, tempers, and . . . distempers." [156] He agreed that the mother must beware of corrupting the soul of the child by indulging his animal appetites. For Bushnell, to allow the child merely to exist "in the senses" in his early years, without the aid of suitable guidance,

151. *Ibid.*, p. 236.
152. *Ibid.*, p. 237.
153. Humphrey, *op. cit.*, p. 64.
154. *Ibid.*, chap. viii.
155. *Ibid.*, p. 65.
156. Bushnell, *Christian Nurture*, p. 272.

was perilously near to letting it live "in the sensualities." [157] But Bushnell's philosophy of "nurture" made one very important departure from that of Humphrey. And this was with reference to the child's native equipment. To Bushnell, the child's original nature was a pure, not a corrupt one. The mother who exerted an immediate guardianship over her child's mind and body had not, therefore, the problem of restraining his natural tendencies. This had important consequences for his attitude toward outdoor play and active employments. Play, he declared, "wants no motive but play." [158] The frisking, carefree spirit of children was to him a symbol of "Christian Liberty." [159] It did not have to be justified as a means of hardening the constitution. It was an end in itself, or, rather, it was an end known to and sanctioned by the Creator.

Samuel Goodrich likewise accepted the child's active nature for its own sake. He declared that, up to the age of ten, the child should be freed by his parents to "develop the animal powers, to secure and establish good health, good spirits, and a good constitution." [160] In other words, he advocated following nature or observing natural laws of growth. Except in matters of food, drink, and the like, he did not emphasize restraints.

It is evident that Dr. Alcott saw the discrepancy between the conservative revival of the Lockian hardening process, and the newer doctrine of natural development, for he included a chapter on this subject in his text for mothers. According to Alcott, the purpose of taking children abroad is not so much to harden their constitutions as "to give them a more free access to air and light than they can have at home; and . . . to cultivate the faculties of attention, comparison, etc." [161] He believed that an important part of physical education was the cultivation of the five senses and that the environment was an accessory to this cultivation. To strengthen the physical constitution was only part of the task of the mother. She had, in making use of the world beyond the nursery, to aid her child in serving an apprenticeship to his senses. We noted above [162] that the Reverend T. H. Gallaudet made acquaintance with the outdoor world a means of instructing the child about his own soul. Alcott granted the value of lessons, but

157. *Ibid.*, p. 279.
158. *Ibid.*, p. 340.
159. *Ibid.*, pp. 339–40.
160. Goodrich, *op. cit.*, p. 292.
161. Alcott, *op. cit.*, p. 293.
162. Cf. *ante*, p. 91.

his main plea was for "unrestrained pastimes and gambols of the young on the green grass, or beside the rippling stream, . . . unrepressed by those who are set over them." [163]

In all these approaches to child activity, we see a new affirmation of man's physical nature, and of certain laws, whether "natural" or divine, which regulate this nature.

To be simple and moderate in diet and dress, to give growing space to the organs of the body, and activity to its muscles, and finally, to make use of the environment to cultivate the senses, all these doctrines were logical and acceptable to the reformer of the period.

For a brief time, in this pre-Darwinian era, the purposes of those who denied and those who affirmed the demands of the flesh were at one. And the reason for this may be found in the fact there was no one group of theorists who were entirely free from the dogma of another group. Humphrey's ascetic spirit, for example, owed something, not only to the recrudescence of an earlier Puritanism, but also to humanistic and scientific stresses which invoked the same simple laws. Proponents of "natural laws," on the other hand, were careful to build an acceptable religious framework upon which to base their theories of human growth.[164]

Their common denominator was the immediate task at hand, the communication to mothers of their great responsibility for the guardianship of the precious temple of the immortal spirit.

163. Alcott, *op. cit.*, p. 238.
164. See Appendix D.

CHAPTER VII

GENTLE RULER

THE mighty river of society must be fed by two streams, said a Maine writer, in 1835:

The one may bear itself along in the rush of the waterfall, or in the roar of the cataract, as if conscious that nothing can stay its course; the other winds itself in gentle murmurings amidst vale and glen . . . until both are united in one common flood. The mill and the manufacturing establishment may mingle their harsh discords with the rushing waters of one; but the voice of singing birds, and of innocent children at their play . . . will blend in a rich and beautiful harmony with the low deep melody of the other.

The first of these streams may be judged to typify the masculine sphere, in which the turmoil of the business world is reflected. The second represents the domain of the keeper-at-home, the woman, who, this writer further declares, may "in her *lowliest* lot . . . hold as important a station in the moral universe as the monarch of a thousand hills." [1]

This characterization of the two distinct roles of the sexes in midcentury society may be seen, particularly when related to the illumination and elevation of the feminine function, as part of a popular reaction against the crudities of the masculine world of business. This reaction came not alone from conservative ministers and moralists of the period. George Combe hit squarely upon the sore spot of the popular conscience when he accused business men of dedicating their "whole powers and energies to the production of the mere *means of living*," while benumbing those faculties which call into play "the affections; . . . the enjoyment of the splendid loveliness of nature . . . the expansion of the intellect in the pursuits of science . . . refinement of manners . . . and . . . adoration . . . of our most bounteous Creator." [2] This dissatisfaction with the unworthy goals of mercan-

1. "Woman's Sphere," *Ladies' Magazine*, 8:263, May, 1835.
2. George Combe, *Moral Philosophy* (New York, William H. Colyer; Boston, Lewis & Sampson, 1844), p. 184.

tile endeavor was part and parcel of the emotional ferment in New England which sent many of the younger generation in the cities thronging to lyceums and poetry readings, to escape the sordid realities of the counting house.[3] It fed the fire of transcendentalism and of humanitarian reform. For the common man who had, perforce, to continue engaging on six days of the week in base and lucrative toil, there was devised a somewhat simpler solution.

"The mother sways the dominion of the heart, the father that of the intellect."

This was the fashioning of the concept of the home as a sanctuary [4] or retreat, beyond the pale of the outside world, where the husband might soothe his harassed spirit and breathe fresh life into his benumbed faculties.

The virtues of the ideal home celebrated in the pictures, song, and literature of the period, testify to the popularity of this concept. This home, or retreat, dignified by its ideal members, was de-

3. Brooks, *The Flowering of New England,* chap. ix.
4. Cf. "Introductory Address," *Parent's Magazine,* 1:7–8, September, 1840.

scribed as a place " 'where every word is kindness, and every look affection,' " [5] and where "the best feelings of the heart expand," [6] as contrasted with the painful scenes of the world of business and pleasure where, we read, "the heart is sensible to a desolation of feeling," [7] where "even the dictates of common honesty" are disregarded, and the general good is "sacrificed to the advancement of personal interest." [8] That this view of the home was widespread is evidenced by a comment made by William Thayer in 1857. He declared that too much emphasis had been placed upon the retreat or "refuge" aspect of home life. The father's affections, he believed, might delight in the home circle, but they should also seek to identify themselves with the creative force which operates to mold the social structure outside the home.[9]

The stress upon the "affections" or the rule of love as essential to the regenerative atmosphere of the home may be seen as complementary to the ascendancy of the softer Christian virtues in midcentury society.[10] It owed much also to the emotional appeals of humanitarian reform. One is reminded of the Dickens vogue [11] during this period, and the immortal characters which emerged from his fiction, Tiny Tim, Little Nell, and especially Ebenezer Scrooge, who was regenerated by the Christmas spirit of love and kindness. It may be judged that the songs of Stephen Foster, which appeared in the 'fifties, caught and held national attention by their "heart appeal," and their sentimentalization of the home theme.[12] The Susan Warner novels came in, likewise, on this effusive tide, winning unheard-of recognition in the world of feminine letters.[13] Sentimental verse and pictures of the period will be forever identified with the decade known as the "feminine fifties," and the span of decades described as "the sentimental years." [14] The ruling principle underlying all this expression was love, and love as embodied and interpreted by the

5. "The Duties of Woman," in *The Young Woman's Gift*, Cotesworth Pinckney, editor (Boston, J. Buffum, 1851), p. 51.
6. "Home," *Ladies' Magazine*, 3:217, May, 1830.
7. *Ibid.*, p. 218.
8. *Loc. cit.*
9. Thayer, *Life at the Fireside*, pp. 4–5.
10. Cf. *ante*, p. 75.
11. Fred Lewis Pattee, *The Feminine Fifties* (New York and London, D. Appleton–Century Company, Inc., 1940), chap. vi.
12. Cf. Gabriel, *The Course of American Democratic Thought*, pp. 6–7.
13. Pattee, *op. cit.*, p. 57.
14. See especially chap. vi in Branch, *The Sentimental Years*.

"genteel female" of the time. Lydia Maria Child called music
" 'the feminine principle, the heart of the universe,' " because,
she declared, " 'it is the voice of love.' " [15] Once more we recall
the caption used by Goodrich in *Fireside Education,* "The mother
sways the dominion of the heart. . . ." [16] Woman, the wife, the
mother, was regarded as peculiarly fitted by her tender nature
not only to render her home happy, but, in shedding "a soothing
influence over man's coarser nature" to regenerate her husband,
to win him "from those dark and besetting vices which assail
him in his conflict with the world." [17]

All this is important to an understanding of the power vested
by reformers in the maternal role in the midnineteenth century
family. We have been too prone from our twentieth century van-
tage point to dismiss the sentiment of this period as a surface expression of feminine vapidity and frailty,[18] an emotional effusion
irrelevant to the social emergence and emancipation of women in
our western society.

Analysis shows that there was a deeper significance to this
emphasis upon sentiment, or the "love principle," and that it
tended to hasten rather than to retard the "emancipation" of
women.

William Alcott wrote in 1837:

The nations, instead of being controlled by fear, are ere long to
be controlled by the law of love and kindness. In this . . . revolution . . . woman is to perform a most important, if not the principal part. She is to wield the sceptre, first over her husband, and
next over the children whom God may give her.
Let her understand, then, fully, the efficacy of kindness. . . .[19]

Here was something far different from the passive role of the
woman submissive to her husband's domination and satisfied
merely to cater to his whims. "Wielding the sceptre" implied an
active role of molding, changing, ruling by the affections. Daniel

15. Branch, *op. cit.,* p. 183, citing the *Broadway Journal.*
16. See illustration p. 150.
17. Mrs. Sarah E. Goodhue, "The Oak and the Vine," *Mother's Assistant,*
13:140, November, 1848.
18. Cf. Inez H. Irwin, *Angels and Amazons* (Garden City, N. Y., Doubleday
Doran & Co., Inc., 1933), pp. 16–20, and Furness, *The Genteel Female,*
pp. 3–22.
19. Alcott, *The Young Wife,* p. 37.

Webster called mothers "the affectionate and effective teachers of the human race."[20]

With this background, we may proceed, then, to a consideration of the concepts which had to do with the mother's use of this power to mold her young children. There were two schools of thought with regard to the mother's basic equipment for the expression of affection. Phrenologists held the disquieting belief that the woman possessing a small bump of "philoprogenitiveness," or "attachment to one's own offspring" was an unmotherly type, while the good mother type was possessed of a correspondingly large protuberance on the skull.[21] This placed a definite limitation upon the mother not gifted with this desirable propensity. The other school of thought spoke in more general terms of the maternal instinct of affection [22] as an emotion common to all mothers. According to the Reverend David Strong, writing in 1851, no person could have so intense an interest in the welfare of a child as its mother. "No one," he wrote, "can administer to its wants with so much tenderness. No one can watch over him, from day to day, with such care. No one can bear his petulance with so much patience. . . ." [23] Another writer observed that "the endurance of a mother's love appears to be the result of the divine intention." [24] Washington Irving addressed himself to this theme exclaiming, "Oh! There is an enduring tenderness in the love of a mother to a son that transcends all other affections of the heart." [25] This more generalized and romantic approach had one important point in common with the pseudo scientific approach of the phrenologists. It admitted, as George Combe pointed out, "the Love of Children as an instinctive propensity of the human mind." [26] Phrenology helped to intensify interest in this

20. Daniel Webster, "Influence of Woman," in Griswold, *Prose Writers of America*, p. 185.

21. O. S. and L. N. Fowler, *Self Instructor in Phrenology and Physiology* (New York, Fowlers & Wells, 1855), pp. 54–56.

22. Sigourney, *Letters to Mothers*, p. 48. See also Harriet Martineau, *Household Education* (Philadelphia, Lea & Blanchard, 1849), p. 89.

23. Reverend David A. Strong, "Maternal Responsibility," *Mother's Assistant*, 1851, p. 97.

24. O. P. Farrington, "Maternal Relation," *Mother's Assistant*, 23:48, August, 1852.

25. Washington Irving, "The Love of a Mother," in Griswold, *Prose Writers of America*, p. 218.

26. George Combe, *A System of Phrenology* (2d ed. Edinburgh, John Anderson, 1825), p. 76.

propensity by calling attention to the various manifestations of the feeling,[27] so that, in the long run, the moral or mental philosophers and the phrenologists were talking the same educational language. Thus, when the moralists objected to pampering and overindulgence of children on the score of selfishness and misguided affection, the phrenologists agreed, but added the useful explanation that the excessively indulgent or fond mother was one who had her bump of philoprogenitiveness overdeveloped.[28] Here, as elsewhere in this study, we recognize that a middle position or common ground was found for purposes of childhood education. In this case it was made possible by two attitudes, one, that the domestic affections are vitally important in molding childhood, and two, that these affections can be guided, or directed into proper channels by intelligent mothers. The resulting popular attitude is reflected in the following sentiment expressed by a contributor to the *Ladies' Magazine:* "The mother holds . . . the hearts of her children in her hand. . . . But, in order to give them the right impress, she must feel that the maternal relation involves subjects of no minor interest." [29]

Thus, the mother instinct of love and affection was seen as paramount to the redemption of a worldly minded society. When the *Parent's Magazine* was begun in 1840, its introductory address set this important keynote. Mother love was portrayed as the direct antithesis of selfishness, particularly in its manifestations upon the newborn infant. The editors called attention to the attitude of a young mother toward her infant: "She anticipates its wants, runs at every cry, raises the whole family to assist her, soothes her darling by her tones, calls it by a thousand endearing names . . . ," [30] and for all this trouble, said the editors, "she feels herself, day by day, fully repaid." [31] Indeed, she would perform these offices even though she were assured that the child would not live. "What," we read, "but a strong instinctive affection could enable the mother to set a value so high, upon an object, which, so far as her own *profit* is concerned, is altogether worthless . . . ?" [32]

27. *Loc. cit.*
28. Branch, *op. cit.*, p. 222, citing O. S. Fowler.
29. "Woman's Sphere," *Ladies' Magazine*, 8:264–65, May, 1835.
30. The Editors, "Introductory Address," *Parent's Magazine*, 1:5, September, 1840.
31. *Loc. cit.*
32. *Ibid.*, p. 6.

Physicians of the period, who preached of the necessity for the health of the mother during pregnancy, hinted definitely at the close connection between the mother's feelings or "temper" and the resulting disposition of her offspring. Thus, Dr. Andrew Combe declared that "the temper and turn of mind in the child are often a legible transcript of the mother's condition and feelings during pregnancy." [33] From this statement it may be inferred that the instinctive affection of the mother was viewed by some as operable even before the birth of the child. To cultivate the higher affections in her offspring, the mother had to stand as guardian over her own mental condition and emotions during pregnancy.[34] For purposes of this study, observations will be confined to the relationship which began at birth between the mother and child, but it is well to note, in passing, the impetus given to this doctrine of the affections by medical speculations upon the importance of the prenatal relationship.

Beginning, then, with the newborn infant, the mother's first duty in her "rule by affection" was seen as that of exhibiting consistent gentleness, fondness, and affection in her own character. Reference was made above to the emphasis placed by preachers and moralists on the power of maternal example. The "loving" aspect of this example was given specific attention. Mrs. Child, for example, gave an entire chapter in her *Mother's Book* to "The Affections." [35] Mrs. Sigourney entitled a chapter in her *Letters to Mothers,* "Maternal Love." [36]

Mrs. Child specified that the very first rule of education is "that a mother govern her own feelings," [37] and that the rule for developing good affections in children is that they never be allowed "to see or feel the influence of bad passions." [38] Taking a realistic view of the matter, she observed that while "a mother's instinct teaches fondness," there is the difficulty that "mothers are sometimes fond by fits and starts—they follow impulse, not principle." [39] The good mother, on the other hand, is consistent. She is also constant in her attentions. If in the same room with her in-

33. Andrew Combe, *A Treatise on the Physiological and Moral Management of Infancy,* p. 81.
34. *Ibid.,* p. 82; cf. Sigourney, *Letters to Mothers,* p. 28.
35. Child, *The Mother's Book,* chapter ii, pp. 6–9.
36. Sigourney, *op. cit.,* Letter v, pp. 47–55.
37. Child, *op. cit.,* p. 4.
38. *Ibid.,* p. 9.
39. *Ibid.,* p. 5.

fant, she bestows upon it smiles and looks of fondness from time
to time. If in an adjoining room, she allows "some of the endearing appellations to which he has been accustomed" [40] to meet the
ear of her infant. The result of this sort of demonstration is that
the child is given a sense "of safety and protection alike conducive to his happiness and beneficial to his temper." [41]

Mrs. Sigourney urged mothers to mingle their teachings "with
smiles, and the dialect of love." [42] "Guard . . . ," she wrote,
"serenity of spirit, for the child is still a part of yourself, as the
blossom of the plant, from whose root it gathers sustenance.
Breathe over it the atmosphere of happy and benevolent affections." [43] She regarded love as the religion of the infant, to be
taught by a mother's accents and countenance, and whole deportment.

Both Mrs. Child and Mrs. Sigourney regarded infancy as a
period of unfoldment [44] during which the exercise of gentleness
and love act upon the child's soul like sunshine upon a rosebud. To
turn the duties of this relationship over to a nurse or servant at
such a crucial stage of the child's development was to "degrade
its essence or its mission." [45]

Waterston, speaking before the American Institute of Instruction in 1835, advocated that the parent cherish a "calm and
well-balanced affection" in his heart, since "Love begets love." [46]
He believed that if this important influence was missing from the
home, the school could do little for a child.[47] On the other hand,
if it has been present in the early days of childhood, the parent
himself may die, but his example lives on.[48]

In addition to this emphasis upon maternal love as the germinat-
ing power for the unfoldment of innate goodness, there were two
other approaches to the subject of maternal example which,
although noted in previous chapters, are worthy of repetition in
this connection. Humphrey, we will recall, was reluctant to admit the spotless innocence of childhood. For this reason he re-

40. *Ibid.*, p. 4.
41. *Ibid.*, p. 5.
42. Sigourney, *op. cit.*, p. 45.
43. *Ibid.*, p. 31.
44. *Ibid.*, p. 28; cf. Child, *op. cit.*, p. 2.
45. Sigourney, *op. cit.*, p. 55.
46. Waterston, *Moral and Spiritual Culture*, p. 203.
47. *Ibid.*, p. 208.
48. *Ibid.*, p. 209.

garded parental love as a constraint or "sweet control" [49] which acts from the birth of the child onward as a deterrent to the development of the corrupt passions. He was, therefore, wary of the romantic press poetry of the day which prattled about "the angelic sweetness of infancy" and "the ever-gushing purity of maternal love." [50] In his opinion, the maternal instinct of love was not just an all-pervasive warmth to promote growth of good qualities, but was rather an intelligently directed check to innate corruption. Yet Humphrey acknowledged the instinct [51] of the mother, and his emphasis upon example was as emphatic as that of the romanticists.

The other approach may be termed "scientific," though it had its roots in moral philosophy as well as in the more objective scientific study of the period. Dr. Amariah Brigham claimed that the importance of example lies in the fact that it is the natural propensity of the child to imitate. If parents wish therefore "to have their children possess a spirit of benevolence, kindness or humility, they must cherish and cultivate these virtues in themselves." [52] In speaking of this principle of imitation, Dr. Brigham called attention to a work on the human mind written by the Scotch philosopher, Dugald Stewart, who devoted one section in this work to the "Principle of (Sympathetic) Imitation." [53]

This appeal to the "law" of learning is also seen in the work of Madame de Saussure translated for the edification of Americans by Mrs. Willard and Mrs. Phelps in 1835.[54] Madame de Saussure included in her *Progressive Education* a chapter on the "Influence of Sympathy," [55] in which she stated as an argument for the "sweet exchange of sentiments" [56] that "the instinct of imitation is stronger in children than fear." [57]

Fowler, the American phrenologist, gave two reasons for ad-

49. Humphrey, *Domestic Education*, p. 47.

50. *Ibid.*, p. 48.

51. *Ibid.*, p. 42.

52. Brigham, *Influence of Mental Cultivation and Mental Excitement upon Health*, p. 91.

53. *Ibid.*, p. 90, citing Dugald Stewart, *Elements of the Philosophy of the Human Mind* (Edinburgh, T. & T. Clark, 1877), I, 35. Note that this reference occurs in a section of Stewart's book designated as *Outlines of Moral Philosophy*, a section not included in earliest editions of *Elements*.

54. Cf. *ante*, p. 58.

55. De Saussure, *Progressive Education*, chap. v.

56. *Ibid.*, p. 178.

57. *Ibid.*, p. 179.

vocating attention to parental example: one, that the faculty of imitation is always large in children; and two, that the action of the organ of imitation stimulates and enlarges that organ.[58] It should be noted, however, that he classed "sympathy" with "active kindness" as two portions of one organ, "Benevolence," which, he declared, "does not appear in infants, but begins to be developed at about two years old, when it augments very rapidly," [59] and which becomes large when kindled by parental kindness and benevolence.

Objectivity is the chief contribution of this approach to the subject of parental example. It focused attention on "laws" governing the mind, and, in giving sanction to the controlled use of maternal fondness in education of offspring, called attention to certain specific duties in the mother-child relationship.

We come then to a consideration of the first and most obvious duty in the mother's rule by affection. This concerned her overt expression of love for her child. An engraving in the frontispiece of one of the early gift books of the period shows a mother seated in a chair with her small daughter cradled in her arms, her head bent to kiss the child. The sub-title is "Affection." [60] This is typical of many sentimental prints of the day featuring demonstrative tenderness in the family circle.[61] Mrs. Sigourney began her *Letters to Mothers* with the words: "You are sitting with your child in your arms. So am I. And I have never been as happy before. . . . How this new affection seems to spread a soft, fresh green over the soul. . . . What a loss, had we passed through the world without tasting this purest, most exquisite fount of love." [62] A poem entitled "A Mother's Love" elaborates on this sentiment. The following verses are excerpts:

> Lightly a soft cheek presses hers,
> The first and fond caress;
> And through her thrilling bosom stirs,
> The mother's tenderness.

[And further],

> How still she sits beside his bed,

58. Fowler, *Education and Self-Improvement*, p. 250.
59. *Ibid.*, p. 237.
60. *The Visitor* (Boston, Peirce & Williams, 1829), frontispiece.
61. Cf. Furness, *The Genteel Female*, print entitled "A Mother's Counsels," p. 208.
62. Sigourney, *op. cit.*, p. vii.

And watches o'er his rest!
And oft his little helpless head
She pillows on her breast.[63]

The filial response to this affection is seen in the following verses taken from a poem eulogizing a departed mother:

There was a kiss, the mind could calm,
Its sweets I loved to sip,
As't fell like some celestial balm,
Upon the ruby lip.

'Twas not a formal fondness shrine;
But all replete with bliss,
And left a pleasing charm behind;
It was my mother's kiss.[64]

Mothers were reminded of great men like the "immortal Newton" who, engulfed in dissipation in his later life, yet was redeemed when he felt again upon his head "the gentle pressure of his mother's hand." [65] The physical contact, the caress, the outward expression of affection, were considered important in the molding of character. It is interesting to note that even the practical Harriet Martineau had something to say about this expression as a means of developing "strong affections" in a child. But she also warned that "the sweetness of these caresses will be lost when they cease to be spontaneous," [66] that the mother must never ask more than the child can give. Madame de Saussure also warned against excess of such expression, quoting Maria Edgeworth, and also the testimony of physicians.[67] That these writers mention the subject at all is evidence that the operation of the "love" principle was a matter of discussion among domestic reformers of England and France as well as in the United States of the sentimental era.

Perhaps the most surprising of all comments on this tender topic comes from the pen of Theodore Dwight, Jr., in his *Father's Book*. He described as a simple measure for discipline or government of children, that of training the infant "to signify his wants

63. "A Mother's Love," *The Visitor*, pp. 12–13.
64. "My Mother," *The Young Woman's Gift*, pp. 40–41.
65. Mrs. Isaac Hatch, "Single and Married," *Mother's Assistant*, 9:20–21, July, 1846.
66. Martineau, *op. cit.*, p. 93.
67. De Saussure, *op. cit.*, pp. 177–78.

by kissing instead of crying," giving an example of a family in which three children had been thus trained from the age of eight months. He wrote: ". . . Although one of them was peculiarly unwilling to be kissed, and long resisted teaching; it became habituated to it by mild and persevering management, and practised it with pleasure as long as it remained unable to express itself otherwise." [68] His instruction to the parent was therefore to pay no heed to an infant's cries, "but after bringing its lips to your own, yield to its desires and . . . you will perceive that he begins to be affected by the experience he thus receives." [69]

Theodore Dwight would no doubt have objected to the use of demonstrativeness for spoiling or pampering children, but he saw it as a means for calling the higher sentiments into play. Likewise Heman Humphrey who, insistent as he was upon firm management of children, believed that "the most obedient and affectionate children are those that have been accustomed from their cradle, to regard every wish of their mother, as a law of love, and rather to anticipate her desires, than to wait for any less gentle demonstration of her authority." [70]

Today, in the 1940's, this "silken cord" relationship between the mother and child has been so long in disrepute that child study specialists are finding it necessary to revive the practice of showing normal tenderness in the handling of children. Children, they say, need the security of expressed parental affection. Furthermore, the infant who has had the close physical contact of breast feeding and cuddling, is likely to be better adjusted than the formula-fed infant. [71] The "hands off" approach, carefully cultivated by some of the earlier nursery school specialists, has given way to the more natural approach of an earlier day, with the important provision that the "mothering" given be not of the "smothering" variety. [72] The nineteenth century sought more than "security" for its individuals through this tender means. It sought, particularly in New England, to stir the sluggish heart and affections of a society long chilled by the stern dictates of

68. Dwight, *The Father's Book*, p. 32.

69. *Ibid.*, p. 33.

70. Humphrey, *op. cit.*, p. 46.

71. Frank, "The Fundamental Needs of the Child," *Mental Hygiene*, 22:359, July, 1938. See also Benjamin Spock, M. D., *The Common Sense Book of Baby and Child Care* (New York, Duell, Sloan & Pearce, 1945), p. 33.

72. Lorine Pruette, *The Parent and the Happy Child* (New York, Henry Holt & Co., 1932), pp. 54–55.

Calvinism and Puritanism. According to Calhoun, Europeans who visited the new world in the midnineteenth century were impressed by coolness in American family relations,[73] particularly relations between wives and husbands. The word "compensation" was not in use then, in its modern psychiatric interpretation of the word, but a commentator on New England life noted the intensity of maternal affection, and attributed this to the lessening of family endearment caused by paternal preoccupation [74] with the affairs of the business world.

Whatever the explanation is for the excess of sentimentality in this period, it is important to this study for the part it plays in modifying concepts of childhood education.

Most important of the controversies centered in the maternal "rule by affection," was that concerned with the control of child behavior. Thus far in this chapter we have considered the mother's basic equipment for the affectionate mode of control, the example set by her own behavior, and her initial means of awakening the desired responses. The practical disciplining of the behavior of growing children was the end to which these means were directed.

Conservative educators gave serious attention to the question of maternal authority in the home, attributing much of the lawlessness and recklessness of the growing republic to the breaking down of old traditions in family government. Thus, Humphrey wrote: "It is more difficult than it was, half, or even a quarter of a century ago, for parents to 'command their household after them.'" The boy, he claimed, "wants to be 'his own man' long before his wisdom teeth are cut; and the danger lies in conceding the point to him under the notion, that our fathers were quite too rigid and that a more indulgent domestic policy, corresponding with the 'spirit of the age' is better." [75]

It is helpful to review here, briefly, the factors which contributed to this lax "domestic policy." There was the practical factor of the removal of paternal authority from the minute affairs of the home. There was the economic factor of increased opportunity for the young American boy, which took him prematurely away from the reins of parental control. In the lower sectors of society, child labor was removing children at an unbelievably early age from the relatively more controlled environ-

73. Calhoun, *Social History of the American Family*, II, 132.
74. *Ibid.*, p. 133.
75. Humphrey, *op. cit.*, p. 23; cf. Thayer, *op. cit.*, p. 23.

ment of the family circle. There were, in addition to these practical factors, many trends of thought contributing to the "spirit of the age." Several of these bore directly upon methods in family government. The eighteenth century had stressed the authority of human "reason," thus weakening the stress upon divinely constituted parental authority.[76] One may judge from anecdotes of the middle period on child management that the "appeal to reason" used somewhat loosely on young children, met with little success. There was also the "laissez-faire"[77] attitude toward early discipline, compounded in part of the belief that children must reach a certain age in order to become moral agents,[78] and in part of the Rousseau philosophy which gave considerable freedom to children up to the age of twelve. Finally, superimposed upon all these concepts were those ushered in at the beginning of the mid-nineteenth century, concepts which focused attention on the very young child as a socially important being; scientific concepts which influenced attitudes toward growth and learning, and romantic concepts of child nature emphasizing the flawless, almost divine characteristics of the human infant.[79]

In the midst of all this change and confusion, the midcentury mother was faced with the necessity for exercising an authority in the family to which she was unaccustomed by nature and tradition. And domestic reformers, observing her inadequacies and perplexities, had much analysis to give to a definition of her proper role. The greatest part of their task was to reconcile the ascendancy of the "feminine" or "love" principle with a sturdy and consistent formula for keeping society in order.

The Reverend John Abbott gave two chapters in his volume *The Mother at Home* to "Maternal Authority."[80] In stressing the necessity for obedience, Abbott cited the case of a little girl who refused to take the medicine prescribed for her. The following dialogue ensued between the mother and child:

76. e.g., Mary Wollstonecraft, *A Vindication of the Rights of Women* (3d ed. London, J. Johnson, 1796), I, 354. "A slavish bondage to parents cramps every faculty of the mind . . . ," and, 356, "Children cannot be taught too early to submit to reason. . . ."

77. Horace Bushnell described this as the "ostrich nurture," *Christian Nurture*, chapter iii.

78. Humphrey, *op. cit.*, pp. 27–28.

79. Cf. *ante*, p. 18.

80. Abbott, *The Mother at Home*, chapters ii and iii.

"Yes, my dear, do take it, for it will make you feel better."

"No it won't, mother, I don't want it."

"Yes, it will, my child, the doctor says it will."

"Well it don't taste good, and I don't want it."

The mother continues her persuasions [Abbott wrote] and the child persists in its refusal. After a long and wearisome conflict, the mother is compelled either to throw the medicine away, or to resort to compulsion, and force down the unpalatable drug. Thus, instead of appealing to her own supreme authority, she is appealing to the *reason of the child,* and, under these circumstances, the child of course refuses to submit.[81]

It is evident from this passage that John Abbott rejected appeal to reason and placed conservative emphasis upon parental authority as "supreme." It is significant that he granted this supremacy to the mother, however.

In another anecdote he reveals the way in which he would employ the "affections" to aid in securing control. An instance is given [82] of a little girl, Mary, who in spite of her mother's mild but firm command not to play with the Bible, pulls it from its pedestal and plays with it. The mother, acting immediately, but tenderly and sorrowfully, "inflicts real pain" upon the child, saying, " 'Mary, it makes mother very unhappy to have to punish you. She loves her little daughter, and wishes to have her a good girl.' " She then leaves her in solitude to "deepen the impression" and returns later to ask if the child is ready to ask God to forgive her. "The mother then kneels with her daughter, and offers a simple prayer for forgiveness, and the return of peace and happiness. . . . At night, just before she goes to sleep, she mildly and affectionately reminds her of her disobedience, and advises her to ask God's forgiveness again." [83]

In this example, love and affection are used to appeal to the conscience, their purpose being to subdue the child's will by gentle means. The new element here is not only the absence of harshness, but the use of the personal relationship to ensure a kind of emotional bondage to the sense of duty. We may judge that the phrase "this hurts me more than it does you" was initiated during this period in our American history. The personal, emotional aspect of this philosophy was out of keeping with the older Calvin-

81. *Ibid.,* p. 28.
82. *Ibid.,* pp. 33–35.
83. *Ibid.,* pp. 34–35.

ism of New England. It shows, as does Abbott's approval of the Nathan Dickerman biography,[84] a close sympathy with the revivalistic methods of evangelical Protestantism.

Contributors to the *Parent's Magazine* which, we will recall, reflected on the whole a rural point of view in education, showed themselves in harmony with Abbott's philosophy. One writer insisted that disobedience of children be condemned as a sin against God, and that the parents' appeal to a higher authority "cultivates conscience, and tends to make obedience willing and sincere." [85] But, he declared, "The pleasure of obedience may be heightened by the maternal smile, . . . the little culprit may be made to kneel down before God, and the soft hand may be placed on his head, while the heavenly Father is implored to forgive his sins. . . ." One scene of this sort "conducted with becoming seriousness" exceeds that of "many chidings and chastenings." [86] This same writer recognized in another article the fact that young children like to be "free as air" but that they also need rules, and if rules are given justly and kindly, the child heart is softened, and sin is removed.[87]

It is surprising to find the "little culprit" approach, or the appeal to conscience featured in a prize essay [88] which was noted above for its "progressive" view of child nature. We may recall here Mrs. Robinson, the mother of the "Restored Family," who turned her children out of doors to play, and who took a thoroughly objective view of the bodies and intellects of her children.[89] Mrs. Robinson considered the use of the rod "perverting to the moral feelings of the child," [90] but on extreme occasions she was forced to resort to it. At such times, she made her methods ceremonious and impressive, to deepen a sense of repentance in the offender. When Willie, her small son, was guilty of a grave misdemeanor, she "called him to her, and with the greatest gravity explained his offence, and informed him of the penalty, appointing

84. *Ibid.*, pp. 142–44.

85. H. Rood, "No. 2—Obedience in Children," *Parent's Magazine*, 1:78, December, 1840.

86. *Ibid.*, p. 79.

87. H. Rood, "Government of Children," *Parent's Magazine*, 1:106–7, January, 1841.

88. Mrs. M. O. Stearns, "The Restored Family," *Mother's Assistant*, 4:97–119, May, 1844.

89. *Ibid.*, pp. 102–3.

90. *Ibid.*, p. 104.

an hour of the following day for its infliction." Meanwhile, Willie's sister was sent to procure a rod, and "on returning with the rod in her hand, and tears in her eyes, affectionately kissed the little offender." The rod was then hung in a prominent place where Willie could see it and repent of his sins. At the appointed time his mother "took him to her chamber, and holding him affectionately in her lap, discussed at length his offence. She read and explained to him the account of Eli's death saying, 'Would you rather have God punish your mother, or have her punish you?' " Willie of course chose to be punished. "Before inflicting the chastisement, she knelt and prayed with him. . . ." [91]

This example shows that the stress upon guilt and repentance was deeply rooted even among those who romanticized child nature. The new emphasis upon maternal control of discipline tended, in some instances, to combine the worst features of religiosity and romanticism.

The real center of the controversy over modes of control lay in the use of the rod or of corporal punishment in child government. In the examples given above, a modified use of the rod was prescribed, and the old severity replaced by maternal tenderness.

Humphrey wrote of the prevailing "doctrine of very modern date" which rejected the use of the rod even in extreme cases.[92] The Boston schoolmasters who answered Horace Mann's report complained ". . . it is quite offensive now-a-days to ears polite, to talk of authority, and command, and injunction. We must persuade, and invite, and win." [93] Goodrich wrote, ". . . the birchen rod is almost banished from society. Children, it is said, must be drawn by the cords of love." [94] Hubbard Winslow, preaching against dangerous innovations in education, commented on the "strange notion of modern time" that subjugation of the will is undesirable, and on the failure of moderns to recognize the "indispensable virtues of the rod." [95]

To get at the root of this rejection of the rod we must examine briefly into the school controversy which raged at this time. When Lyman Cobb published his book on the *Evil Tendencies of Cor-*

91. *Loc. cit.*
92. Humphrey, *op. cit.*, p. 56.
93. Association of Masters of the Boston Public Schools, *Remarks on the Seventh Annual Report of the Honorable Horace Mann*, p. 128.
94. Goodrich, *op. cit.*
95. Winslow, "On the Dangerous Tendency to Innovations and Extremes in Education," Lect. 7, *American Institute of Instruction*, 5:182–83, 1835.

poral Punishment in New York in 1847, he included the opinions of several prominent New England educators in the appendix. Thus, he quoted Jacob Abbott, brother of John, as saying " 'I think . . . that corporal punishment ought to be limited to *"extreme* cases of *wilful, deliberate,* and *malicious* DISOBEDIENCE, as the *ultimatum,* or *last* RESORT *only."* . . .' " [96] Gallaudet expressed it as his belief that the rod should be used "only as the last resort," but he objected to giving it up entirely, since used in the right "spirit, manner, and place" it need not be an "instrument of evil." [97] The most thorough analysis of the problem was passed on to Cobb by Horace Mann, whose views were reprinted from his "Lectures on Education." Mann condemned corporal punishment for its undesirable effects upon child character. Punishment, he said, excites fear, and fear "is a most debasing, dementalizing passion." [98] He said, further, that to make an issue of bodily pain is ignoble, since the intrepid child should be contemptuous of bodily pain. Corporal punishment could, therefore, bring about only two results and both of these were undesirable; one, to make the weak child weaker and more fearful, and two, to make the bold and fearless child more reckless, and contemptuous of authority.[99]

It was this new attitude of Mann's which alarmed such conservers of tradition as the Boston schoolmasters and the Reverend Hubbard Winslow. This rejection of the fear motive seemed a dangerous philosophy to them. Even Goodrich, who stood midway between the old and the new ways of thinking and whose appeals were not based on religious dogma, upheld "the principle of fear" and complained of those who defined fear as "a motive which may influence a brute." [100]

At the extreme left of the school controversy stood Bronson Alcott, who declared that "harshness and restraint, fear, and interdiction, arbitrary reward and punishment, where the laws of affection, order, and conscience, generally prevail, will not be often required." [101] This much of his philosophy might have been

96. Cobb, *The Evil Tendencies of Corporal Punishment,* p. 228.
97. *Ibid.,* pp. 237–38.
98. Horace Mann, extract from "Lectures on Education," in Cobb, *op. cit.,* p. 245.
99. *Ibid.,* p. 246.
100. Goodrich, *op. cit.,* p. 121.
101. Amos Bronson Alcott, *Observations on the Principles and Methods of Infant Instruction* (Boston, Carter & Hendee, 1830), p. 22.

acceptable to some progressives, but he went beyond this and stated that under such conditions "the child becomes a law to himself." [102] In making this sort of statement, Alcott placed himself definitely outside the pale of the immediate controversy.

There can be little doubt that this school discussion of discipline influenced those who were speculating on proper modes of family government. Those who were agreed on avoiding extremes of leniency or harshness were forced to define when, where, and how the rod should be employed, if at all. The result of this was the formulation of various sets of rules to be followed by mothers in the correction of their children. We have seen the effects of this upon the followers of the John Abbott philosophy. As the midcentury period progressed, the tendency was to put less emphasis upon the appeal to the child's conscience, and more upon the mother's use of common sense and understanding, in meting out punishments. In short, moralists and educators learned more about young children, and began to realize that the rod itself was merely a symbol, and not entirely a suitable one for controlling the destiny of so important a being as the growing American citizen.

Since Jacob Abbott, author of the Rollo books, made gentle training of the young a lifelong interest, it is helpful to trace the progressive steps in his thinking on discipline. When the Boston schoolmasters objected to Horace Mann's views on punishment, they quoted Jacob Abbott on the shortcomings of the "gentle winning influence of moral suasion." [103] Abbott had, in an address given before the American Institute of Instruction in 1831, used as an illustration the case of a mother who had exhausted her "stores of rhetoric and logic" [104] in pleading with a child to get him to bed. Abbott used this example to emphasize the necessity of "arbitrary command" [105] and of absolute authority on the part of the mother or teacher. As quoted in this connection he was taken to agree with the masters, that a child should obey his mother "not, from sympathy, and affection, and harmony of opinion," [106] but from the authority residing in the mother. Ab-

102. *Loc. cit.*
103. Association of Masters of the Boston Public Schools, *Remarks on the Seventh Annual Report of the Honorable Horace Mann*, pp. 130–31.
104. Jacob Abbott, "On Moral Education," Lect. 2, *American Institute of Instruction*, 2:48, August, 1831.
105. *Loc. cit.*
106. Association of Masters . . . , *op. cit.*, p. 129,

bott was thus classed as being conservative in his philosophy of punishment.

Ten years later, in 1841, Abbott contributed an article to the *Mother's Assistant* entitled *"Punishments,"* [107] in which he analyzed proper modes to be employed with young children. In this article is cited the hypothetical case of a little girl, four years old, "who has acquired the habit of falling down upon the floor, with loud outcries of sorrow and passion, when any thing displeases her." [108] According to Abbott, the mother may do one of three things to control this situation:

First [he wrote], there is bodily punishment. Her mother may wait until the fit is over, and then take her into her room by herself and . . . punish her with a rod. This course steadily pursued, will as certainly cure the fault, as water will extinguish fire. Secondly, she may adopt a milder mode. She may take the child up and carry her away to another room (not leaving her in the dark, or alone under such circumstances as to frighten her), and confine her there for ten minutes after such offence.[109]

This second method, Abbott declared, will likewise cure the fault, but will take longer. The third punishment is one of an even milder variety. The mother may leave the child on the floor "taking no notice of her whatever." When the outcries have subsided "and she comes to her mother of her own accord," the mother may treat her with "gentle displeasure" for a half hour or so after the offence, and stimulate the child's conscience "to a continual reproof." This method, which takes more time than either of the other two, says Abbott, will certainly, "if steadily and invariably administered," wear out the disease.[110]

In commenting on these three modes, Abbott stated that "the kind of punishment is not very essential." The first method is quickest, but "makes a sacrifice of the maternal feelings," the last takes leisure and "great perseverance." All three are successful if administered in the right spirit, and this spirit consists in adherence to three general principles to be observed by the mother. First, the administration of punishment must be *uniform;* second, punishments should be *mildly* administered; third, and per-

107. Jacob Abbott, "Punishments," *Mother's Assistant*, 1:74–77, February, 1841.
108. *Ibid.*, p. 74.
109. *Loc. cit.*
110. *Loc. cit.*

haps most significant, "parents should be very cautious how they punish faults, the commission of which bring any special . . . inconvenience to themselves." [111] Not once in this article does Abbott use the word "authority." He is concerned more with the effectiveness and justice of the method than with preserving the sanctity of parental command. In elaborating on the principle of mildness he declares that "the ordinary child faults may be corrected by means of a course of punishment which will not even disturb the common flow of good humor and hilarity." [112] In principle three, he intimates that the mother is not always right and that justice to the child must take precedence over parental impulse.[113] Abbott's comment on leaving the child in the dark is also significant as indicating a regard for the child's mental health, and repudiation of a method which increases fear.

Abbott's final and most complete work on child management did not appear until after the midcentury period, in 1872,[114] but since it marks a culmination in his thinking, growing out of his observations of the middle period, it is of interest to this study. Despite the fact that Abbott reiterates in this volume all his earliest statements about the precedence of parental authority over reason and affection, he goes into an even more complete exposition of the philosophy set forth in his article of 1841, and in this analysis "gentle measures" win out. In order to see the full effects of an ameliorated view of punishment upon his thinking, let us examine an anecdote he employs, entitled "The Little Runaway." [115]

A small boy, three or four years of age, was given to running out into the street instead of staying in his own yard to play. His mother, instead of chastising him or "subjecting him to any . . . inconvenience or privation having no obvious connection with the fault," simply required him, without anger, to remain in the house within her sight.[116] Abbott, who had stated that reason and affection should not prevail over authority, put these explanatory words into the mother's mouth:

111. *Ibid.*, pp. 75–76.
112. *Loc. cit.*
113. Cf. with this view, article entitled "Don't Be So Troublesome," *Parent's Magazine*, 2:218–19, June, 1842.
114. Jacob Abbott, *Gentle Measures in the Management of the Young* (New York, Harper & Bros., 1872).
115. *Ibid.*, pp. 76–79.
116. *Ibid.*, p. 79.

"I am very sorry . . . to have to keep you in the house . . . I don't blame you very much for running away. It is what foolish little children, as little as you, very often do. I suppose you thought it would be good fun . . . but it is not safe. By-and-by, when you grow a little larger, you won't be so foolish, and then I can trust you in the yard at any time. . . . And now what can I get for you to amuse you while you stay in the house with me?" [117]

This, from the author of the Rollo books, and written a half century before the advent of American "techniques" of preschool and parental education! Jacob Abbott's progress of ideas is of especial interest here because it is such a good exposé of the "middle way" of the New England reformer of his period. Unable to break totally with the old concepts of conscience and of authority, and somewhat distrustful of an extravagant espousal of the "rule of love," Abbott hit upon a careful compromise which reconciled the best features of both. Through his own love and understanding of little children, he fell in line with many of the more progressive attitudes toward child nature. He came a long way from the morbidly religious approach of his brother John Abbott. No one can follow the progress of his thinking without gaining a new respect for the forces which created that little prig, Rollo.

The same sort of progress may be noted in the writings of other educators of the period, whose approach in other matters was essentially a conservative one. The Reverend Harvey Newcomb revealed a growing recognition of the needs of child nature in his "rules for family government," among which are such statements as:

Give your reasons frequently enough. . . . Avoid giving needless occasion for the exercise of authority, by bringing the disposition of the child to unnecessary trial. . . . To correct peevishness, in a child, avoid the causes which excite it. . . . Treat them with tenderness at those times when they are most irritable. Different dispositions require as various treatment as different physical constitutions. . . .[118]

Humphrey admitted, in spite of his brief for the use of the rod, that *"affectionate persuasion, addressed to the understanding, the*

117. *Loc. cit.*
118. Harvey Newcomb, "Rules for Family Government," *Parent's Magazine*, 2:96, December, 1841.

conscience and the heart, is the grand instrument to be employed in family government." [119]

Goodrich recommended the ameliorated methods of control [120] advocated by Miss Sedgwick in her volume entitled *Home*, stating at the same time that a child "will not long resist patient kindness, tender remonstrance, affectionate counsel." [121]

During the decade of the 'fifties, the Reverend A. B. Muzzey and Reverend William Thayer, both conservers, rather than innovators in domestic reform, gave considerable treatment in their texts [122] to analysis of modes of control, in each case evolving a set of principles akin to those of Jacob Abbott. Thayer attempted, in addition to this, to analyze the pitfalls of parental indulgence or "spoiling" of children. Some mothers, he said, rule solely by love, and in place of a "wise and affectionate commandment" substitute an ineffectual kind of "loving consultation." [123] Other parents, such as the mother of Byron, employ severity which is crushing to "young and tender affections." Still a third group spoil their children by alternating love with severity, being lenient one day and harsh the next. In place of all these Thayer recommended the sweet blending of justice and love.[124]

The kind of family government or "rule" resulting from all this analysis of disciplinary modes tended, instead of reinstating paternalistic methods in the home, to put additional responsibility upon the shoulders of the mother. Under the older regime, punishment of a misdemeanor could be deferred until the father, as head of the household, could administer the necessary retribution. Punishment was a penalty or fine imposed upon the child for an offence or violation of authority. Just as soon as other considerations entered into the situation, consideration of the mother's mood, and the child's disposition, of the motives underlying behavior, and the immediate ends in view in applying corrective methods, the matter of discipline became too complex to be held over for the father's attention. Thus, for example, Abbott's anecdote of the little girl given to having temper tantrums was told to convey the importance of the mother's consistent action in episodes of this sort. His story of the "little runaway" would have

119. Humphrey, *op. cit.*, p. 43.
120. Goodrich, *op. cit.*, pp. 106–16.
121. *Ibid.*, p. 106.
122. Muzzey, *The Fireside*, chaps. vi–xii; Thayer, *op. cit.*, chap. iii.
123. Thayer, *op. cit.*, p. 77.
124. *Ibid.*, pp. 77–78.

been pointless had it not included the mother's policy of fitting the punishment immediately to the crime.

It is interesting to note here the comment of Lyman Cobb on the matter of transferred punishment. He referred to the case of the mother who "spends a considerable portion of her leisure time, while her husband is at home, in complaining to him of the faults of her children" with the result that the father whips the children "without the least investigation." Cobb exclaimed ". . . *can* a MOTHER do this? . . . I answer; it is ONLY the case where all the *finer* and *nobler* feelings of a MOTHER have become blunted by an EXCESSIVE use of VERY STRONG *tea* or *coffee*, or of *wine* or *brandy*, . . . or when the LOVE OF PLEASURE and GAYETY has taken full possession of her mind, instead of the LOVE of DOMESTIC HAPPINESS!" [125] While Cobb was not necessarily condemning here the deferral of punishment, he was implying the very definite responsibility of the dutiful mother in securing just treatment for her children.

The idea of Christian nurture, of the gradual strengthening of moral character through daily growth in the gentler affections, was taking hold upon midnineteenth century society. In a former period such growth had concerned the soul alone, and rewards were viewed as residing in a future world. But when moral growth came to be concerned with man's body and his mind and his heart, there had to be a whole new set of values. Flesh was no longer to be mortified, but respected as being part of man. The mind and heart were no longer to be dominated by fear and a heavy conscience. The mother, as the most constant attendant upon the progress of the growing individual, was seen as the logical one to nurture the body, and through the use of gentle measures of control, to point the way to a state of mind in which "perfect love casteth out fear." Thus Catherine Beecher wrote, ". . . we do find from universal experience, that *affection* can govern the human mind with a sway more powerful than the authority of reason, or the voice of conscience," [126] and "the world is no longer to be governed by *physical* force, but by *the influence which mind exerts over mind.*" [127] This was the ideal visualized by some of the reformers of the period, but for many decades the "sense of sin" was to hold its place clamorously in this kingdom of love.

125. Cobb, *op. cit.*, p. 33.
126. Catherine Beecher, *Suggestions Respecting Improvements in Education*, pp. 45–46.
127. *Ibid.*, p. 52.

PART THREE

RETROSPECT

CHAPTER VIII

SUMMARY AND CONCLUSIONS

IN drawing conclusions from this study it is helpful to look backward over the ground covered in defining the mother's role as educator. We will recall that her duties with respect to religious and moral guidance were approached, broadly, from two points of view. One was that of the social conservator who, alarmed by increasing indifference to religious and moral values in New England society, appealed to mothers for aid in checking this indifference at its source, by bringing up the new generation in "the nurture and admonition of the Lord." The second was that of the romantic and the "progressive" who, admitting the necessity for restoring the status quo, nevertheless went beyond this, granting an almost divine, creative power to the mother as an exponent of progress, or instrument in bringing about the millennium. Frequently underlying these two approaches were fundamentally different views of child nature and of the goals to be sought in religious and moral education. Differences were nevertheless reconciled by domestic reformers, who were able to discover a common ground in their agreement regarding the importance of early impressions in the education of the young child. On this common ground there was oneness of opinion as to the significance of the mother's example, diligence, and activity in the spiritual nurture of her children, whether this education was grounded in piety and religiosity, or in enlightened morality.

With respect to the intellectual cultivation of children, the mother's unique function received emphasis for two general reasons. One was that fathers had increasingly little time to give to the instruction of children, because of the pressure of business which kept them away from the home; the other that new and liberal views of mental culture tended to regard learning as a continuous process which could be most logically fostered by the person associated closely and constantly with the child, namely, the mother.

Reformers were united in their reaction against the unnatural forcing process of the eighteenth century, which had put a premium upon intellectual precocity in children. In this point of view, they were influenced, in part by a resurgence of pietism, which feared overcultivation of the intellect as a menace to the cultivation of the moral and religious sentiments, in part by naturalistic concepts of child nature, which emphasized growth as unfoldment, and in part by the findings of the sciences and the pseudo sciences with respect to the body and the mind and their close interrelationship.

As learning became associated with something more than instruction and the formal discipline of an earlier period, simple daily events in the child's life were seen as occasions for promoting mental growth, and the role of the mother was described as that of interpreter, guide, and widener of horizons. This put a premium upon maternal education and intelligence, and yet, at the same time gave prestige to the untutored mother whose limited knowledge could be put to daily and hourly use at the level of the child's experience.

Interest in the mother's role as guardian of her child's physical well-being was intensified by discoveries which placed remedies for the physical ailments of society within the control of intelligent individuals. When it was recognized that human ignorance and not Providence was frequently the cause of sickness and death, women were faced with a new and weighty set of responsibilities involving cognizance of, and obedience to, the laws of health and of growth.

In the field of domestic reform, the ideal of the frail and genteel mother was, therefore, replaced with that of the healthy, well-informed, domestic woman, equally capable of mastering the affairs of her kitchen and nursery, and of assimilating knowledge which would qualify her for her important custodianship.

What lent dignity to this erstwhile prosaic domestic role was not, however, the practical health message alone, with its implications for maternal responsibility, but more particularly the moral significance attached by domestic reformers to concerns of the flesh. This involved a new set of attitudes toward the body as an instrument capable of moral use, and glorified as "the temple of the soul." When the body, the mind, and the soul were seen as interdependent in their functioning, the physical education of children was given a fresh emphasis, and the minor affairs of eating, drinking, dressing, and so forth, were associated with the formation of character. During this pre-Darwinian era it was possible even for the phrenologists, whose postulates were basically materialistic, to give physical education this spiritual superstructure. At the other end of the scale, reformers of a transcendentalist bent carried this exaltation of the concerns of the flesh to a pantheistic extreme.

Finally, with respect to her mode of control over child behavior, the mother was called upon to aid in the general uplift of society by her exercise of the love principle or rule by the affections. This principle was called into play partially as a result of popular reaction against the crudities and selfishness of the masculine world of business. Emphasis was placed upon the two distinct roles of the sexes, and the feminine role was identified as that of the standard-bearer for the milder Christian virtues of kindliness, benevolence, and the "domestic" affections. This stress was consistent with the drive toward moral and religious perfection, which granted to mothers power to check the evils of materialism and to restore society to a state of moral excellence.

The role of "gentle ruler," although outwardly of a mild and submissive character calculated to keep women in their appropriate sphere, implied also a certain amount of positive power to change, to mold, and to control human beings by means of appealing to their "higher sentiments."

Mothers were considered as divinely constituted to carry out this role by virtue of "maternal instinct" or native endowment for the exercise of the tender sentiments. While phrenologists implied a limit to maternal power in this respect by calling attention to the deficiency of the domestic affections or propensities in some women, they nevertheless joined forces with other reformers to dictate an active role for mothers in the molding of young children.

When the application of the love principle conflicted with older views of punishment by means of the rod, a system of ameliorated punishments was evolved which tended to reduce emphasis upon the supreme authority and infallibility of the parent and to place a premium upon understanding of children and common sense modes of control. Domestic reformers of the period were largely responsible for the evolution of this modified system, but here, again, they were successful because they discovered a common ground where old and new views of child nature and of parental authority could be utilized simultaneously. On this ground they sought to maintain a just balance between older repressive methods of discipline, with their appeal to fear, and the newer romantic approach which tended in its extremes to exercise a weak and ineffectual type of "suasion." The mother was regarded as the mediator between these two extremes.

Turning, then, to a statement of conclusions, the most important observation which can be made about the findings as a whole is that they have uncovered an area of social and philosophical thought which extends beyond the radius of the proposed problem, with significant results for the definition of the problem itself. The chief result concerns a definition of the term "education." Unless we can understand what the midnineteenth century idealist meant by education, this study will seem, particularly in its emphasis upon backgrounds, to have fallen into the very error for which the nineteenth century has been condemned—that of generalization, or of straying beyond the confines of a given problem. But since this investigation has dealt in midnineteenth century concepts, it must consider the semantics of these concepts. Domestic education, for example, was defined as pertaining to all the "rights and duties of parents in the government and instruction of their families." [1] Humphrey, the author of the phrase, meant rights and duties with respect to a perfect education, one so perfect that it might "never be realized, even in the millennium." [2] He saw education as a term more comprehensive "than law, or politics—than government or religion." [3] Dr. William Alcott also strove to give education this broader meaning, declaring that it meant not "mere instruction," but "the formation of character, physical, intellectual, social, moral and religious— . . . both for time and for eternity." [4] Another remark of Alcott's gives an interesting clue to the midcentury shift of attitude toward education. He complained that many people of his time turned away in disgust "at the idea of studying education as a science," believing that skill to train up the young was one acquired accidentally or as a "peculiar gift of Heaven bestowed on a few." [5]

Their view of education as a "science" based upon a definite set of principles to be followed purposefully is suggestive of the phrenological emphasis upon laws and principles. We will recall

1. Humphrey, *Domestic Education*, p. 15.
2. *Ibid.*, p. 13.
3. *Ibid.*, p. 11.
4. Alcott, *The Young Wife*, p. 319.
5. *Loc. cit.*

that Alcott placed Combe's *Constitution of Man* on his required list for parents.[6] Combe had stated in the preface to this work that the only novelty of his contribution lay in its emphasis upon "the relations which acknowledged truths hold to each other," that no one, so far as he knew, had coordinated physical, organic, and moral laws in their application to man.[7] Yet Alcott's zeal for coordination went even beyond that of Combe. He placed Paley's *Theology* on the reading list for parents, presumably to add spiritual laws to the categories proposed by phrenologists. Thus, for him, education had come to mean that department of knowledge which embraces all laws affecting man's growth for time, and for eternity.

This interpretation of Alcott's seems typical of the position taken by the domestic reformer during this period. The tendency was to seize upon all that the so-called scientists had to offer on man's sojourn in the here and now, giving full significance to observance of "natural laws," but to retain fast hold upon the tenets of religious faith, upon the importance of divine law, and of the hereafter, incorporating both into a system of education consistent with the three major doctrines of the democratic faith in the midnineteenth century. These doctrines, referred to in various ways throughout this study, have been described by Gabriel as the doctrine of the fundamental law, made up of both moral and natural law, the doctrine of the free individual, which placed the means of man's power in his own hands, and finally the doctrine of "the mission of America." [8] Obviously, the perfect education figured in all these. Humphrey was careful to point out that "a perfect education is not to be hoped for in the present world." But, he declared, "we can conceive what it would be, and the conception may be of use to us." [9]

In each chapter of this investigation, there has had to be a reconstruction of the specific problems of fireside education in the light of social and scientific developments, and of democratic ideals current in the midcentury years. Every aspect of this education took on importance because of its relation to forces operating in the American scene as a whole. This, as we have seen, gave a peculiar emphasis to the maternal role, and seemed to

6. Alcott, *op. cit.*, p. 314.
7. George Combe, *Constitution of Man*, p. vii.
8. Gabriel, *The Course of American Democratic Thought*, pp. 16, 19, 22.
9. Humphrey, *op. cit.*, p. 12.

bestow on women, in theory at least, the control of the mainspring of social progress. Before elaborating on the doctrines derived from this emphasis, it is necessary to set forth a second general conclusion which concerns a classification of the literature examined in this study.

A superficial glance at this vein of didactic literature dealing with mothers and young children might lead a student of American thought to deduce the following: that domestic education was part of a broader movement toward domestic reform; that this reform sprang chiefly from conservative alarm at the rapid onward movement of a democratic society; that maternal and fireside influence were highlighted for two reasons, one, to check feminism and keep women in the home, and the other, to control social evils at their source by prescribing a firm course of government for the rising generation; or, more briefly, that the principal message of this literature is a conservative one, acting as a cross-current or even backwash against the mainstream of social progress.

There is just enough truth in this set of hasty observations to make the conclusions of a more thorough study seem paradoxical. Thus, it is possible to construe the movement toward domestic reform as being on the whole a conservative one. It was Harriet Martineau's contention, for example, that women were held back to some extent by the "persuasion that there are virtues which are peculiarly masculine, and others which are peculiarly feminine." [10] The church frequently used women for its own ends, and, according to Miss Bertha Stearns, many of the ministers who collaborated with women in the publication of domestic literature did so with the purpose of keeping the world in order.[11] Much of the emphasis upon the softer Christian virtues of love, meekness, and self-denial was doubtless due to a conservative desire to keep women submissive, and to soft pedal their alarming propensities toward intellectual cultivation and unbecoming loquaciousness on social questions. As for children and their early education, the fireside was considered by some conservatives as the only place safe from the unsettling influences of the democratic spirit, which was identified with overweening individualism, recklessness, and lawlessness. To such reactionaries, even the common

10. Martineau, *Society in America*, III, 115.
11. Cf. *ante*, p. 42.

school and the Sabbath school were menaces to an aristocratic order, and the rise of the middle classes a social development to be deplored.

Yet a closer examination of this literature has revealed a set of ideas which run directly counter to this backward trend. It has appeared in this study that domestic reform in general, and domestic education in particular, demanded that women be released from old bonds of submission, that mothers be provided with better intellectual advantages, that they rule by the softer virtues, rather than be enslaved by them, and that they be adequately aware of their own peculiar contributions to the solution of social problems. For children, the movement to strengthen fireside education has seemed to demand that certain desirable educational innovations be brought into the home, and that every aspect of education be enlivened by its connection with the goals of democratic progress.

The resolution of the paradox is seen in the middle ground found by reformers who were able to forget their fundamental differences in the discovery of a common task, the improvement of society. Through the interaction of their ideas, brought about by the many-sided attack on domestic reform, conservatives were liberalized, and liberals were led to weigh and consider before discarding old values.

We come, then, to a set of conclusions which concern the mother, and the consequences for her which followed upon the new definition of education. First of all, mothers were granted during these years a position of singular moral responsibility in carrying out the purposes of a democratic society. The best summary of this position was expressed by Catherine Beecher in 1842:

The success of democratic institutions, as is conceded by all, depends upon the intellectual and moral character of the mass of the people. If they are intelligent and virtuous, democracy is a blessing; but if they are ignorant and wicked, it is only a curse. . . . It is equally conceded, that the formation of the moral and intellectual character of the young is committed mainly to the female hand. The mother forms the character of the future man, . . . the wife sways the heart, whose energies may turn for good or for evil the destinies of a nation. . . . If this be so, as none will deny, then to American women, more than to any others on earth,

is committed the exalted privilege of extending over the world
those blessed influences, which are to renovate degraded man, and
"clothe all climes with beauty." [12]

This passage shows the way in which the ideals of conservatives
and liberals merged in the solution of the problems of a democratic
society. Conservative alarm at the rise of the "masses" resolved
itself into faith in the potentialities of the masses under proper
guidance. The question of political and civil rights for women
paled into insignificance in the light of this great responsibility
which made them moral agents for the carrying out of democratic
purposes. This was the mother's part in the "mission of America."

A second doctrine concerns the mother's part as an exponent
of the "middle way" of non-aggression, or in a sense, of compromise, in the control of society. The best expression of this is
seen in the philosophy set forth in Chapter VII on the mother's
rule by affection and suasion. The social implications of the application of the "law of love" are apparent. A perfect society was
visualized in which neither aggression nor soft indulgence should
hold sway, where human beings might be controlled with firmness but without resort to injustice and brute force. Again, the
most telling example of the mother's relation to this new kind of
government comes from the pen of Catherine Beecher. And since
Miss Beecher was herself the product of a highly conservative
Calvinistic background, the progress of her reasoning here is of
especial note. In her volume on the slavery question she voiced
objections to the harsh methods employed by the Abolitionists,
and this was her argument against them:

In the nursery, if the child does wrong, the finger of scorn, the
taunting rebuke, or even the fair and deserved reproof of equals
will make the young culprit only frown with rage, and perhaps
repeat and increase the injury. But the voice of maternal love, or
even the gentle remonstrances of an elder sister, may bring tears
of sorrow and contrition.

So in society. Let a man's enemies, or those who have no interest in his welfare, join to rebuke and rail at his offences, and
no signs of penitence will be seen. But let the . . . bosom friend
approach him, with kindness, forbearance and true sincerity, and
all that is possible to human agency will be effected. [13]

12. Beecher, *A Treatise on Domestic Economy*, pp. 36–37.

13. Catherine E. Beecher, *An Essay on Slavery and Abolitionism* (Philadelphia, Henry Perkins; Boston, Perkins & Marvin, 1837), pp. 54–55.

This conciliatory approach had, to Miss Beecher, the trifold sanction of Christian principles, of democratic principles, and of the laws of the mind, these three sets of principles being harmoniously interrelated. The Abolitionists violated democratic principles because they failed to preserve the spirit of free discussion by taking "every possible means to soothe exasperated feelings," and "to avoid all those offensive peculiarities that in their nature tend to inflame and offend." [14] They went against a law of mind "first seen in the nursery and school, afterwards developed in society" that a person excited by passion is "least likely to judge correctly of truth, and least likely to yield to duty." [15]

The way in which this approach was tied in with maternal example may be illustrated by reference to a different sort of instance. Mrs. Lydia Child, who, we will recall, belonged to the Antislavery party, and drew down censure upon herself by her association with agitators, yet revealed in her *Mother's Book* an attitude toward women which agrees fundamentally with Miss Beecher's philosophy. She mentioned the rare case of the woman caught in an unfortunate marriage and thwarted in her endeavors to rule her children wisely by the influence of a husband not to be trusted. The only course left open to such a mother was, she declared, to win her husband to a sense of duty by "patience, humility and love," [16] or, this failing, by renewed vigilance for the good of her children and by prayer. This was the accepted "womanly way," and a way on which such reformers as Miss Beecher and Mrs. Child could agree. They were both affirming the efficacy of compromise, because they opposed coercive or antagonistic measures of control. Mrs. Child, even when she was zealous in the cause of Antislavery, expressed the faith that "Divine Providence *always* opens the way for the removal of evils, individual or national, whenever man is sincerely willing to have them removed." [17]

These examples may serve to show the way in which the maternal role was related to wider social problems. The middle way was really the principle of "nurture" or the slow growth and guidance process of the nursery applied to society. It implied a

14. Beecher, *ibid.,* pp. 138–39.
15. *Ibid.,* p. 54.
16. Child, *The Mother's Book,* p. 51.
17. Lydia M. Child, *An Appeal in Favor of That Class of Americans Called Africans* (Boston, Allen & Ticknor, 1833), p. 151.

faith in the capacity of the masses to respond to this nurture and to grow in self-control, and it insisted upon Christian wisdom and understanding in those who were prescribing for social ills.

A third and final socially important doctrine suggested by this study is one implied in both of the others, namely, that of the activity of the mother. The moral agent of democracy, the exponent of the "middle way," could not lead an existence which was merely idle, or delicate, or fashionable. Regardless of conditions of wealth or of poverty, of health or frailty, of higher learning or of little education, the ideal mother, as viewed by reformers, was never excused from the responsibility of action based upon intelligent thought. Midnineteenth century New England possessed an ardent faith in remedies. Every conceivable mental, physical, and moral ill was prescribed for, and there was common agreement that maternal indifference or inactivity was an inexcusable error.

Fowler, the phrenologist, gives us an amusing instance of the sort of attack directed at the apathetic woman of the period. To his injunction that women improve their intellects by putting them to use, one reply came to Fowler, " 'But I've nothing to think *about.*' " "Poor soul," he wrote, in Carlylean fashion, "you *are* to be pitied. A world of wonders even within yourself, and yet, barren heath, you've nothing to think about! . . . all nature around you teeming with events, every one of which has its cause, and most of them within your reach, and yet, thought-starved mortal, you've nothing to think about! Poor thing, you should have a name and place among other idiots." When another answer came to Fowler from a woman complaining that she had "not sufficient *time* even to eat and sleep," he answered, "Then no matter, but you *must* find time to *die* the sooner for *not* thinking. . . ." [18] This is typical of the sort of incentive to action used upon mothers. Thus, if their offspring were sickly, they were told that they had the cause and the remedies within their reach. If ills were spiritual they were informed that they had in their hands the power to restore purity. If the lack was intellectual, all nature "teeming with events" lay before them as Fowler said, to be understood and transmitted to their children.

It is interesting to speculate on what the Civil War and ensuing developments of the later nineteenth century did to these Utopian hopes for the mother's role in American society. The

18. Fowler, *Fowler on Memory*, p. 48.

great conflict itself brought the sad realization that the middle way of compromise was not an acceptable one to the majority of the people. Furthermore, the moral agency of the individual was seen as a paltry force after all, when Darwinian science opened its door upon the long, unfathomable, impersonal process of human growth. The "mission of America" was a persisting dream, but this mission became identified with a complexity far too vast to be concerned with such minor matters as the molding of fireside morals. Finally, as woman's activity was demanded in other spheres, her crowning task of the nurture of the young was minimized. With increased expansion in business production, the number of occupations open to women increased, holding out inducements not only at the lower levels of society, but in more refined circles where the higher education of females had done its work to produce a "new woman." This new woman was eager to make use of her knowledge, and horizons opened for her which would have been inconceivable to her mother. Gradually barriers were broken down which had excluded her from the professions. Teaching, always acceptable to the woman who could make her way by no other means, was dignified and labeled as a sphere for which women were eminently fitted. And in all this activity the primary function of woman as mother was receding into the background. As schools were improved and teaching was feminized, the nurture of the young was considered to a certain extent transferable to agencies other than the home. The change of status of women in general made the mother's educational role, as such, dwindle in importance.

An interesting by-product of this study is the light which it throws upon the issues which underlay the so-called feminist or Woman's Rights movement in America. And here again we encounter a need for semantic clarity. "Feminism," although it is defined as the "theory, cult or practice of those who advocate such legal and social changes as will establish political, economic and social equality of the sexes" [19] has come to be identified with the entire movement toward emancipation of women. This investigation has revealed that the midnineteenth century approached the subject of woman's emancipation in two distinct ways. On the one hand, feminists in the sense just defined interpreted *rights* primarily in terms of political and social equality. The philosophy

19. *Webster's New International Dictionary of the English Language* (2d ed. unabridged), p. 930.

which motivated this group was a radical one embracing the doctrine of expediency. On the other hand, a group equally concerned with the elevation of women in society defined emancipation in terms of *responsibilities,* believing that rights were attained through increased capacity to mold the minds of men and of the rising generation. The doctrine of the "middle way" of gradual progress was preached as eloquently by this group as that of immediate action was demonstrated by the other. The second group, as we have seen, was in close harmony with the goals of domestic reform and fireside education. The first group by virtue of its motivation was opposed to any development which might retard its own progress.

This study has helped to clarify the stand taken by those social reformers who opposed militant feminism. The real conflict lay, not between views which dictated female submission on the one hand and female freedom on the other, but in a definition of woman's primary function in a democratic society. The militant feminists felt it necessary to decry the domestic function in their zeal to make a clean break with the old order. The other group felt that the only "emancipation" which was worth while was that which gave first emphasis to the vocation of the wife and mother.

There is evidence in modern literature that the conservative aspect of the woman movement has been subject to some misinterpretation. Schmalhausen and Calverton wrote, for example, that "woman in the nineteenth century was as much a slave of man as in the fifteenth or sixteenth." [20] To illustrate their point, they selected a passage containing the following sentiment, penned by Mrs. Graves in 1858, " 'She [a good woman] has no desire to rule where she feels it to be her duty, as it is her highest pleasure "to love, honor and obey"; and she submits with cheerful acquiescence to that order in the conjugal relation which God and nature have established.' " "Such sentiments," we read, in this modern study, "rendered women impotent by virtue of their deception. They paralysed their minds, and inhibited their emotions." "No *new woman*" it is stated, "could have emerged from such an environment. . . ." [21] These authors had apparently not read all of Mrs. Graves' book or they would have recognized their

20. Samuel D. Schmalhausen and V. F. Calverton, editors, *Woman's Coming of Age* (New York, Horace Liveright, Inc., 1931), p. xiv.
21. *Ibid.,* p. xv.

conclusions as half-truths. For Mrs. Graves predicted in this same volume "glorious results" from the "revolution going on in the female mind at the present day." [22] Women, she declared, were "beginning to put forth their exertions in the great cause of female improvement." [23] Mrs. Graves lauded this exertion, but she lamented the erratic course of many female reformers of her time who had "inflicted deep injury where they intended good, by drawing woman away from . . . domestic life." [24] She believed that redress of woman's wrongs would come from a "gradual awakening to a sense of justice and a more enlightened public opinion." [25] Thus, it would appear that the total import of this message, seen in its context, was somewhat different from the one implied by Schmalhausen and Calverton. Mrs. Graves was herself a "new woman" of her day, writing, like her contemporaries Sarah Hale and Catherine Beecher, to prod her apathetic and fashionable sisters into an awareness of their social responsibilities. The contention submitted here is that these "active conservatives" contributed as definitely to the cause of female enlightenment as did the more militant feminists.

If "feminism" were a dead subject today, this double aspect of its nineteenth century development would be of doubtful relevance to us, but the issues which were brought into sharp relief a century ago are once more coming into focus. By dipping briefly into this contemporary controversy we may perhaps determine whether the nineteenth century arguments have any modern application.

Within the last decade there have been expressions of dissatisfaction with the gains which have been made as a result of the successful crusade of the militant feminists. Women, it is said, have established themselves in the business and social world on a basis of equality with men, but their achievements have not brought the expected liberation, contentment, and fulfilment for the sex as a whole which was predicted by the early feminists. This failure has caused a reaction in recent years. At one extreme, conservatives who are almost more conservative than their nineteenth century predecessors would put women back into the home, forgetting, as one modern writer points out "the curtail-

22. Graves, *Woman in America*, p. xiv.
23. *Ibid.*, p. xvii.
24. *Ibid.*, p. xiv.
25. *Ibid.*, p. 179.

ment of women's work in the home, with the limitations in size of families and the transference of the greater part of home production to outside industry." [26] At the other extreme, those who find fault with our social order would build a brave new world, where the emancipation of women can go on still further, emancipation being interpreted as further release from the limitations of the home environment. Thus we read, "In the new society the parent will no longer be a parent: he will be merely a human being." [27] and, "The time will come when most children will be brought up by professional educators." [28] The home itself is regarded, according to this philosophy, not as a great social agency, but "from a more cosmic viewpoint" as "the great anti-social agency." [29] Fortunately, neither of these extreme opinions prevails widely.

In recent years, a sane view of the woman problem has been emerging which admits neither the complete decline of "feminism" nor the worthlessness of the traditional family roles. And this balanced approach comes from those who would solve simultaneously the problems of women and of the home. Thus Dr. Una B. Sait wrote in 1938, "We have now reached a stage where a more balanced estimate is possible of the values involved in the conflicting interests of women." [30] There can be no turning back, she declared.[31] No problem would be solved by putting women back into the home. Indeed, it is not the working classes of women who retard the advance of their sex. "Rather," she affirmed, is it "those women who are willing to remain immature dependents, to be lazily lapped in security, to let others shoulder their responsibilities, and to accept special privileges without making an adequate return." [32] This group, said Dr. Sait, must learn the responsibilities involved in their improved status. Furthermore, it becomes apparent, she stated that "if a woman chooses to become

26. Una B. Sait, *New Horizons for the Family* (New York, Macmillan Company, 1938), p. 499. By permission of the Macmillan Company, publishers.

27. Samuel D. Schmalhausen, "Family Life: A Study in Pathology" in *The New Generation*, V. F. Calverton and S. D. Schmalhausen, editors (New York, Macaulay Company, 1930), p. 294.

28. B. Liber, "The Pathos of Parenthood," in *The New Generation*, p. 311.

29. Schmalhausen, *op. cit.*, p. 294.

30. Sait, *op. cit.*, p. 501. By permission of the Macmillan Company, publishers.

31. *Ibid.*, p. 499.

32. *Ibid.*, pp. 499–501.

a mother, her primary responsibility lies within this most significant of all human relationships." [33] And so, once more we are witnessing a re-evaluation of woman's role in terms of her primary responsibilities to society.

Another modern writer has thrown a revealing light on the condition of women today by attempting to define "why women fail." Miss Pruette has suggested that one of the chief reasons for the "failure" of modern woman is that she has lost her sense of importance in the one province "that is so peculiarly hers," [34] that of child bearing and child rearing. Once, she said, childbirth had to be done in the face of great dangers, and woman experienced a sense of triumph in meeting these dangers unaided. Today, modern medicine has removed these hazards and by a mere whiff of anaesthetic has put a veil of oblivion between women and one of the "few significant experiences in their lives." [35] In child rearing, according to Miss Pruette:

the severe criticism of the average mother's way with her children, coming from social workers, psychiatrists, educators and psychologists, has helped to destroy a great part of complacency which was formerly the young mother's protection. When she hears all the things she has done so dreadfully to her children, by loving them too much, by not loving them enough, her maternal activities seem to become invested with a futility and a danger that make it sometimes appear the wisest course for her to do nothing at all. The dictum that mother knows best and the dogma of the natural instincts of motherhood have so fallen into disfavor as to be available refuges only for the ignorant or the stubborn.[36]

One thing the midnineteenth century can surely offer the midtwentieth, is to suggest ways in which maternal self-confidence may be restored. Miss Pruette believes that women fail because they do not have to succeed, and because they consider their efforts insignificant. There was small chance for this defeatist attitude during those years when every slightest mood and gesture of the mother was thought to be influential in the formation of child character, when the very food she prepared was deemed capable of leading astray or of purifying the appetites, and when her in-

33. *Ibid.*, p. 501.
34. Lorine Pruette, "Why Women Fail," in *Woman's Coming of Age*, p. 247.
35. *Ibid.*, pp. 246–47.
36. *Ibid.*, p. 247.

cessant activity and vigilance with respect to her children and her household was believed essential to the carrying out of democratic purposes.

To go back to the dogma that "mother knows best" would of course be impossible, but to reiterate the importance of early home influences upon childhood would be only to concur with the most recent scientific emphases in the study of personality. To endow food with moral properties and to speak of the body as the "temple of the soul" would be considered naïve pantheism today, and yet we come perilously close to such an attitude when we support unqualified advertising of the morale-boosting qualities in certain vitamins. To assert once more that the future of democracy depends upon the activity and vigilance of parents in the education of young children is to discount the prime importance of armies and of atomic weapons in our warring world. Yet there are those who believe that the only effective way to preserve the democratic spirit and to remove fear and greed from society is to foster impulses of " 'understanding, love, and altruism' " [37] in the new generation.

37. Sait, *op. cit.*, p. 503, citing Beatrice Hinkle.

CHAPTER IX

A CHAPTER ON BIBLIOGRAPHY

BIBLIOGRAPHICAL information in this chapter is divided into two parts, the first being a descriptive section on selected sources, designed to aid the reader who wishes to do further research, and the second a complete bibliography of works consulted in this study. The two parts may be used together, and supplemented by information given in Chapter III.

I. NOTES ON SOURCES

A. *Backgrounds: Social, historical and intellectual.*

Primary sources which yield valuable data on social conditions and cultural developments in midnineteenth century New England are of several types. Comments on the social scene up to 1835, and factual evidence presented by a native New Englander may be found in Abbott's *New England and Her Institutions* (1835). More discursive and perhaps biased on conditions in America are the writings of English visitors to this country, Martineau's *Society in America* (1849), Bunn's *Old England and New England* (1853), and Mackay's *The Western World* (1849). The first of these is particularly helpful because of Miss Martineau's interest in domestic reform and her comments on education, which reveal liberal views of the times. For complete details on these volumes written by travelers see Berger's *The British Traveller in America, 1836–1860* (1943).

A historical sketch of developments in the churches of New England is included in an account by Henry Barnard entitled "The Growth and Progress of Religious Denominations in the United States for the Past Hundred Years." This appeared as an Appendix to Barnard's contribution "Educational Development" in the 1873 edition of the work *First Century of National Existence.* Also useful on religious backgrounds are chapters iii through vi in Munger's *Horace Bushnell, Preacher and Theologian* (1899).

Three firsthand sources of information on the "woman question" of the day are Mansfield's *Legal Rights, Liabilities and Du-*

ties of Women (1845), Graves' *Woman in America* (1843) and Margaret Fuller Ossoli's *Woman in the Nineteenth Century* (1874). Mrs. Graves' volume, being didactic in purpose, has little value as a factual account, but it throws considerable light on domestic problems of the period, the troublesome "servant question" and the evils caused by "fashionable follies." Margaret Fuller Ossoli's work, published originally in 1845 is of interest as the first statement of feminism made by an American. Its predecessor was Mary Wollstonecraft's *Vindication of the Rights of Women* (1796).

Fiction of the midcentury years, particularly of the semididactic variety written by Catherine Sedgwick, is useful in delineating family practices of the times. Her domestic tales, said to have the "real flavor of New England," present a fertile field for the scholar interested in inferring domestic customs from situations portrayed in moralized fiction.

The autobiographical work by Goodrich, *Recollections of a Lifetime* (1856) is of value for the facts it gives on book production in the first half of the nineteenth century. Titles of books published in America between 1820 and 1852 are listed in Roorbach's *Bibliotheca Americana* (1939), a catalogue which, while not exhaustive, is a useful guide, particularly when employed in connection with information on authors provided by the *Dictionary of American Biography* and other biographical sources.

An estimate of the popularity of many of the didactic volumes which appeared in the midcentury may be found in literary notices and book reviews printed in periodicals used in this study. See particularly the *Ladies' Magazine* and the education periodicals. Excerpts from currently popular works, quoted as separate articles in magazines were also an index of popularity. For example, the piece entitled "Causes of Insanity," *Ladies' Magazine* (1834) was taken from Brigham's book entitled *Remarks on the Influence of Mental Cultivation and Mental Excitement upon Health* (1833).

Among the secondary writings which treat of the American scene and of the status of women and children in nineteenth century society, the most useful is Volume II of Calhoun's *Social History of the American Family* (1918). This text, the only one of its kind which has been written, covers too wide a territory geographically to be very thorough on regional data, but it contains a helpful analysis of the forces which modified family customs.

Essential in a different way is Branch's *The Sentimental Years* (1934), a popularized account of the passing scene and cultural developments which affected the American public during the years 1836 to 1860. This book has a broader scope and is more comprehensive than other popularly written works such as Pattee's *The Feminine Fifties* (1940), concerned largely with literary developments of one decade, and Irwin's *Angels and Amazons* (1933), which treats of the struggle of women to attain recognition and rights. Furness' anthology entitled *The Genteel Female* (1931) contains a helpful introductory chapter and bibliography. All of these works contribute to an understanding of modes, manners and concepts of the times.

Intellectual histories which explain the progress of democratic thought and of trends, religious, political, educational and industrial affecting the common man in nineteenth century society are indispensable background sources. Brooks' *The Flowering of New England* (1940) emphasizes the renaissance of learning in New England during the period under consideration. Gabriel's *The Course of American Democratic Thought* (1940), Parrington's *Main Currents in American Thought,* Volume II (1927), and Fish's *The Rise of the Common Man* (1929) are excellent general texts on democratic progress. For information on the religious setting of the period, Chapter xxviii on "The Complex Faith of New England" in Bates' *An American Faith* (1940), and Fleming's *Children and Puritanism* (1933), a history of children in the life and thought of the New England churches, are important. Also useful in this connection is the essay entitled "Divines and Moralists" in the *Cambridge History of American Literature,* Volume II (1918).

B. *Biographical Materials*

Primary sources on biography which merit notice are: Hale's *Woman's Record* (1870), Griswold's *Prose Writers of America* (1847), and Hart's *Female Prose Writers of America* (1852). Mrs. Hale's comments on distinguished women of the period, involving either praise or gentle rebuke, are occasionally enlightening on conservative versus liberal controversies of the period. Abbott's *Young Christian* (1882), a memorial volume of Jacob Abbott written by his son, contains biographical data and other useful background material. A biographical note on Catherine

Sedgwick which stresses her interest in the "home" theme may be found in the work entitled *Homes of American Authors* (1853).

The fact that President Humphrey of Amherst wrote *The Life and Labors of Reverend T. H. Gallaudet* (1857) has significance in this study. In consulting these sources, one asks the question why certain biographical works were undertaken. It is evident, for example, that Mrs. Hale wrote her *Woman's Record* because the theme was of vital importance in her crusade for public recognition of the importance of women to society. Mrs. Child's *Good Wives* (1833), as well as Burns' *Mothers of the Wise and Good* (1851) are likewise informative with respect to the ideals of domestic reform.

Among the secondary sources on biography, Bolzau's *Almira Hart Lincoln Phelps* (1936), Harveson's *Catherine Esther Beecher, Pioneer Educator* (1932), and McCuskey's *Bronson Alcott, Teacher* (1940) are studies containing helpful references. Popularized accounts such as Finley's *Lady of Godey's* (1931), the story of Sarah Hale, and Haight's *Mrs. Sigourney, the Sweet Singer of Hartford* (1930) include good background detail.

C. *Literature for Parents*

Didactic literature addressed to parents and either written by New Englanders or published in New England during the years 1830 to 1860 was the central focus of all the research done in this study. Background works were used to provide a setting and supplementary didactic writings to explain the concepts revealed by this literature.

In singling out significant books and articles in this group it is helpful to note in the bibliography those authors whose names are affixed to more than one work. Most of these were responsible for at least one title in the parent literature of the period. Among their writings, books most worthy of examination are John S. C. Abbott's *The Mother at Home* (1833), William A. Alcott's *The Young Mother* (1836), Child's *The Mother's Book* (1831), Goodrich's *Fireside Education* (1838), Humphrey's *Domestic Education* (1840), Phelps' *Observations upon an Infant* (1835), Sigourney's *Letters to Mothers* (1838), and Thayer's *Life at the Fireside* (1857). Arthur's *The Mother* (1846) is also of interest, as semi-fiction by the temperance reformer. Two texts which emphasize the father's part in education are Dwight's *The Father's Book* (1834) and Hall's *On the Education of Children* (1836).

Practical methods in the instruction of young children are given in Gallaudet's *Child's Book on the Soul* (1831), and Jacob Abbott's *Little Philosopher* (1830), both of which show the influence on Americans of European systems of learning of the object lesson variety. Also important for methods employed with children are Abbott's *Gentle Measures in the Training of the Young* (1872), Mrs. Horace Mann's *Moral Culture of Infancy* (1863) and Fowler's *On Memory* (1842). The latter is included here because of its exhortations to mothers and its suggestions for the application of phrenology to a science of education.

Periodical articles for parents listed under the *Ladies' Magazine, The Mother's Assistant,* and the *Parent's Magazine* are of particular interest for further research, reflecting as they do a variety of points of view on methods and philosophies of the period. To be noted especially are the articles written by authors whose names appear elsewhere in this study.

D. *Young Ladies and Their Education*

A second set of didactic writings worthy of examination are the manuals, guidebooks, and moral essays of midcentury New England which had as their purpose the instruction of prospective wives and homemakers. William Alcott's *Young Wife* (1837) and *Young Housekeeper* (1839), Beecher's *Treatise on Domestic Economy* (1842), Newcomb's *Young Lady's Guide* (1853), Phelps' *Female Student* (1840), Tuthill's *Young Lady's Home* (1839), Sigourney's *Letters to Young Ladies* (1833), Wise's *Young Lady's Counsellor* (1851), and Winslow and Sandford's *Lady's Manual of Moral and Intellectual Culture* (1854) are works of some substance, while the *Ladies' Almanac* (1856), the *Mother's and Young Lady's Annual* (1853), and the *Young Woman's Gift* (1851) are lighter volumes containing various types of essays and poems. All of these aid in defining current concepts of the role of women and of mothers in American society. A study in itself would be educational philosophies revealed by the guidebooks which were issued in such quantity at this time.

E. *General Didactic Works*

Certain writings addressed to the public at large stand out as being especially significant to this study. Bushnell's *Christian Nurture* ranks first as an influence in the field of religious and moral development of the young. Although this work was not published in its enlarged form until 1861 it was existent as a treatise in 1847 and was printed, according to Roorbach's listing, at least as early as the 1850's under the title *Views of Christian Nurture*. That it was known to educators is evidenced by Mrs. Horace Mann's recommendation of it in her *Moral Culture of Infancy,* a work which was written in 1843 and published in 1863.

Waterston's *Thoughts on Moral and Spiritual Culture* (1842), Lunt's pamphlet on *Moral Education* (1838), Jacob Abbott's lecture "On Moral Education" (1831) and Combe's *Moral Philosophy* (1844) reveal trends of the times with respect to moral goals and philosophies.

George Combe's *Constitution of Man* (1838) was a forerunner of several phrenological works designed to improve mankind. Other writings listed under his name and that of Orson Squire Fowler are of note for the reader interested in the relationship between phrenology and education in the nineteenth century. The article entitled "Phrenology" in the *North American Review* (1833) gives a comprehensive evaluation of this pseudo science as viewed by a critic of the period. A modern estimate of phrenology and its place in the development of psychology may be found in Boring's *A History of Experimental Psychology* (1929).

Mention was made in Chapter III of the health literature of the period, and of William Alcott's contributions in this field. Catherine Beecher's *Letters to the People on Health and Happiness* (1855) also merits notice. A work which influenced William Alcott and many other health reformers of the time was Sylvester Graham's *The Science of Human Life* (1839), a treatise of special interest in connection with this study because of its vegetarian teachings and influence on popular food habits and attitudes.

Educational controversies and philosophies of the midcentury are reflected in Horace Mann's *Annual Reports* (1839, 1841, 1844) listed under Massachusetts Board of Education, and in the *Remarks on the Seventh Annual Report of the Honorable Horace Mann* (1844) by the Association of Boston Schoolmasters. Also of note is Cobb's *The Evil Tendencies of Corporal Punishment* (1847) which influenced current attitudes toward discipline, and Brigham's *Remarks on the Influence of Mental Cultivation and Mental Excitement upon Health* (1833) which contributed to the general reaction of the times against educational precocity. Winslow's article entitled "On the Dangerous Tendency to Innovations and Extremes in Education" (1835) is interesting as portraying conservative concepts of the period, while De Saussure's *Progressive Education* (1835), translated from the French, mirrors, as Horace Mann's reports do, liberalizing influences at work in the field of education.

F. *European Influences*

While no attempt is made in this book to trace the "fireside education" theme to European origins, a number of clues have come to light in the course of the study which are useful for the student concerned with this development. The work *Progressive Education,* mentioned above, by Madame Necker de Saussure, is of great importance as a precursor of scientific American writings on the early education of children. Mrs. Willard's preface to the translation of this work quoting correspondence which passed between her and Madame de Saussure is illuminating on French concepts with respect to the role of women in society during the confused period following the French revolution. A book entitled *The French Tradition in Education* (1922) by Howard C. Barnard devotes a chapter to Madame de Saussure's influence, and her indebtedness to Rousseau. Another text of interest in this connection is *The Education of Mothers of Families* (1842) mentioned in the American preface of *Progressive Education.* This text, translated from the French of M. Aimé-Martin by Edwin Lee was published in London.

Two writings of the Swiss educator, Pestalozzi, should be noted as possible influences on American thought. One is his *Mother's Book,* mentioned as such in the *American Journal of Education* (Vol. IV, p. 100, March, 1839) and recommended to the public. The other is the English translation of his *Letters on Early Education* addressed to J. P. Greaves. An American adaptation of the latter was published in Boston under the title *Letters of Pestalozzi on the Education of Infancy* (1830). This little volume and a French translation of the *Mother's Book* entitled *Manuel des Mères de*

Pestalozzi (1821) are obtainable in the Sterling Library at Yale University. Other clues to Pestalozzian influence, as was stated previously in Chapter III, may be found in the writings of Amos Bronson Alcott, and the Reverend T. H. Gallaudet, both of whom were influenced by the Swiss educator.

Among the English writings on fireside education which appear to have had some recognition in America are: *Hints for the Improvement of Early Education* by Mrs. Louisa Hoare, which ran through fifteen editions in London and was published in New York in 1820; *Home Education* (1838) by Isaac Taylor, a work by a British author published both in New York and in London; and *Household Education* (1849) by Harriet Martineau, which was published in London and in Philadelphia. In estimating English influence, attention should also be given to the writings of Maria Edgeworth, one of Rousseau's disciples in England whose works were known and read in America in the early part of the nineteenth century. *Practical Education* by Maria and Richard L. Edgeworth appeared in the first American edition in New York in 1801. A second edition was being printed in Boston in 1815. A small volume by an American writer which shows acquaintance with Maria Edgeworth as well as with other European concepts of education is entitled *Thoughts on Domestic Education,* by a Mother, published in Boston in 1829.

II. BIBLIOGRAPHY

NOTE: Periodical articles are designated by an asterisk. In the case of three periodicals used extensively, i.e., the *Ladies' Magazine, Parent's Magazine,* and *Mother's Assistant,* articles are grouped together under the title of the periodical itself rather than listed alphabetically according to author or subject.

ABBOTT, E., et al. *Abbott's Young Christian.* Memorial ed. New York, Harper & Bros., 1882.

ABBOTT, GORHAM D. *Memoir of Nathan Dickerman* bound with Abbott, John S. C. *The Mother at Home* and *The Child at Home.* New York, American Tract Society, 1833.

ABBOTT, JACOB. *Gentle Measures in the Management of the Young.* New York, Harper & Bros., 1872.

—— *The Little Philosopher.* Boston, Carter & Hendee, 1830.

*—— "On Moral Education," Lect. 2. *American Institute of Instruction,* 2:45–64, August, 1831.

—— *New England and Her Institutions.* Boston, John Allen & Co., 1835.

—— *The Rollo Code of Morals.* Boston, Crocker & Brewster, 1841.

ABBOTT, JOHN S. C. *The Mother at Home.* 2d ed. Boston, Crocker & Brewster, 1833.

ADAMS, NEHEMIAH. *The Baptized Child.* 2d ed. Boston, William Peirce, 1836.

AIMÉ-MARTIN, M. *The Education of Mothers of Families.* Trans. from the 3d Paris ed. with remarks . . . by Edwin Lee. London, Whittaker & Co., 1842.

ALCOTT, AMOS BRONSON. *Conversations with Children on the Gospels.* 2 vols. Boston, James Munroe & Co., 1836–37.

*—— "Maternal Influence," Art. 2. *American Annals of Education and Instruction,* 3:16–24, January, 1833.

*[——] "Maternal Instruction, Hints to Parents," Art. 6, *American Journal of Education,* 4:53–58, January, 1829.

—— *Observations on the Principles and Methods of Infant Instruction.* Pamphlet. Boston, Carter & Hendee, 1830.

*ALCOTT, WILLIAM A. "Editor's Address," *The Moral Reformer,* 1:5, January, 1835.

—— *The Home Book of Life and Health.* Boston, Phillips, Sampson & Co., 1856.

—— *The House I Live In.* Boston, Light & Stearns, 1837.

—— *The Laws of Health.* Boston, John P. Jewett & Co., 1857.

—— *Vegetable Diet.* Boston, Marsh, Capen & Lyon, 1838.

—— *The Young Housekeeper.* 4th ed. Boston, George W. Light, 1839.

—— *The Young Mother.* Boston, Light & Stearns, 1836.

—— *The Young Wife.* Boston, George W. Light, 1837.

American Authors, 1600–1900. A Biographical Dictionary. Kunitz, S. J. and Haycraft, H., editors. New York, H. W. Wilson Company, 1938. See "William H. McGuffey," pp. 495–96.

ARTHUR, T. S. *The Mother.* Boston, S. Colman, 1846.

Association of Masters of the Boston Public Schools. *Remarks on the Seventh Annual Report of the Honorable Horace Mann.* Boston, Charles C. Little & James Brown, 1844.

BAILEY, EBENEZER. *The Young Ladies Class Book.* 21st ed. Boston, Gould, Kendall, & Lincoln, 1839. See especially "Childhood," pp. 239–44; "Maternal Influence," by Lydia Sigourney, pp. 263–64; "Consumption," by J. G. Percival, pp. 58–60.

BARNARD, HENRY. *Educational Development,* republished from *First Century of National Existence.* Hartford, L. Stebbins, 1873. See Appendix: "The Growth and Progress of Religious Denominations in the United States for the Past Hundred Years," pp. 590–665.

BARNARD, HOWARD C. *The French Tradition in Education.* Ramus to Mme. Necker de Saussure. Cambridge, University Press, 1922.

BARNES, GILBERT H. *The Antislavery Impulse,* 1830–1844. New York & London, D. Appleton–Century Company, Inc., 1933.

BATES, ERNEST S. *An American Faith.* New York, W. W. Norton & Co., Inc., 1940.

BEECHER, CATHERINE E., and STOWE, HARRIET B. *The American Woman's Home.* New York, J. B. Ford & Co., 1869.

BEECHER, CATHERINE E. *The Duty of American Women to Their Country.* New York, Harper & Bros., 1845.

BEECHER, CATHERINE E. *An Essay on Slavery and Abolitionism*. Philadelphia, Henry Perkins, and Boston, Perkins & Marvin, 1837.

—— *Evils Suffered by American Women and American Children*. New York, Harper & Bros., 1846.

—— *Letters to the People on Health and Happiness*. New York, Harper & Bros., 1855.

—— *Suggestions Respecting Improvements in Education*. Pamphlet. Hartford, Packard & Butler, 1829.

—— *A Treatise on Domestic Economy*. Revised ed. Boston, Thomas H. Webb & Co., 1842.

—— *The True Remedy for the Wrongs of Woman*. Boston, 1851.

BEECHER, HENRY WARD. *Life Thoughts*. Edna Dean Proctor, editor. Boston, Phillips, Sampson & Co., 1858.

BERGER, MAX. *The British Traveller in America, 1836–1860*. New York, Columbia University Press, 1943.

BOAS, LOUISE S. *Woman's Education Begins*. Norton, Mass., Wheaton College Press, 1935.

BOLZAU, EMMA LYDIA. *Almira Hart Lincoln Phelps*. Philadelphia (Lancaster, Pa.), Science Press Printing Company, 1936.

BORING, EDWIN G. *A History of Experimental Psychology*. New York and London, Century Company, 1929. (Copyright, 1929, D. Appleton–Century Company, Inc.)

BRANCH, E. DOUGLAS. *The Sentimental Years, 1836–1860*. New York, D. Appleton–Century Company, Inc., 1934.

BRIGHAM, AMARIAH. *Remarks on the Influence of Mental Cultivation and Mental Excitement upon Health*. Boston, Marsh, Capen & Lyon, 1833.

BROOKS, VAN WYCK. *The Flowering of New England*. New York, E. P. Dutton & Co., 1940.

BRUBACHER, JOHN S., editor. *Henry Barnard on Education*. New York & London, McGraw-Hill Book Company, Inc., 1931.

BUNN, ALFRED. *Old England and New England*. London, R. Bentley; Philadelphia, reprinted by A. Hart, 1853.

BURNS, JABEZ. *Mothers of the Wise and Good*. 4th ed. Boston, Gould & Lincoln, 1851.

BUSHNELL, HORACE. *Christian Nurture*. New York, Charles Scribner & Co., 1867.

CALHOUN, ARTHUR W. *A Social History of the American Family*. 2 vols. Cleveland, Arthur H. Clark Company, 1918.

CALVERTON, V. F., and SCHMALHAUSEN, SAMUEL D., editors. *The New Generation*. New York, Macaulay Company, 1930.

See "Family Life: A Study in Pathology" by S. D. Schmalhausen, pp. 275–303; and "The Pathos of Parenthood" by B. Liber, pp. 304–329.

CHILD, LYDIA M. *The American Frugal Housewife*. Boston, American Stationers' Company, 1836.

—— *An Appeal in Favor of That Class of Americans Called Africans*. Boston, Allen & Ticknor, 1833.

—— *Brief History of the Condition of Women in Various Ages and Nations*. 5th ed. 2 vols. in one. New York, C. S. Francis & Co., 1845.

—— *Good Wives.* Boston, Carter, Hendee & Co., 1833.

—— *The Mother's Book.* 2d ed. Boston, Carter & Hendee, 1831.

COBB, LYMAN. *The Evil Tendencies of Corporal Punishment.* New York, Mark H. Newman & Co., 1847.

COMBE, ANDREW. *The Physiology of Digestion.* 1st American ed. Boston, Marsh, Capen & Lyon, 1836.

—— *The Principles of Physiology Applied to the Preservation of Health.* New York, Harper & Bros., 1834.

—— *A Treatise on the Physiological and Moral Management of Infancy.* 2d ed. Edinburgh, Maclachlan, Stewart & Co., 1841.

COMBE, GEORGE. *The Constitution of Man.* Boston, William D. Ticknor, 1838.

—— *Lectures on Popular Education.* 1st American ed. Boston, Marsh, Capen & Lyon, 1834.

—— *Moral Philosophy.* New York, William H. Colyer; Boston, Lewis & Sampson, 1844.

—— *A System of Phrenology.* 2d ed. Edinburgh, John Anderson, 1825.

DE BOW, J. D. B., *Mortality Statistics of the Seventh Census of the U. S., 1850.* Washington, A. O. P. Nicholson, 1855.

DE SAUSSURE, MADAME NECKER. *Progressive Education.* Trans. from the French: with notes and an appendix by Emma Willard and Almira H. L. Phelps. Boston, William D. Ticknor, 1835.

DE TOCQUEVILLE, ALEXIS. *Democracy in America.* H. Reeve, trans. 3d American ed. New York, George Adlard, 1839.

DEWEES, WILLIAM P. *A Treatise on the Physical and Medical Treatment of Children.* 4th ed. Philadelphia, Carey & Lea, 1832.

*DICK. "Clothing of Children," *Family Magazine*, 4:461–62, 1837.

Dictionary of American Biography. 20 vols. New York, C. Scribner's, 1928–44.

    See especially "Jacob Abbott," I, 21–22; "John S. C. Abbott," I, 22–23; "Nehemiah Adams," I, 93–94; "William A. Alcott," I, 142–43; "Harvey Newcomb," XIII, 450–51; "Hubbard Winslow," XX, 396; "Daniel Wise," XX, 422–23.

* "Dissertation on the Sinfulness of Infants," *Christian Disciple*, 2:245–50, August, 1814.

* "Dresses for Infants," *Godey's Lady's Book*, 40:142, February, 1850.

DWIGHT, THEODORE. *The Father's Book.* Springfield, G. and C. Merriam, 1834.

EDGEWORTH, MARIA and RICHARD L. *On Practical Education.* 2d American ed. 2 vols. Boston, T. B. Wait & Sons, 1815.

FERN, FANNY (MRS. SARAH P. PARTON). *Fresh Leaves.* New York, Mason Brothers, 1857.

FINLEY, RUTH E. *The Lady of Godey's.* Philadelphia and London, J. B. Lippincott Company, 1931.

FISH, CARL R. *The Rise of the Common Man, 1830–1850.* A. M. Schlesinger and D. R. Fox, editors, *A History of American Life*, Vol. VI. New York, Macmillan Company, 1929.

FLEMING, SANDFORD. *Children and Puritanism.* New Haven, Yale University Press, 1933.

FOWLER, ORSON SQUIRE. *Education and Self-Improvement.* Founded on Phrenology. 2d ed. enlarged. New York, O. S. and L. N. Fowler, 1844.

FOWLER, ORSON SQUIRE. *Fowler on Memory*, or Phrenology Applied to the Cultivation of Memory . . . 2d ed. enlarged. New York, O. S. and L. N. Fowler, 1842.

—— *Hereditary Descent.* New York, Fowlers & Wells, 1854.

FOWLER, O. S. and L. N. *Self Instructor in Phrenology and Physiology.* New York, Fowlers & Wells, 1855.

*FRANK, LAWRENCE K. "The Fundamental Needs of the Child," *Mental Hygiene*, 22:353–79, July, 1938.

FURNESS, CLIFTON J., editor. *The Genteel Female.* New York, Alfred A. Knopf, 1931.

GABRIEL, RALPH H. *The Course of American Democratic Thought.* New York, Ronald Press Company, 1940.

GALLAUDET, T. H. *Child's Book on the Soul.* Parts 1 and 2. Hartford, Cooke & Co., 1831.

GESELL, ARNOLD. *The Guidance of Mental Growth in Infant and Child.* New York, Macmillan Company, 1930.

GOODRICH, SAMUEL G. *Fireside Education.* New York, F. J. Huntington & Co., 1838.

—— *Recollections of a Lifetime.* 2 vols. New York and Auburn, Miller, Orton & Mulligan, 1856.

GOODSELL, WILLYSTINE. *A History of Marriage and the Family.* New York, Macmillan Company, 1934.

GRAHAM, SYLVESTER. *Lectures on the Science of Human Life.* London, William L. Orsell, 1839.

GRAVES, MRS. A. J. *Woman in America.* New York, Harper & Bros., 1843.

GRISWOLD, R. G. *The Prose Writers of America.* 2d ed. Philadelphia, Carey & Hart, 1847.
  See especially "Influence of Woman" by Daniel Webster, p. 185; and "The Love of a Mother" by Washington Irving, p. 218.

GROVES, ERNEST R. *The American Woman.* New York, Greenberg, 1937. [2d ed. New York, Emerson Books, Inc., copyright, 1944.]

HAIGHT, GORDON S. *Mrs. Sigourney, the Sweet Singer of Hartford.* New Haven, Yale University Press, 1930.

HALE, SARAH J. *Woman's Record.* 3d ed., revised. New York, Harper & Bros., 1870.
  See especially "Harriet Martineau," pp. 739–42; "Mary Wollstonecraft Shelley," pp. 780–81; "Sarah Margaret Fuller," pp. 665–70; "Madame de Stael," pp. 517–19, and "Madame de Saussure," p. 886.

HALL, JOHN. *On the Education of Children.* 2d ed. Hartford, Canfield & Robins, 1836.

HART, JOHN S. *The Female Prose Writers of America.* Philadelphia, E. H. Butler & Co., 1852.
  See especially, "Catherine Sedgwick," pp. 17–25; "Sarah G. Hale," pp. 93–99; "Louisa C. Tuthill," pp. 100–104; "Lydia M. Child," pp. 116–27; Ann E. Porter's "Cousin Helen's Baby," pp. 346–52.

HARVESON, MAE ELIZABETH. *Catherine Esther Beecher, Pioneer Educator.* Dissertation, University of Pennsylvania, Philadelphia, 1932.

HINSDALE, B. A. *Horace Mann and the Common School Revival in the United States.* New York, Charles Scribner's Sons, 1937.

HOARE, MRS. LOUISA. *Hints for the Improvement of Early Education.* New York, Collins & Co., 1820.

Homes of American Authors. New York, G. P. Putnam & Co., 1853.
See especially, Catherine Sedgwick, pp. 159–76.

HUMPHREY, HEMAN. *Domestic Education.* Amherst, J. S. and C. Adams, 1840.

—— *The Life and Labors of the Reverend T. H. Gallaudet.* New York, Robert Carter & Bros., 1857.

* "Infant Schools," Art. 2, *American Annals of Education and Instruction,* 3:296–304, July, 1833.

IRWIN, INEZ HAYNES. *Angels and Amazons.* Garden City, N. Y., Doubleday Doran & Co., Inc., 1933.

KISSAM, RICHARD S. *The Nurses' Manual and Young Mother's Guide.* Hartford, Cooke & Co., 1834.

Ladies Almanac. Boston, Shepard, Clark & Brown, 1856.
See especially, "Hints to Young Mothers on the Physical Management of Children," p. 80.

*Ladies' Magazine. Boston, 1828–1836. Variant titles are *The Ladies' Magazine and Literary Gazette* and *The American Ladies' Magazine.*
Important for the following articles:
"American Institute of Instruction," 6:422–23, September, 1833; "American Manners," 8:507–9, September, 1835; "Beauty," 3:31–35, January, 1830; "Boarding Schools," 4:145–54, April, 1831; Books and Authors, reviewing Combe's *Lectures on Popular Education,* 7:376–79, July, 1834; "Causes of Insanity," quoted from Amariah Brigham, 7:79, January, 1834; "A Chapter from 'The Book of Marriage,'" 6:261–65, June, 1833; "Children's Dresses," 6:463, October, 1833; "Fashion," by Mathew Carey, 7:148–52, April, 1834; "Fashion," by L. E., 3:311–15, July, 1830; "Fashionable Follies," 3:181–87, April, 1830; "Female Biography," 7:41, January, 1834; "From a Mother's Diary," 4:128–30, January, 1831; "The Good Dinner," 6:38–40, January, 1833; "Dr. Grigg's Lecture," 4:514–18, November, 1831; "Hints to Young Mothers," 7:52, February, 1834; "Home" by L. E., 3:217–20, May, 1830; "Infant Schools," 3:224–26, November, 1830; "Infant Schools," 5:179–82, April, 1832; "The Influence of Women on Society," by Bolles, 4:256–69, May, 1831; Literary Notice on A. B. Alcott's *Observations on the Principles and Methods of Infant Instruction,* 3:533, November, 1830; Literary Notice on Lydia M. Child's *Good Wives,* 6:237–39, May, 1833; Literary Notice on *Incidents in the Life of President Dwight,* 4:335, July, 1831; "The Mode," 4:193–96, May, 1831; "A Mother's Journal," extracts from Phelps' *Observations upon an Infant,* 8:441–49, August, 1835; "The Mother," by Sarah J. Hale, 7:567–70, December, 1834; "The Mother of Washington," 4:385–94, September, 1831; "Physical Education of Women," 4:30–36, January, 1831; "A Plea for Children," by C. Sedgwick, 8:93–99, February, 1835; "The Pledge," 7:134, March, 1834; "Principles and Influence of Taste," 3:80–85, February, 1830; "Privileges of American Ladies," 3:40–41, January, 1830; "The Question," 7:476–78, October, 1834; "Religion Is the Strength of Woman," 7:222–28, May, 1834; "Should Females Be Employed in Cookery?" 7:481–87, November, 1834; "Sentiment" by Spurzheim, 6:423,

September, 1833; "A Sketch from Life," 6:258–60, June, 1833; "A Supplement to a Plea for Children," 8:597–604, November, 1835; "What Good Will Phrenology Do the Ladies?" by Sarah J. Hale, 5:474, October, 1832; "Mrs. Willard on Female Education," 7:163–73, April, 1834; "Woman's Sphere," 8:262–67, May, 1835; "The Worth of Money," 3:49–55, February, 1830.

LARCOM, LUCY. *A New England Girlhood.* Boston, New York and Chicago, Houghton Mifflin & Co., 1889.

LESLEY, SUSAN I. *Recollections of My Mother.* Boston and New York, Houghton Mifflin & Co., 1899.

Letters of Pestalozzi on the Education of Infancy. Boston, Carter & Hendee, 1830.

LIVERMORE, GEORGE. *The Origin, History and Character of the New England Primer.* New York, Charles Fred Heartman, 1915.

LUNT, WILLIAM P. *Moral Education.* Pamphlet. Quincy, John A. Green, 1838.

MACKAY, ALEXANDER. *The Western World, or Travels in the U. S. in 1846–47.* 2 vols. Philadelphia, Lea & Blanchard, 1849.

MANN, HORACE. *Annual Reports* (see Massachusetts Board of Education).

*—— "Editor's Address," *Common School Journal,* 7:3–21, January, 1845.

*—— "Intellectual Education," *Common School Journal,* 1:11–13, November, 1838.

*—— "Value and Necessity of Education," *Common School Journal,* 1:4, November, 1838.

MANN, MRS. HORACE, and PEABODY, ELIZABETH P. *Moral Culture of Infancy, and Kindergarten Guide.* Boston, T. O. H. P. Burnham, 1863.

MANSFIELD, EDWARD D. *The Legal Rights, Liabilities, and Duties of Women.* Salem, John P. Jewett & Co., 1845.

Manuel des Meres de Pestalozzi traduit de l'Allemand. Geneve et Paris, J. J. Paschond, 1821.

MARTINEAU, HARRIET. *Household Education.* Philadelphia, Lea & Blanchard, 1849.

—— *Society in America.* 3 vols. London, Saunders & Otley, 1837.

Massachusetts Board of Education. *Annual Reports.* Boston, Dutton & Wentworth, 1838–47.
    Important for the following:
Horace Mann, *Second Annual Report of the Secretary of the Board of Education,* 1839; *Fourth Annual Report . . . ,* 1841; and *Seventh Annual Report . . . ,* 1844.

MCCUSKEY, DOROTHY. *Bronson Alcott, Teacher.* New York, Macmillan Company, 1940.

Mother's Assistant. Boston, 1841–63(?). Variant titles are *Mother's Assistant, Young Ladies' Friend and Family Manuel; Mother's Assistant and Fireside Miscellany* and *Mother's Assistant and Child's Friend.*
    Important for the following articles:
"Advantages of Maternal Associations," by Harvey Newcomb, 3:197–200, September, 1843; "Cheap Publications," by Reverend F. P. Tracy, 3:175–76, August, 1843; "Common Sense and Daily Events," by Reverend A. P. Peabody, 5:31–32, August, 1844; "The Conversion of

My Little Daughter," 4:74–81, April, 1844; "Culture of the Passions," editorial, pp. 143–45, 1853; "Did You Ever Take Me in Your Arms to Christ?" by Reverend P. C. Headly, pp. 153–54, 1853; "Domestic Education," by Mrs. H. F. Hunt, 10:50–53, July, 1850; "The Emigrant's Daughter," by Mrs. S. P. Clark, 9:39–43, August, 1846; "The Era for Mothers," by William M. Thayer, pp. 129–46, May, 1851; "Exactness, a Family Conversation," editorial, pp. 127–33, 1853; "Example," 3:13, January, 1843; "The Family School," by Charles Holden, 3:247–49, November, 1843; "Female Culture," by Miss S. C. Edgarton, 3:94–95, April, 1843; "Female Heroism," by Catherine Leicester, 23:119, October, 1852; "Form and Principle," by J. S. Lunt, 9:73–80, 97–107, November, 1846; "Frequency of Nursing," by Andrew Combe, M. D., 3:11–13, January, 1843; "Health," editorial, pp. 174–81, 1853; "How Children May Make Their Parents Happy," 9:121–38, December, 1846; "How to Train Your Children Aright," by Mrs. L. Pillsbury, 8:1–6, January, 1846; "Influence of Female Literature on Female Character," by Reverend Andrew A. Lipscomb, 7:61–69, September, 1845; "Introductory Address," by the editors, 1:1–8, September, 1840; "Leading Children to God," 9:141–42, December, 1846; "Lessons of Benevolence," by William A. Alcott, 4:30–31, February, 1844; "Maternal Relation," by O. P. Farrington, 23:48, August, 1852; "Maternal Responsibility," by Reverend David A. Strong, pp. 97–101, April, 1851; "Mothers Can Do Great Things," by Reverend S. J. Prime, 3:227, October, 1843; "The Oak and the Vine," by Mrs. Sarah E. Goodhue, 13:140, November, 1848; "Paternal Duty," by President Wayland, 12:110, May, 1848; "Providence," poem, p. 116, 1853; "Punishments," by Jacob Abbott, 1:74–77, February, 1841; "Responsibility of Authors and Readers," by S. G. Goodrich, 1:33–35, February, 1841; "The Restored Family," by Mrs. M. O. Stevens, 4:97–119, May, 1844; "Rewards and Punishments," by Harvey Newcomb, 3:29–32, February, 1843; "Single and Married," by Mrs. Isaac Hatch, 9:11–23, July, 1846; "There Is No School Like the Family School," by William A. Alcott, 3:1–3, January, 1843; "The Toilet," p. 188, July, 1851; "Truth Triumphant, or the Bible Vindicated," by Reverend Matlack, 12:1–13, 25–37, January, 1848; "Was It Providence?" by Miss Sedgwick, 5:71–72, September, 1844; "A Word with Mothers," by Susan A. Tucker, 3:145–50, July, 1843.

Mother's and Young Lady's Annual. Boston, Cyrus Stone, 1853.

MUNGER, THEODORE T. *Horace Bushnell, Preacher and Theologian.* Boston and New York, Houghton Mifflin & Co., 1899.

* "The Murder of the Innocents," *Atlantic Monthly*, 4:345–56, September, 1859.

MUZZEY, REVEREND A. B. *The Fireside.* Boston, Crosby, Nichols & Co., 1856.

NEWCOMB, HARVEY. *First Question Book.* Revised ed. Vol. I. Boston, Massachusetts Sabbath School Society, 1837.

—— *The Young Lady's Guide to the Harmonious Development of Christian Character.* 5th ed. revised. Boston, 1843.

* "On the Influence of Education as a Source of Error," *Christian Disciple*, 2:264–67, September, 1814.

OSSOLI, MARGARET FULLER. *Woman in the Nineteenth Century* in "Works of Margaret Fuller," Vol. III. Boston, Roberts Brothers, 1874.

Parent's Magazine. Gilmanton and Concord, N. H., 1840–1850(?). Variant titles are *Parent's Monitor and Young Peoples' Friend* and *Parent's Magazine and Young Peoples' Friend.*

Important for the following articles:

"The Abuse of Works on Education," 2:145–47, March, 1842; "Bearing of Parental Fidelity on the Millennium," 1:52–57, 73–77, November, December, 1840; "Causes of Indifference and Neglect among Parents," by Reverend S. R. Hall, 1:37–41, October, 1840; "Caution to Parents," 1:203–5, May, 1841; "Christian Education," 1:199–203, May, 1841; "On Cultivating a Benevolent Spirit in Children," 2:195–97, May, 1842; "Domestic Happiness," 1:258–59, July, 1841; "Don't Be So Troublesome," 2:218–19, June, 1842; "Early Discipline," by Harvey Newcomb, 2:271–72, August, 1842; "Education of Young Ladies," by Willis G. Clark, 2:149–51, March, 1842; "End of Insubordination," 2:105–6, January, 1842; "Extracts from the Report of the N. H. Maternal Association," by A. C. Curtis, 1:81–85, December, 1840; "Family Scenes, No. 1," 2:12–13, September, 1841; "Family Scenes, No. 2," 2:80–81, December, 1841; "Family Worship," 1:121–26, February, 1841; "The Father," 2:174–75, April, 1842; "For What Is a Mother Responsible?" 1:220–22, June, 1841; "Formation of Habits," 2:272–74, August, 1842; "The Government of Children," by H. Rood, 1:105–7, January, 1841; "The Ground of Parental Obligation, No. 6," 2:235–36, June, 1842; "An Interview with Convicts in the N. H. State Prison," 1:234–38, June, 1841; "List of Books Recommended for the Library of a Maternal Association," 1:282–83, August, 1841; "The Little Foot," by Miss H. F. Gould, 1:71–72, December, 1840; "The Little Hand," by Lydia Sigourney, 1:95, December, 1840; "Maternal Associations," 1:205–7, May, 1841; "To Mothers and Nurses," 1:245–46, July, 1841; "A Mother's Prayers Are Not Easily Forgotten," 1:145–47, January, 1841; "Management of Infants," 2:3–4, September, 1841; "My Mother," 1:168, March, 1841; "No. 2—Obedience in Children," by H. Rood, 1:77–80, December, 1840; "On Physical Education," 2:217–18, June, 1842; "Our Country," by Mr. Welch, 2:25–26, October, 1841; "Paternal Neglect," by John S. C. Abbott, 2:147–49, March, 1842; "Responsibility of the Mother," 1:154–56, March, 1841; "Rules for Family Government," by Harvey Newcomb, 2:96, December, 1841; "A Sailor's Mother," 1:115–16, January, 1841; "Self-Discipline," 2:257, July, 1842; "Stinginess," 2:118, January, 1842; "Teething," 2:167–68, March, 1842; "Temperance," by Reverend E. N. Kirk, 1:21–22, September, 1840; "The Time to Begin," 1:162–63, March, 1841; "To the Editors of the Parent's Magazine," 1:129–30, February, 1841; "Topics of Conversation at Maternal Meetings," 1:283–87, August, 1841.

PARRINGTON, VERNON L. *Main Currents in American Thought.* 3 vols. New York, Harcourt Brace & Co., 1927–30.

PARTON, JAMES, GREELEY, HORACE, et al. *Eminent Women of the Age.* Hartford, S. M. Betts & Co., 1868.

See especially, "Fanny Fern—Mrs. Parton" by Grace Greenwood, pp. 66–84.

PATTEE, FRED LEWIS. *The Feminine Fifties.* New York & London, D. Appleton-Century Company, 1940.

PHELPS, ALMIRA H. L. *Female Student,* or Lectures to Young Ladies on Female Education. 2d ed. New York, Leavitt, Lord & Co.; Boston, Crocker & Brewster, 1836.

—— "Observations upon an Infant," pp. 323–48, Appendix in De Saussure, *Progressive Education.*

—— "Remarks on the Education of Girls," *Godey's Lady's Book,* 18:253–55, June, 1839.

"Phrenology," *Encyclopaedia Britannica,* 11th ed. XXI, 534–41.

"Phrenology," *New International Encyclopedia,* 2d ed. XVIII, 568–69.

* "Phrenology," Art. 3. *North American Review,* 37:59–83, July, 1833.

PRUETTE, LORINE. *The Parent and the Happy Child.* New York, Henry Holt & Co., 1932.

READ, THOMAS B. *The Female Poets of America.* 6th ed. revised. Philadelphia, E. H. Butler & Co., 1855.

* "Recent Publications," *Spirit of the Pilgrims,* 5:122, February, 1832.

* "Review of Spurzheim on Education," Art. 3. *American Annals of Education and Instruction,* 3:122–28, March, 1833.

ROLLER, BERT. *Children in American Poetry, 1610–1900.* George Peabody College for Teachers, Nashville, Tenn., 1930.

Roorbach, O. A. *Bibliotheca Americana, 1820–1852.* Catalogue of American Publications. New York, Peter Smith, 1939.

RUSSELL, WILLIAM. Prospectus, *American Journal of Education,* 1:3, January, 1826.

SAIT, UNA B. *New Horizons for the Family.* New York, Macmillan Company, 1938.

SCHMALHAUSEN, SAMUEL D., and CALVERTON, V. F., editors. *Woman's Coming of Age.* New York, Horace Liveright, Inc., 1931.

    See especially, "Why Women Fail" by Lorine Pruette, pp. 240–59.

SEDGWICK, CATHERINE M. *Home.* New ed. Cambridge, John Wilson & Son, 1875.

—— *Live and Let Live.* New York, Harper & Bros., 1837.

—— *The Morals of Manners.* New ed. revised. New York, J. Miller, 1864.

—— *Redwood.* Revised ed. New York, George P. Putnam, 1850.

*SEDGWICK, THEODORE. "Causes of Poverty in the United States," *Family Magazine,* 5:213–14, November, 1837.

*—— "Poverty of the Manufacturing Class," *The Family Magazine,* 5:254–56, December, 1837.

SHEPARD, ODELL, editor. *The Journals of Bronson Alcott.* Boston, Little, Brown, & Co., 1938.

SIGOURNEY, LYDIA H. *Letters to Mothers.* Hartford, Hudson & Skinner, 1838.

—— *Letters to Young Ladies.* Hartford, P. Canfield, 1833.

—— *The Daily Counsellor.* 3d ed. Hartford, Brown & Gross, 1859.

—— *The Girl's Reading Book.* 9th ed. New York, J. O. Taylor, 1839.

SPOCK, BENJAMIN, M. D. *The Common Sense Book of Baby and Child Care.* New York, Duell, Sloan & Pearce, 1945.

STEARNS, BERTHA M. "New England Magazines for Ladies," *The New England Quarterly,* 3:627–56, October, 1930.

STEWART, DUGALD. *Elements of the Philosophy of the Human Mind.* 2 vols. Edinburgh, T. and T. Clark, 1877.

STOWE, HARRIET BEECHER. *Oldtown Folks.* Boston, Fields, Osgood & Co., 1869.

TAYLOR, ISAAC. *Home Education.* New York, D. Appleton & Co., 1838.

*THAYER, WILLIAM M. "Editor's Address," *Happy Home and Parlor Magazine,* 7:15–16, January, 1858.

—— *Life at the Fireside.* Boston, Congregational Board of Publications, 1857.

Thoughts on Domestic Education by a Mother. Boston, Carter & Hendee, 1829.

TRENT, W. P., et al., editors. *Cambridge History of American Literature.* 4 vols. New York, G. P. Putnam's Sons; Cambridge, England, University Press, 1918.

    See "Divines and Moralists" by Samuel Wolff, II, 196–223; and "Books for Children" by Algernon Tassin, II, 396–409.

The True History of the Late Division in the Anti-Slavery Societies, from *Second Annual Report of the Massachusetts Abolition Society.* Pamphlet. Boston, David H. Ela, 1841.

TUTHILL, LOUISA C. *The Young Lady's Home.* New Haven, S. Babcock, 1839.

*—— "Letter to a Young Mother," *Happy Home and Parlor Magazine,* 7:363–66, 1858.

The Visitor. Boston, Peirce & Williams, 1829.

WADE, MASON, *Margaret Fuller, Whetstone of Genius.* New York, Viking Press, 1940.

WARNER, SUSAN (pseud. ELIZABETH WETHERELL). *The Wide Wide World.* New York, George P. Putnam, 1851.

WATERSTON, R. C. *Thoughts on Moral and Spiritual Culture.* Boston, Crocker & Ruggles, 1842.

WEBER, MAX. *The Protestant Ethic.* London, Allen & Unwin, Ltd., 1930.

WELSH, SISTER MARY MICHAEL. *Catherine Maria Sedgwick.* Washington, Catholic University of America, 1937.

WILLARD, EMMA. *A Treatise on the Motive Powers Which Produce the Circulation of the Blood.* New York and London, Wiley & Putnam, 1846.

*WINSLOW, HUBBARD. "On the Dangerous Tendency to Innovations and Extremes in Education," Lect. 7. *American Institute of Instruction,* Vol. V. Boston, Carter, Hendee & Co., 1835.

—— and SANDFORD, MRS. JOHN. *The Lady's Manual of Moral and Intellectual Culture.* (Other title, *The Benison,* a gift book.) New York, Leavitt & Allen, 1854.

—— *Woman as She Should Be.* 2d London ed. Boston, T. H. Carter, 1838.

WISE, DANIEL. *The Young Lady's Counsellor.* New York, Eaton & Mains, 1851.

WOLLSTONECRAFT, MARY. *A Vindication of the Rights of Woman.* 3d ed. London, J. Johnson, 1796.

*WOODBRIDGE, WILLIAM C. "Editor's Address," *American Annals of Education and Instruction.* New series. 1:325–32, August, 1830.

The Young Woman's Gift. Cotesworth Pinckney, editor. Boston, J. Buffum, 1851.

    See especially, "The Duties of Woman," pp. 48–54, and "My Mother," pp. 40–41.

APPENDIX A

A Kinship of Reform

THE web of relationships which drew some of the domestic reformers of New England together throws an interesting side-light on the interaction of their ideas. This is especially revealing as it touches upon the activities of the transcendental group, the educational innovators, and the religious group, composed of orthodox and semi-orthodox reformers.

The first two groups were interrelated, in Boston and Cambridge, especially by ties of blood, of marriage, of friendship, and of ideas. Consider, for example, the following facts: Margaret Fuller's "Conversations" attracted, and exposed to transcendental ideas, the Peabody sisters, Elizabeth and Mary, and Lydia Maria Child,[1] all of whom were concerned with the nurture of young children. Elizabeth Peabody had assisted Bronson Alcott in his Temple School, as had also Margaret Fuller.[2] Mary Peabody produced her letters on the *Moral Culture of Infancy* during these years [3] and was presumably influenced by the liberal ideas of her associates. Since she was shortly to become the second wife of Horace Mann, this connection with the transcendentalist group is of some significance. Mann, it is said, was a devotee of Emerson.[4]

Mrs. Child had written her *Mother's Book* some years earlier and doubtless furthered the domestic cause in this group. She and Margaret Fuller had studied Locke together in their student days.[5]

Bronson Alcott and Dr. William Alcott were cousins. This relationship between the transcendentalist educator and the more orthodox crusader for physical reforms was a fruitful one according to Odell Shepard, who states, "there is a sense in which nearly everything that Bronson wrote and did is attributable to William. Presumably because of Bronson's early abandonment of orthodox religious faith, the two drifted slowly apart, but the effects of their close association in boyhood and youth were never obliterated." [6]

William Alcott may also be judged to have absorbed some of Bronson's ideas which he fed into the stream of orthodox thought together with new phrenological concepts. His comment on Bronson's much talked of "Record of a School" would indicate that he did not reject all of the ideas of his

1. Wade, Margaret Fuller, *Whetstone of Genius*, p. 75.
2. *Ibid.*, p. 35.
3. This work did not come out in book form until 1863, twenty years after it was written. Cf. Mann and Peabody, *Moral Culture of Infancy, and Kindergarten Guide*, p. iv.
4. *D. A. B.*, XII, 243.
5. Wade, *op. cit.*, p. 15.
6. Odell Shepard, editor, *The Journals of Bronson Alcott* (Boston, Little, Brown & Co., 1938), p. xv.

criticized cousin. "We say the book is not just such a book as we should make," William declared, "and yet we are by no means sure that it does not contain more excellencies than any which we could prepare, as well as fewer faults. It certainly affords many capital hints, and cannot but be valuable to every teacher who THINKS." [7]

Another center of interest from the point of view of relationships was Amherst, Massachusetts. Heman Humphrey was president of Amherst College when Jacob Abbott came there as a young instructor.[8] Gorham Abbott was also in Amherst at this time as director of the Academy. Amherst was a stronghold of religious orthodoxy but it drew something of liberalism from the breadth of view of its president, who was at this time leading classes in mental and moral philosophy. It is interesting to note that Mrs. Jacob Abbott was corresponding, during this Amherst period with her dear friend, Mary Peabody.[9] Of the three Abbott brothers, Jacob was the one who was to draw praise, in later years, from Horace Mann and to cross the bridge from narrow orthodoxy to a qualified liberalism. In the interim between the time he left Amherst and his later period of ripening, he was associated with the conservative Hubbard Winslow, and with Nehemiah Adams as co-editor of *The Religious Magazine*.[10]

Of Humphrey himself and the progress of his ideas, a relationship of especial interest was that which he sustained with T. H. Gallaudet, the Hartford educator and divine. Humphrey published his *Life and Labors of the Reverend T. H. Gallaudet* in 1857.

Catherine Beecher's Female Seminary was located in Hartford. That Gallaudet was in sympathy with her ideas may be judged from his inscription on a copy of her pamphlet entitled *Suggestions Respecting Improvements in Education*.[11]

In the Beecher family, Catherine and her sister Harriet collaborated in the writing of *The American Woman's Home*. However their ideas may have differed on the slavery question, they were united on the subject of domestic reform. It should be noted of Henry Ward Beecher, their brother, that he was at one time associated with Orson Squire Fowler, the phrenologist.[12]

Emma Willard was the sister of Almira Phelps and together they translated Madame De Saussure's *Progressive Education*. Of this work, William Alcott said, "we can discover but one prominent fault in it; which is that it is too solid and excellent to be valued by the present generation of superficial readers." [13]

7. William Alcott, "Books and Periodicals," *Moral Reformer*, 1:383–84, December, 1835.
8. E. Abbott et al., *Abbott's Young Christian*, p. 28.
9. *Ibid.*, pp. 34–38.
10. *D. A. B.*, XX, 396.
11. This inscribed pamphlet is in the possession of the Sterling Memorial Library, Yale University.
12. Branch, *The Sentimental Years*, p. 278.
13. William Alcott, "Books and Periodicals," *Moral Reformer*, 1:260, August, 1835.

Boston and the Open Mind

R. C. Waterston, Boston author, Sunday school teacher, and educational theorist recommended that teachers engage in group discussions on the subject of moral education. The preparation for these discussions, as he suggested it, seems to express the Boston spirit of eclecticism in reform. "Would it not be well," he said, "for teachers to have in their library whatever books there may be of this nature? Todd's, Abbott's, Wayland's, Gallaudet's; Phrenological or Transcendental; on Morals, on the Soul, on Nature, on Revelation. Let them be read and studied; the good retained, the bad rejected. Even that which does not answer the wishes of the teacher, may suggest to him a good he might otherwise never have found." [14]

Harriet Martineau, commenting on the Boston temper some years earlier had noted a readiness to accept new ideas, but deplored the lack of balance which led to fanatic extremes in the application of these ideas: "The good people of Boston are more fond of excitement than of consistency. . . . When Spurzheim was there, the brain was everything; and his wise and benevolent remonstrances about the neglect or abuse of the bodily powers were received with great candour, and with much apparent conviction. Short as the interval has been, a considerable number of his disciples have gone directly over to the opposite philosophy; and in their spiritualism out-herod Herod. They frame their theory and practice on the principle that human beings are created perfect spirits in an infant body. Some go further back than this, and actually teach little children dogmatically that spirit makes body; and that their own bodies are the result of the efforts of their spirits to manifest themselves. . . . There is a school in Boston . . . conducted on this principle. The master presupposes his little pupils possessed of all truth, in philosophy and morals; and that his business is . . . to help the outward life to conform to the inner light . . . those who survive the neglect of bodily exercises and over-excitement of brain, will be found the first to throw off moral restraints, on perceiving at length that their moral guide had been employing their early years in the pursuit of shadows and the contempt of realities." [15]

APPENDIX B

Notes on the Child

Horace Mann on Nature and Nurture. "Consider then his condition when first ushered into life. He is encompassed by a universe of relations, each one of which will prove a blessing or a curse, just according to the position which he may sustain towards it, and yet in regard to all these relations it is to him a universe of darkness. All his faculties and powers are susceptible of a right direction and control, and, if obedient to them, blessings innumerable and inexhaustible will be lavished upon him. But all his powers and faculties are also liable to a wrong direction and control; and, obedient to them, he

14. Waterston, *Thoughts on Moral and Spiritual Culture*, p. 169.
15. Martineau, *Society in America*, III, 174–76. There can be little doubt that Miss Martineau was referring, here, to Bronson Alcott's Temple School.

becomes a living wound, and the universe of encompassing relations presses upon him only to torture him. And yet into this universe of opportunities for happiness on the one hand, and of dangers and temptations on the other, he is brought, without any knowledge whither he should go or what he should do, —by what means he shall secure happiness or avert misery. To leave such a being physically alone, that is, to refuse to provide nourishment, raiment, protection against the seasons and the elements, would be to ensure his destruction. But such abandonment would be mercy, compared with leaving him alone intellectually and morally. Nor is it guidance merely that he needs; for his guides will be soon removed in the course of nature, when he will be left with the dreadful heritage only of an enlarged consciousness of wants with equal inability to supply them. . . . Before, then, his natural protectors and guardians and teachers are removed, they will leave their work undone if he have not been prepared to protect and guide and teach himself. Nay, if the generation that is, do not raise above their own level the generation that is to be, the race must remain stationary, and the sublime law of human progression be defeated." [16]

Peter Parley's Appeal to a Mother. "You have a child on your knee. Listen a moment. Do you know what that child is? It is an immortal being; destined to live forever! It is destined to be happy or miserable! And who is to make it happy or miserable? You—the mother! You, who gave it birth, the mother of its body, are also the mother of its soul for good or ill. Its character is yet undecided; its destiny is placed in your hands. What shall it be? That child may be a liar. You can prevent it. It may be a drunkard. You can prevent it. It may be a thief. You can prevent it. It may be an atheist. You can prevent it. It may live a life of misery to itself and mischief to others. You can prevent it. It may descend into the grave with an evil memory behind and dread before. You can prevent it. Yes, you, the mother, can prevent all these things. Will you, or will you not? Look at the innocent! Tell me again, will you save it? Will you watch over it, will you teach it, warn it, discipline it, subdue it, pray for it? Or will you, in the vain search of pleasure, or in gayety, or fashion or folly, or in the chase of some other bauble, or even in household cares, neglect the soul of your child, and leave the little immortal to take wing alone, exposed to evil, to temptation, to ruin? Look again at the infant! Place your hand on its little heart! Shall that heart be deserted by its mother, to beat perchance in sorrow, disappointment, wretchedness and despair? Place your ear on its side and hear that heart beat! How rapid and vigorous the strokes! How the blood is thrown through the little veins! Think of it; that heart, in its vigor now, is the emblem of a spirit that will work with ceaseless pulsation, for sorrow or joy, forever." [17]

Mrs. Sigourney on the Infant. "But young mother, what do you hold in your arms? A machine of exquisite symmetry, the blue veins revealing the mysterious life-tide through an almost transparent surface, . . . such a form as the art of man has never equalled, and such a union of matter with mind, as his highest reason fails to comprehend. You embrace a being, whose developments may yet astonish you, who may perhaps sway the destiny of

16. Horace Mann, "Value and Necessity of Education," *Common School Journal*, 1:4, November, 1838.

17. Goodrich, *Fireside Education*, pp. 169–70.

others, whose gatherings of knowledge you can neither foresee or limit, and whose checquered lot of sorrow or of joy, are known only to the Omnipotence which fashioned him." [18]

Mrs. Tuthill on the Genteel Baby. "Another reason the baby had for crying under your inexperienced hands was, because you tried to make him trim and genteel. A genteel baby! I should as soon think of a genteel lily, or a genteel angel. The sweet, innocent unconsciousness of babyhood, is an antipodal to gentility. . . .

"Bear with my honest warmth . . . ; many a poor child has suffered torture, and some have lost their precious lives to gratify a mother's vanity." [19]

Fanny Fern's "House without a Baby." "There was not a child in the house, not one; I was sure of it, when I first went in. Such a spick-and-span look as it had! Chairs—grown-up chairs, plastered straight up against the wall; books arranged by rule and compass; no dear little careless finger-marks on furniture, doors, or window-glass; no hoop, or ball, or doll, or mitten, or basket, or picture-book on the premises. . . . I sat down at the well-polished window, and looked across the street. At the upper window of a wooden house opposite, I saw a little bald baby, tied into a high chair, speculating upon the panorama in the street, while its little fat hands frantically essayed to grab distant pedestrians on the sidewalk. Its mother sat sewing diligently by its side. Happy woman! she has a baby! She thought so, too; for by-and-by she threw down her work . . . took the child from its prison-house; and covered it with kisses." [20]

APPENDIX C

List of Books Recommended for the Library of a Maternal Association [21]

The Mother's Magazine, bound vols.
The Parent's Magazine.
The Father's Book. By Dwight.
Abbott's Mother at Home.
Babington on Education.
Meditations of a Christian Mother.
Hall's Lectures on Religious Education.
Christian Education. American Tract Society.
The Family Monitor. By Rev. J. A. James.
Mrs. Sigourney's Letters to Mothers.
Hannah More's Strictures on Female Education.
The Young Mother. By Dr. Alcott.
Payson's Sermons for Christian Families.

18. Sigourney, *Letters to Mothers*, p. 24.
19. Louisa Tuthill, "Letter to a Young Mother," *Happy Home and Parlor Magazine*, 7:364, 1858.
20. Fanny Fern, *Fresh Leaves*, p. 232.
21. *Parent's Magazine*, 1:282–83, August, 1841.

Cotton Mather's Essay to Parents.
Book for Parents.
Mothers' Friend.

[*This list is followed by an outline of "Topics of Conversation at Maternal Meetings"* [22] *with page references given for topics under the headings of "Family Government and Discipline"; "Parental Qualifications"; "Religious Instruction"; "Moral Education"; "Physical Education"; "Errors of Parents"; "Speaking the Truth"; "Dress," and "Children's Amusements."*]

APPENDIX D

Laws

"All the plans of wise men are founded upon the assumption of the regularity and invariableness of nature's laws. . . . When we suffer from the irresistible action of these laws, it is because we have not yet discovered them or are wickedly regardless of them. So in our physical and moral nature, we are subject to the laws of exercise, temperance, veracity, justice, benevolence, piety, and if these are obeyed, it cannot be ill with us. . . . The philosophy or the opinion which refers events that are within our control to an agency beyond it, bereaves man of a power graciously conferred on him by Heaven for the promotion of his welfare." [23]

"There are properly two sets of the Divine laws. One of these is found in the Decalogue, already alluded to, as well as elsewhere, and is called the *moral* law; the other, though alluded to there, is to be chiefly learned by study, and is called the *physical* law. It is found operating both in us and around us. We cannot, if we would, escape from it. It is everywhere.

"Some have thought it not so important as the moral law, because God has not particularly revealed it. But such persons would not, as I suppose, disregard the laws by which water and wind and steam are made available. . . . They would regard them as God's laws. . . ." [24]

"We are apt to neglect or despise the laws of the body, as if the latter were a mere appendage of the mind and soul; or as if they had no bond of connection or sympathy.

"Every parent and educator should fully understand that, in order to secure the best bodily health, the mind should be fully and harmoniously developed, as well as properly cultivated. Here, as I believe, great advantage would accrue to mankind from the study, not of the science of mere 'head feeling,' but of phrenology." [25]

"Physiologists, medical practitioners, and all who take medical aid, admit the existence of *organic laws:* And the sciences of government, legislation,

22. *Ibid.*, pp. 283–87.

23. Horace Mann, "Intellectual Education," *Common School Journal,* 1:12–13, November, 1838.

24. William A. Alcott, *The Laws of Health* (Boston, John P. Jewett & Co., 1857), p. 11.

25. William A. Alcott, *The Home Book of Life and Health*, p. 98.

education, indeed our whole train of conduct through life, proceed upon the admission of laws in morals. Accordingly, the laws of nature have formed an interesting subject of inquiry to philosophers of all ages; but, so far as I am aware, no author has hitherto attempted to point out, in a combined and systematic form, the relations between these laws and the constitution of Man; which must, nevertheless, be done, before our knowledge of them can be beneficially applied: . . ." [26]

APPENDIX E

Notes on Phrenology

An objection to phrenology. "The motto, 'principles not men,' has often served as a decent disguise for the most slavish truckling,—and we believe that it is in like manner possible to refine away our objections to wicked agents into an impersonality of crime, which, as it can have no existence, can excite little horror and no alarm. Everything is to be treated gently. It is wrong to believe that infanticide is a more unnatural crime, than any other murder; because 'the *natural* love of offspring is very weak in some women.' . . .

"In a word, ultra Epicureanism is the most distinguishing trait of phrenological notions of education,—the question is as old as the world,—and we are persuaded that the experience of mankind is altogether against this system." [27]

Phrenology applied to a philosophy of education. "As parents, you are, no doubt, troubled, in a greater or less degree, by the exhibition of anger, stubbornness, irritability and other evil and unamiable traits of character in your children. . . .

"But do not despair. . . .

"These passions in childhood are not indicative of such depravity of heart as is indicated by falsehood, theft, etc. They are the natural impulses, inseparable from the season of childhood and youth. You must bear in mind that this season is one of great activity and energy; . . . and that all the passions are inflammable, and ready to take fire at the least friction. . . .

"You must not, therefore, aim to eradicate these elementary principles of the mind, but only . . . to take them off the wrong track and put them on the right; or, what is better still, never suffer them to enter the wrong. But having assumed the wrong form, you will, by pursuing a process of mental transformation, see the *stubbornness* of your children taking the form of *decision of character and fortitude.*

"From anger will come a *hatred* of whatever is *mean and low,* and a *love of truth.* . . .

"From *irritability and a disposition to cry at trifles,* will come *sympathy* for the afflicted, *sensitiveness* and *delicacy* of feeling. . . .

"From *excessive love of play* will spring *activity in business.*

"From *covetousness* will come a desire for the *acquisition of property,*

26. George Combe, *The Constitution of Man,* Preface, pp. vii–viii.
27. "Phrenology," *North American Review,* 37:74, July, 1833.

which is perfectly commendable, if, in the disposition of it, the law of God is observed. . . .

"The word of God and the Holy Spirit will aid you in thus modifying or giving a new and healthful direction to all the evil, unamiable and rude dispositions or propensities of your children." [28]

Phrenology and the Millennium. "This glorious science has only to be spread and studied, completely to revolutionize man civilly, politically, religiously, morally, intellectually, and physically, so that a hundred years hence, he would not be recognized as belonging to the same race. Phrenologists, remember, that, in propagating this science, you, though a mere handful, are doing more good, promoting more happiness, abolishing more vice, and sowing the seeds of virtue, more than all the lawyers, doctors, teachers, clergymen, and religionists, of all christendom, and ten years will prove it by *experiment.* Ten years will turn, and overturn these United States, till the *true* principles of this science leaven society, till existing institutions totter on their basis, and are 'rolled together and pass away as a scroll,' to make way for the principles revealed by this science . . . the first step towards this great and glorious result, and the balance of this work will remodel the *government* and *moral* training of children; which alone will gain the day; and then Phrenology applied to religion, will complete the victory, and renew man *morally* as well as socially, intellectually and physically. Mark these prophecies and place them by the side of 1852." [29]

APPENDIX F

Views on the Body, the Soul, and the Appetites

From Horace Bushnell. "It will not be incredible to any thoughtful person, least of all to any genuinely philosophic person, that the treatment and fare of the body has much to do with the quality of the soul, or mind—its affinities, passions, aspirations, tempers; its powers of thought and sentiment, its imaginations, its moral and religious development. For the body is not only a house to the mind as other houses are, which we may live in for a time with no perceptible effect on our character, but it is a house in the sense of being the mind's own organ; its external life itself, the medium of all its action, the instrument of its thought and feeling, the inlet also of all its knowledges and impressions, and the instigator, by a thousand reactions, of all such spiritual riot and corruption as have had their leaven brewed in as many physical abuses and disorders. . . .

"So important a thing, for the religious life of the soul, is the feeding of the body. Vast multitudes of disciples have no conception of the fact. Living in a swine's body, regularly over-loaded and oppressed every day of their lives, they wonder that so great difficulties and discouragements rise up to hinder the Christian clearness of their soul. Could they but look into Agur's prayer, and take the meaning—feed me with food convenient for me, lest I

28. "Culture of the Passions," editorial, *Mother's Assistant,* 1853, pp. 143–45.

29. Fowler, *Fowler on Memory,* pp. 82–83.

be full, and deny thee, and say, who is the Lord?—they would find a real gospel in it. . . .

"I have spoken, thus briefly, to . . . adult experience, because it is adult conviction which my subject needs to obtain. To simply look on children from without, and tell what effects will be wrought on their religious tempers and habit by their feeding, and the general nurture of their body, will not carry any depth of conviction by itself. . . . And therefore it is that I appeal to parents, in this manner, requiring them to make some observation of themselves; to notice what becomes of them, and their sentiments, and senses of Christ and of God, when they are down under the burdens of an overloaded, or permanently diseased body. . . .

"The child is taken, when his training begins, in a state of naturalness, as respects all the bodily tastes and tempers, and the endeavor should be to keep him in that key; to let no stimulation of excess, or delicacy, disturb the simplicity of nature, and no sensual pleasuring, in the name of food, become a want or expectation of his appetite." [30]

From William Alcott, the *"Moral Argument" for the use of the vegetable diet.* "In one point of view, nearly every argument which can be brought to show the superiority of a vegetable diet over one that includes flesh or fish, is a moral argument.

"Thus, if man is so constituted by his structure and by the laws of his animal economy, that all the functions of the body, and of course all the faculties of the mind, and the affections of the soul, are in better condition—better subserve our own purposes, and the purposes of the great Creator—as well as hold out longer, on the vegetable system—then is it desirable, in a moral point of view, to adopt it. . . .

"How shocking it must be to the inhabitants of Jupiter, or some other planet, who had never before witnessed these sad effects of the ingress of sin among us, to see the carcasses of animals, either whole or by piece-meal, hoisted upon our very tables before the faces of children of all ages, from the infant at the breast, to the child of ten or twelve . . . and carved, and swallowed. . . . What could they—what would they—expect from such an education of the young mind and heart? What, indeed, but mourning, desolation, and wo! . . .

"It cannot be otherwise than that the circumstances of which I have spoken, which so universally surround infancy and childhood, should take off, gradually the keen edge of moral sensibility, and lessen every virtuous or holy sympathy." [31]

Bronson Alcott's class discussion on the "seat of the appetites." [32]

Mr. Alcott: Is the body the eater and drinker?
Several persons: Yes.

30. Bushnell, *Christian Nurture*, pp. 271–76.
31. William A. Alcott, *Vegetable Diet* (Boston, Marsh, Capen & Lyon, 1838), pp. 266–70.
32. Amos Bronson Alcott, *Conversations with Children on the Gospels*, II, 262–63.

Nathan: No; the Spirit.

Charles: Does the spirit eat and drink?

Mr. Alcott: Does a dead body eat and drink?

Francis: No; because the spirit is not there to move the body.

Lucia: I think the spirit eats and drinks through the body.

Mr. Alcott: How?

Francis: The will moves the body.

Charles: The spirit does not eat and drink, I am sure.

Andrew: The spirit makes the body eat, and gets all the good; but it could not eat without a body.

Mr. Alcott. Which is the eater?

Andrew: The body eats, but the spirit sets it in motion.

George K.: The spirit does not eat, it makes the body eat.

Franklin: When the spirit leaves the body, the spirit does not eat.

Mr. Alcott: What hungers?

Several: The Body.

Some: The Spirit.

Mr. Alcott: Does a dead body hunger?

George K.: No; then the spirit must.

Mr. Alcott: Which is the hungerer and thirster and eater?

George K.: Why, I suppose it must be the spirit then.

INDEX